Lokendra Shastri
Department of Computer and Information Science
University of Pennsylvania

Semantic Networks:
An Evidential Formalization and its Connectionist Realization

Pitman, London

Morgan Kaufmann Publishers, Inc., Los Altos, California

PITMAN PUBLISHING
128 Long Acre, London WC2E 9AN

© Lokendra Shastri 1988

First published 1988

Available in the Western Hemisphere from
MORGAN KAUFMANN PUBLISHERS, INC.,
95 First Street, Los Altos, California 94022

ISSN 0268-7526

British Library Cataloguing in Publication Data
Shastri, Lokendra
  Semantic Networks:
  An Evidential Formalization and
  its Connectionist Realization.
  —(Research notes in artificial
  intelligence, ISSN 0268-7526)
  1. Cognition   2. Artificial intelligence
  I. Title II. Series
  153.4   BF311

ISBN 0-273-08779-7

Library of Congress Cataloging in Publication Data
Shastri, Lokendra.
  Semantic Networks:
  An Evidential Formalization and
  its Connectionist Realization.
  (Research notes in artificial intelligence)
  Bibliography: p.
  1. Artificial intelligence. 2. Reasoning.
3. Real-time processing. 4. Machine theory.
I. Title. II. Title: Semantic networks. III. Series:
Research notes in artificial intelligence (London,
England)
Q335.S464 1987   006.3   86-34409
ISBN 0-934613-39-7

Reproduced and printed by photolithography
in Great Britain by Biddles Ltd, Guildford

Contents

Preface

Acknowledgements

1 Introduction   **1**
   1.1 Computational effectiveness: limited inference and parallelism   1
   1.2 Reasoning with incomplete and uncertain information   6
   1.3 From issues to problems   7
   1.4 Representation and retreival: an overview   9
   1.5 Outline of the thesis   12

2 Semantic Networks   **15**
   2.1 Significance of inheritance and recognition   16
   2.2 Semantic networks are notational variants of first-order logic   20
   2.3 Limitations of FOPC based formalizations   21
   2.4 Default properties lead to exceptions and multiple inheritance   23
   2.5 A closer look at exceptions and multiple inheritance   24
   2.6 Semantic networks are equivalent to suitable theories of default logic   27
   2.7 Touretzky's inferential distance ordering   31
   2.8 Evidential nature of knowledge in semantic networks   33
   2.9 An overview of the evidential formalization   34

3 Representation Language   **41**
   3.1 Structure of knowledge   41
   3.2 Concepts and attribute values   45
   3.3 A formal description of the representation language   46
   3.4 Some salient features of the representation language   51
   3.5 Necessary properties versus contingent ones   53
   3.6 Inheritance and recognition problems in terms of the
       representation language   56

4   Evidential Formalization of Inheritance and Recognition   59

   4.1 The problem of combining evidence   60

      4.1.1 Problem formulation   61

      4.1.2 Computing the most probable configuration   63

   4.2 Maximum entropy and the Dempster-Shafer rule   70

   4.3 Maximum entropy and Bayes' rule   72

   4.4 Evidential inheritance   76

      4.4.1 Direct inheritance   77

      4.4.2 Principle of relevance   78

      4.4.3 Multiple inheritance   80

      4.4.4 Evidential inheritance: a summary   93

   4.5 Evidential recognition   97

      4.5.1 Unique relevant concepts   98

      4.5.2 Multiple relevant concepts   99

   4.6 The role of numbers in the theory   102

   4.7 Well-formedness constraints and a proposal for structuring concepts   102

      4.7.1 The Multiple Views Organization   103

      4.7.2 Inheritance in the Multiple Views Organization   106

      4.7.3 Recognition in the Multiple Views Organization   108

5   A Connectionist Realization of the Memory Network   113

   5.1 Need for parallelism   114

   5.2 The Connectionist Model   117

      5.2.1 A brief overview of the brain   117

      5.2.2 Details of the connectionist model   118

      5.2.3 Why a connectionist model of massive parallelism   119

   5.3 Related work on massively parallel models of semantic memory   121

   5.4 Details of the connectionist encoding   123

      5.4.1 Connectivity and node types   124

      5.4.2 Computational properties of nodes   133

      5.4.3 Posing queries and computing solutions   134

   5.5 Examples of network encoding   136

   5.6 Implementation of $\uparrow$ and $\downarrow$ links   145

   5.7 Network behavior: an outline of a proof of correctness   148

   5.8 Simulation results   151

6 Discussion   **167**

   6.1 Structure and inference 167

   6.2 Structure and anomalous inference 169

   6.3 Use of winner-take-all networks for answer extraction 171

   6.4 Representation issues 172

      6.4.1 Finer structure of property values 173

      6.4.2 Representation of relations 175

      6.4.3 Extended inference 178

   6.5 Treatment of evidential information 179

   6.6 Learning 181

   6.7 Biological plausibility 191

   6.8 Conclusion 191

Appendix A   Network Behavior: A Proof of Correctness   **193**

   A.1 Proof of correctness for inheritance 194

      A.1.1 Proof for the local case of inheritance 195

      A.1.2 Proof for the non-local case of inheritance 198

   A.2 Proof of correctness for recognition 208

      A.2.1 Proof for Type recognition 208

      A.2.2 Proof for Token recognition 213

References   **217**

Preface

This book is a revised version of my dissertation carried out at the University of Rochester. It describes how hierarchically structured knowledge about concepts and their properties may be encoded as a massively parallel network of simple processing elements. The proposed *connectionist* semantic memory offers two distinct advantages. First, it solves an interesting class of *inheritance* and *recognition* problems extremely fast - in time proportional to the depth of the conceptual hierarchy. Second, the connectionist encoding is based on an evidential formalization of conceptual knowledge that leads to a principled treatment of *exceptions* and *multiple inheritance* during inheritance, and the *best match* or *partial match* computation during recognition.

This work should be of interest to researchers, both in artificial intelligence and cognitive science, because it formalizes a class of inference that people seemingly perform with extreme facility, and goes on to demonstrate that these inferences may be realized with equal facility using a computational architecture that is inspired, in part, by the architecture of the animal brain.

The research described here was motivated by a desire to arrive at a detailed computational model that would explain how intelligent agents can draw a variety of inferences with remarkable efficiency. We perform a diverse range of cognitive tasks such as visual recognition, language understanding, and commonsense reasoning within a few hundred milliseconds, even though - as the study of artificial intelligence has made abundantly clear - each of these tasks require a large number of complex information processing and inferential steps. The work offers a solution to one component of this complex and central problem.

My search for a solution was strongly biased by the belief that massive parallellism would turn out to be an integral part of any viable solution. This belief was based on the realization that the only existing physical system embodying intelligence - namely, the animal brain - makes pervasive use of massive parallelism. The brain is made up of relatively slow computing elements whose switching times fall in the range of a few milliseconds. And yet, it performs tasks that require millions of individual operations in a few hundred milliseconds! Clearly, when solving these tasks the brain must be carrying out at least a hundred thousand steps in parallel.

Many have been motivated by similar concerns and guided by similar intuitions. The best known example being Scott Fahlman's work on NETL. My goal was to progress beyond NETL; the improvement being targeted along two directions. First, I wanted to employ a more powerful form of parallelism, one in which there was no external controller to direct and control the parallel component of the system. The presence of a central controller in NETL greatly restricted the effective use of parallelism. Second, I wanted to offer a precise account of the reasoning performed by my system. The form of reasoning described as inheritance is confounded by the presence of conflicting information that gives rise to *exceptions* and *multiple inheritance*. In case of recognition, the situation is further complicated because of the need to deal with the partial/best match problem. NETL's behavior was idiosyncratic in the presence of exceptions and multiple inheritance, and it did not deal with partial/best match problems. I wanted my system to solve inheritance and recognition problems in accordance with a semantically *justifiable* formalization of inheritance and recognition. In particular, I wanted the formalization to deal with exceptions and multiple inheritance in a meaningful manner.

I was aware of some ongoing attempts at formalizing inheritance in semantic networks being carried out by David Etherington and Raymond Reiter, and Dave Touretzky. Both these attempts were an improvement over previous formalizations of inheritance in that both offered principled solutions to the problem of exceptions. However, these proposals did not adequately deal with the problem of multiple inheritance - they simply reported an ambiguity in such situations. Even though Touretzky's formalization appeared to handle some cases of multiple inheritance, it turned out that the only cases it could deal with were those that could be reduced to mere cases of exceptions. For reasons discussed in Chapter 2, I adopted an evidential approach that not only lead to principled solutions to the problems of exceptions and multiple inheritance, but also lead to a solution of the partial/best match problem during recognition.

It may be apparent from the above discussion that this work may be described in two independent parts: one part that lays out the evidential formalization of inheritance and recognition, and the other that specifies the connectionist system that realizes the required representation and computation. In the actual research process, however, these two aspects of the work were inextricably linked, and arriving at the connectionist realization was not merely an implementation step. In fact, I believe that I could not have arrived at the evidential formalization without approaching the problem from a connectionist perspective; envisioning a connectionist solution lead to some key insights and provided significant cues that finally lead to the development of the evidential formalization. Some of these points are discussed in Chapter 5.

It has often been argued that a deep understanding of what is intelligence, why is it that we view the world to be structured as we do, and why are we good at certain tasks while inept at some others, will accrue only if we adopt an integrated approach that synthesizes computational, behavioral, as well as neurobiological issues. It is hoped that the work described here is a small step in this direction.

Philadelphia, Pennsylvania   Lokendra Shastri

June, 1987

Acknowledgements

I would like to thank my advisor, Jerry Feldman, for guiding me during my apprenticeship at Rochester, and exposing me to the wonderful world of connectionism. I have learned a great deal from him and this thesis bears testimony to that; but for his guidance, motivation, and support this thesis would not have been possible. I would also like to thank Jerry for creating an unencumbered and intellectually stimulating environment at Rochester and being a constant source of inspiration.

My interactions with James Allen, Dana Ballard, Gary Dell, and Patrick Hayes - members of my thesis committee - have been extremely fruitful. I wish to thank them for lending me their ear, reading numerous rough drafts, and providing valuable feedback. I will long remember the heated arguments with Pat during the course of which I learned a lot. I am indebted to Dana for his critical comments, he was partly responsible for motivating me to seek an evidential formulation of the connectionist semantic memory; his criticism paid rich dividends. James shared with me his insights into semantic networks, offered several helpful suggestions, and asked many crucial questions. Gary provided a refreshing diversity to the committee by offering a psychologist's perspective and directing me to relevant literature in psychology. I am grateful to Henry Kyburg for his comments on my paper on evidential reasoning, and to Steven Small for stimulating discussions on artificial intelligence and connectionism.

I grateful to Shyam Bhaiyya for revealing the power of reasoning to an eight year old by explaining why a ball delivered at 90 mph takes only half a second to reach a batsman at the other end of a cricket pitch. I am also grateful to Subhash for arousing my interest in artificial intelligence and convincing me that I should pursue a career of research - he has remained a constant source of inspiration and ideas.

My stay at Rochester was made pleasant by Addanki, Amit, Diane, Gary, Giannis, Gopalan, Jim, Mark (both B. and M.), Nemo, Ravi, Rich, Sanyal, Sridhar, and Srinivas. Special thanks to Leo who always seems to be around to lend a helping hand; many of the figures appearing in the thesis are his handiwork.

I found the staff at the Department of Computer Science exceptionally warm, friendly, and helpful. Many thanks to Jill Orioli, Rose Peet, Peggy Meeker, Suzanne Bell and Peggy Frantz. Thanks also to Glenda Kent and James Lotkowski at Penn for formatting part of the text, and Jugal Kalita for drawing the figures that Leo didn't.

I wish to thank N.S. Sridharan, the editor of this series, for encouraging me to publish my dissertation, and Pete Brown of Pitman for his extreme patience.

I am grateful to my parents - to whom I dedicate this book - and my brothers and sisters for a happy childhood filled with warm memories. My parents have always encouraged and supported my endeavors and have tried to inculcate in me the desire to excel.

Special thanks to my wife Sadhana for her loving care and understanding - it is difficult to imagine how one could be more supportive and helpful than she is. This dissertation would have taken many more months to finish were it not for her support and sacrifice.

Finally, thanks also to Anjali and Aditi, both of whom are too young to realize what a constant source of amazement and an even greater source of joy they are.

to
Babuji
and Jiji

1 Introduction

The problem of representing and using a large body of knowledge is fundamental to artificial intelligence. It is well recognized that intelligent activity of any significance, whether it be natural language understanding, vision, problem solving, or planning, requires access to a large storehouse of knowledge at all levels of processing. This thesis focuses on two issues that I consider to be crucial to the knowledge representation problem. They are:

- The importance of *computational effectiveness*. Solutions to problems in knowledge representation and inference should satisfy the **real-time** constraint. Human agents take a few hundred milliseconds to perform a broad range of intelligent tasks and we should expect artificially intelligent agents to perform similar tasks in comparable time.

- The need to identify and formalize inference structures that are appropriate for dealing with *incompleteness* and *uncertainty*. An agent cannot maintain complete knowledge about any but the most trivial environment, and therefore, he must be capable of reasoning with incomplete and uncertain information.

1.1 Computational effectiveness: limited inference and parallelism

As the science of artificial intelligence has matured over three decades, it has become apparent that we had underestimated the complexity and intricacy of intelligent behavior. Today we realize that it is one thing to build a system that performs "intelligently" in a limited domain, and yet another to design a system that displays the sort of natural intelligence we take for granted among humans and higher animals. This sharp difference is highlighted by the limitations and brittleness of artificial intelligence (AI) systems developed to understand natural language (English), process visual information, and perform commonsense reasoning. There are programs that "understand" English if the exchange is limited to talk about airplane tickets; there are reliable vision systems that can identify a predefined set of objects presented under carefully controlled conditions; but we have yet to design systems that can recognize objects with the skill of a monkey, or converse with the facility of a five year old.

Given that existing AI systems perform credibly within restricted domains, one may be led to believe that in order to accommodate more complex domains all that is necessary is to encode *more* facts and rules into our programs. But the situation is not so straightforward; it is not as though the existing programs are just miniature versions of larger programs that would perform intelligently in richer domains. The problem is that the solutions do not scale up: the techniques that work in restricted domains are inadequate for dealing with richer and more complex domains. As the domains grow bigger and more complex, we run into the stone wall of computational effectiveness; the performance of the system degrades drastically and it can no longer solve interesting problems in acceptable time-scales. This is not surprising if we recognize that intelligent activity involves very dense interactions between many pieces of information, and in any system that encodes knowledge about a complex domain, these interactions can become too numerous for the system to perform effectively.

If we analyze human behavior we find that in spite of operating with a large knowledge base, human agents take but a few hundred milliseconds to perform a broad range of cognitive tasks such as classifying and recognizing objects, deciphering the meaning of spoken and written words, and making inferences such as: "Tweety is a bird therefore it flies". The human performance data highlights a remarkable property of the representation of conceptual information and the cognitive processes that access it: not only are facts relevant to the task at hand *retrieved* spontaneously, but what is more significant, certain kinds of *inferences* based on conceptual knowledge also get drawn with *extreme efficiency*. Any serious attempt at understanding intelligence must provide a detailed computational account of how such non-trivial operations are performed in a few hundred milliseconds. The real-time constraint becomes sharper if one looks at the computational properties of the biological hardware underlying human cognition. Neurons, the basic information processing elements of the brain, are rather slow computing devices with switching and communication time constants of a few milliseconds. From this it follows that any cognitive activity that takes place in a few hundred milliseconds must essentially be carried out in about a *few hundred time steps* [Feldman & Ballard 82].

Both the real-time constraint and its "hundred step" variant directly apply to cognitive models. But a priori, there is no reason why AI models should mimic the biological architecture and be bound by any limitations imposed by the speed of neuronal elements. One might therefore argue that AI systems do not have to honor the "hundred step" constraint. This argument, however, cannot be offered to skirt the *real-time* constraint, especially if one views it in the following more general form which we will refer to as the **computational effectiveness** constraint.

> To be deemed intelligent, a system must be capable of acting within a specified time frame, and often the specification of an appropriate time frame is not under the agent's control but is laid down by the environment.

The ability to satisfy the computational effectiveness constraint appears to be one of the basic properties of intelligent agents. Success, and at times even the survival of an agent, may depend on his ability to make decisions and choose appropriate actions within a given time frame. In fact, in certain situations we would hesitate to label an activity as being "intelligent" if it takes arbitrarily long. To give an extreme example - if time were not a factor, even a dumb computer could possibly beat the world's greatest chess player at the game by simply enumerating the full search tree and following a path that guaranteed a win. No doubt this would take an aeon, but if time is not a factor this should not be of consequence[2]!

In view of the above, a concern for computational effectiveness is central to AI. From the viewpoint of AI, it does not suffice to offer a computational account of how an agent may solve an interesting set of problems. AI must solve a far more difficult problem: *it must provide a computational account of how an agent may solve*

---

[2]Two caveats are in order. First, we are assuming that a path leading to a forced win exists, but such a path may not exist. Second, in addition to time, space or memory is also a critical resource.

interesting problems in the time frame permitted by the environment?

It is tempting to ignore the computational effectiveness constraint by characterizing it as being merely a matter of efficiency, programming tricks, or an implementation level detail. But doing so would be a mistake; the computational effectiveness constraint is not an *obstacle* in our path to understanding intelligence, on the contrary, I believe that we will understand the principles underlying the organization and use of information in cognitive systems *only if* we tackle the question of computational effectiveness *at the very outset*.

Computational effectiveness places strong constraints on how knowledge may be organized and accessed by cognitive processes. In particular, it clearly rules out a straightforward modeling of an agent's knowledge base as a collection of facts accompanied by a *general purpose* inference engine. Such an account violates the computational effectiveness constraint because any generalized notion of inference is intractable - such a system may take *arbitrarily* long to draw inferences and may even take forever trying to infer what may actually be false!

A possible solution of the computational effectiveness problem lies in a synthesis of the *limited inference* approach and *massive parallelism*.

Limited inference

According to the limited inference strategy, one must identify a limited but interesting class of inference that needs to be performed very fast, and develop appropriate knowledge structuring techniques, algorithms, and computational models to perform this class of inference within an acceptable time frame[3].

The fundamental step in pursuing the limited inference approach is circumscribing the class of inference for which efficient solutions will be found. Several possibilities have been investigated in [Ballard 86][Frisch & Allen 82][Levesque 84][McAllester

---

[3]Such a limited inference system may of course be embedded in a larger system capable of performing more general forms of inference.

80][Vilain 85].

Parallelism

The extremely tight constraint on the time available to perform non-trivial inferences suggests that, in addition to focusing on a restricted class of inference, one will have to resort to parallelism to achieve computational effectiveness. Many cognitive tasks, and certainly all the perceptual ones, that humans can perform in a few hundred milliseconds would require millions of instructions on a serial (von Neumann) computer, and it is obvious that such a computer will be unable to perform these tasks with the desired speed.

A possible solution to this problem suggests itself if one examines the architecture of a traditional von Neumann computer. In such a computer, the computational and the inferential power is concentrated in a single processing unit (the CPU) while the information on which the computations have to be performed is stored in an *inert* memory which simply acts as a repository of the system's knowledge. As a result of the single processor design, only one processing step can be executed at any point in time, and during each processing step the CPU can only access a minuscule fraction of the memory. Therefore, at any given instant, only an insignificant portion of the system's knowledge participates in the processing. On the other hand, intelligent behavior requires dense interactions between many pieces of information, and any computational architecture for intelligent information processing must be capable of supporting such dense interactions. It would therefore seem appropriate to treat each memory cell - not as a mere repository of information, but rather as an *active* processing element capable of *interacting* with other such elements. This would result in a massively parallel computer made up of an extremely large number of simple processing elements - as many as there are memory cells in a traditional computer. The processing capability of such a computer would be *distributed* across its memory, and consequently, such a computer would permit numerous interactions between various pieces of information to occur simultaneously.

In chapter 5 it is argued that the *connectionist* approach provides an appropriate degree of parallelism: one in which a processing element may be assigned to each piece of information and the important *inferential connections* between pieces of information may be directly expressed by *interconnections between the processing elements.*

1.2 Reasoning with incomplete and uncertain information

The computational cost of gathering, processing and storing information about a complex and constantly changing environment makes it impossible for an agent to maintain complete knowledge. Thus, with the exception of some artificially constructed domains, an agent seldom has sufficient information to pin down the *exact state* of the world. Nevertheless, he *must act and make choices on the basis of available information.* In such situations a deductive model of reasoning is inadequate for formalizing the reasoning behavior of an agent. Consider the following example: Assume that an agent *must choose* between actions A and B, where action A is appropriate if hypothesis P is true while action B is appropriate if hypothesis Q is true. Assume that the agent's knowledge is incomplete and although he can deduce "P ∨ Q", he can neither deduce "P" nor "Q". What should an intelligent agent do in such a situation? An excellent strategy would be to make the best use of all available information and try and identify which of the two hypotheses is *more likely* to be true. If P is more likely than Q then he should perform action A else he should perform action B. This form of reasoning is best viewed as *evidential* reasoning, wherein inference does not involve establishing the truth of a proposition, but instead it involves finding the *most likely* hypothesis from among a finite set of alternatives.

In fact, one may argue that the issue of non-monotonicity is best handled by reformulating it in terms of evidential reasoning. If a choice must be made at a certain point in time, the best option available to an agent is to choose the alternative that is most likely given the knowledge at hand, and act as though it *is* the "correct" alternative. Later, if new information becomes available, the likelihoods may change and a different alternative may become most likely. If the agent has to make a choice

6

at this point in time, he should choose the alternative that is now most likely. It the two choices are different, we have a situation akin to non-monotonicity.

Attempts to simulate evidential reasoning as a deductive system without facing up to the issue of likelihood usually end up being mired in consequences such as non-monotonicity or probabilistic truth values. Other alternative approaches such as default logic also do not deal with likelihood and treat the issue of selecting an *extension* as an implementation detail. Likelihood becomes an issue of inference strategy, a quirk of implementation, and at best a fuzzy thing called heuristics.

1.3 From issues to problems

In this thesis I argue that *concept recognition* and *inheritance of conceptual attributes* are important forms of limited inference. Inheritance is the form of reasoning that leads an agent to infer properties of a concept based on the properties of its ancestors. For example, if the agent knows that "birds fly" , then given that "Tweety is a bird", he may infer that "Tweety flies". Recognition is the dual of the inheritance problem and may be described as follows: given a description consisting of a set of properties, find a concept that best matches this description.

I argue that inheritance and recognition are important forms of limited inference and are precursors to more complex reasoning processes. I also argue that a broad range of reasoning tasks that human agents perform effortlessly and extremely fast may be viewed as examples of these.

Given the significance of inheritance and recognition it appears worthwhile to seek a computational account of how these inferences may be drawn with the requisite efficiency. Such an exercise may provide insights into constraints that shape conceptual structures and inferential processes that operate on these structures. However, it has been difficult to arrive at a satisfactory computational account because a satisfactory formalization of semantic networks, inheritance, and recognition has been lacking. Although several formalizations have been proposed, they are limited in their ability to deal with an important aspect of commonsense knowledge namely, the presence of exceptional and conflicting information.

This thesis presents an evidential formalization of semantic networks, inheritance, and recognition wherein the principle of maximum entropy is applied to deal with uncertain and incomplete knowledge. It goes on to demonstrate that this evidential formulation can be realized as an interpreter-free, massively parallel, network of simple processing elements that can solve inheritance and recognition problems extremely efficiently.

The important results of this research are summarized below:

i) The evidential formalization of semantic networks leads to a principled treatment of *exceptions*, *multiple inheritance* and *conflicting information* during inheritance, and the *best match* or *partial match* computation during recognition. This formalization offers semantically justifiable solutions to a larger class of problems than existing formulations based on default logic and the principle of inferential distance ordering.

ii) The above formalization can be realized as a connectionist network that uses controlled spreading activation to solve inheritance and recognition problems in time proportional to the *depth* of the conceptual hierarchy. (This time is independent of the total number of concepts in the conceptual structure.)

iii) The work identifies specific constraints that must be satisfied by the conceptual structure in order to achieve an efficient connectionist realization.

iv) The networks operate without the intervention of a central controller and do not require a distinct interpreter. The knowledge as well as mechanisms for drawing *limited inferences* on it are encoded within the network.

v) The networks can be constructed from a high-level specification of the knowledge to be encoded and the mapping between the knowledge level and the network level is precisely specified.

vi) The solution scales because the design principles are independent of the size of the underlying semantic memory. The number of nodes in the connectionist networks is *at most* quadratic in the number of concepts in the semantic memory.

1.4 Representation and retrieval: an overview

Before we proceed, I would like to provide an overview of the proposed knowledge representation system. An oversimplified description follows:

The system's conceptual knowledge is encoded in a connectionist network referred to as the **Memory Network**. This network is composed of a large number of extremely simple processing elements (nodes) that interact with one another by propagating activation along weighted links. The Memory Network uses controlled spreading activation to solve inheritance and recognition problems in accordance with the evidential formulation presented in this thesis. A problem is posed to the network by activating relevant nodes in it. Once activated the network performs the required inferences *automatically* without the intervention of any external controller. At the end of a specified interval the answer is available implicitly as the levels of activation of a relevant set of nodes. The property of the network whereby nodes achieve an appropriate level of activation derives in part from *built-in* control mechanisms that carefully regulate the spreading of activation, and in part from the rules by which a node combines incoming activation.

In keeping with the connectionist paradigm, the presentation of queries to the Memory Network as well as the subsequent answer extraction is also carried out by connectionist network fragments called **routines**. Routines encode canned procedures for performing specific tasks and are represented as a sequence of nodes connected so that activation can serve to sequence through the routine. In the course of their execution, routines pose queries to the Memory Network by activating appropriate nodes in it. The Memory Network in turn returns the answer to the routine by activating *response* nodes in the routine. The activation returned by a node in the Memory Network is a measure of the evidential support for an answer.

It is assumed that all queries originating in routines are posed with respect to an explicit set of answers and there is a response node for each possible answer. Response nodes compete with one another and the node receiving the maximum activation from the Memory Network dominates and triggers the appropriate action.

Thus computing an answer amounts to choosing the answer that receives the highest evidence *relative* to a set of *potential answers*. The actual answer extraction mechanism explicitly allows for "don't know" as a possible answer. This may happen if there is insufficient evidence for all the choices or if there is no clear cut dominator.

Figure 1.1 depicts the interaction between a fragment of an agent's restaurant routine and a part of his Memory Network. In this routine fragment, the task of deciding on a wine results in a query to the Memory Network about the taste of food and the decision is made on the basis of the answer returned by the Memory Network. Action steps are depicted as oval nodes, queries as hexagonal nodes and response nodes as circular nodes. The Memory Network in the example encodes the following information: Concepts in the example domain are characterized by two properties, has-taste and has-color. HAM and PEA are two concepts in the domain. HAM is SALTY in taste and is PINK in color, PEA is SWEET in taste and is GREEN in color.

The arcs in the Memory Network represent weighted links. The triangular nodes (called binder nodes) associate objects, properties and property values. Each node is an active element and when in an "active" state sends out activation to all the nodes connected to it. The weight on a link modulates the activation as it propagates along the link. While a rectangular node becomes active on receiving activation from any node, a binder node becomes active only on receiving simultaneous activation from a pair of nodes.

To find the taste of HAM a routine would activate the nodes has-taste and HAM. The binder node b1 linking has-taste and HAM to SALTY will receive coincident activation along two of its links and become active. As a result, it will transmit activation to SALTY which will then become active.

Similarly, if some routine needs to find an object that has a salty taste it would activate the nodes has-taste and SALTY. This will cause the appropriate binder node to become active and transmit activation to HAM. Eventually, HAM will become active completing the retrieval.

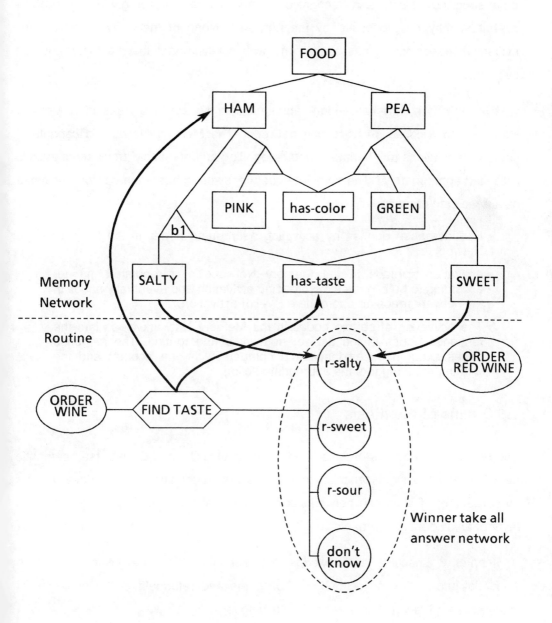

Figure 1.1: Connectionist retrieval system

11

These two cases roughly correspond to how inheritance (finding property-values of a specified object) and recognition (identifying an object given some of its attributes) may be processed by the network. None of the above involved any evidential reasoning or inheritance, and was solely meant to give the reader an overview.

To summarize, the knowledge representation system comprises of a Memory Network and a collection of routine networks. The Memory Network is capable of computing solutions to inheritance and recognition autonomously provided its state is initialized appropriately. The complete query answering operation can be described as a three step process:

- Routines pose queries by activating appropriate nodes in the Memory Network.
- Activation spreads in the Memory Network in a regulated manner according to built-in rules of spreading activation and eventually nodes in the network reach an appropriate level of activation.
- The activation of certain nodes in the Memory Network feeds into the response nodes in the answer network of the routine. The response nodes accumulate evidence and compete with one another and the winning node triggers the appropriate action.

1.5 Outline of the thesis

The rest of the thesis is organized into 5 chapters. Chapter 2 discusses semantic networks and the significance of inheritance and recognition. It describes various formalizations of semantic networks, points out their shortcomings, and argues in favor of an evidential approach.

Chapter 3 specifies a knowledge representation language for capturing the evidential information associated with concepts and reformulates the problems of inheritance and recognition in terms of this language.

The evidential formulation and its application to inheritance and recognition are developed in chapter 4. Section 4.1 derives an evidence combination rule based on the principle of maximum entropy. Sections 4.2 and 4.3 compare this approach to the

Dempster-Shafer evidence combination rule and the Bayes' rule for computing conditional probabilities. Sections 4.4 and 4.5 develop solutions to the problems of inheritance and recognition based on the results derived in section 4.1. These sections also specify the exact conditions that must be satisfied by the conceptual structure in order for the solutions to apply. Chapter 4 concludes with a suggestion for a particular conceptual organization. This organization obeys certain structural restrictions that simplify the evidential reasoning process during inheritance and recognition.

The solutions developed in chapter 4 may be realized as a connectionist network of simple processing elements connected via weighted links. Chapter 5 begins with a description of the connectionist model of computation. It examines the reasons underlying the growing interest in this paradigm and evaluates its relevance to knowledge representation and inference. Section 5.3 reviews some related work on massively parallel models of semantic networks. The connectionist encoding itself is described in section 5.4, wherein, the interconnectivity and computational characteristics of various types of nodes are specified. Section 5.5 presents some examples to illustrate the details of the connectionist encoding while section 5.6 elaborates some implementation details. It can be proved that the proposed networks solve the inheritance and recognition problem in accordance with the evidential formulation and in time proportional to the depth of the conceptual hierarchy. Section 5.7 presents an outline of this proof and discusses some additional constraints that need to be placed on the conceptual structure in order to arrive at an efficient parallel solution. The detailed proof is given in Appendix A. Section 5.8 describes how the proposed system has been simulated on a conventional computer and presents the results of simulating several examples that are often cited in knowledge representation literature as being problematic.

Chapter 6 discusses some significant features of this work, points out its limitations, and lists some unresolved issues. It also indicates possible directions that may be taken in pursuing the line of research described in this thesis.

2 Semantic Networks

Since their introduction by Quillian [Quillian 68], semantic networks have played a significant role in knowledge representation research. Semantic networks express knowledge in terms of concepts, their properties, and the hierarchical sub/superclass relationship between concepts. Each concept is represented by a node and the hierarchical relationship between concepts is depicted by connecting appropriate concept nodes via *IS-A* or *INSTANCE-OF* links[4]. Nodes at the lowest level in the *IS-A* hierarchy denote individuals (Tokens) while nodes at higher levels denote classes or categories of individuals (Types). Concepts get more abstract as one moves up the *IS-A* hierarchy. Properties are also represented by nodes, and the fact that a property applies to a concept is represented by connecting the property node and the concept node via an appropriately labeled link. Typically, a property is attached at the highest concept in the conceptual hierarchy to which the property applies, and if a property is attached to a node C, it is *assumed* that it applies to all nodes that are descendants of C[5].

The term "semantic networks" has been used in a far more general sense in the knowledge representation literature than what has been described above. We will, however, only focus on those aspects of semantic networks that have been mentioned above, namely, the description of concepts in terms of their properties and the organization of concepts using the *IS-A* hierarchy. This characterization is broad enough to capture the basic organizational principle underlying frame-based representation languages such as FRL [Roberts & Goldstein 77], KRL [Bobrow & Winograd 77], and KL-ONE [Brachman & Schmolze 85].

---

[4]For convenience, we will suppress the distinction between *IS-A* and *INSTANCE-OF* links and refer to both as *IS-A*.

[5]As discussed below, this is not always the case.

The organization and structuring of information in a semantic network often leads to an efficient realization of two kinds of inferences which we will refer to as *inheritance* and *recognition*.

2.1 Significance of inheritance and recognition

Inheritance is the form of reasoning that leads an agent to infer properties of a concept based on the properties of its ancestors. For example, if the agent knows that "birds fly" , then given that "Tweety is a bird", he may infer that "Tweety flies". This kind of reasoning, often referred to as default reasoning, is commonplace and one can even argue that it is the quintessence of commonsense reasoning. In general, inheritance may be defined as the process of determining properties of a concept, C, by looking up properties locally attached to C, and if such local information is not available, by looking up properties attached to concepts that lie above C in the conceptual hierarchy.

Recognition is the dual of the inheritance problem. While inheritance seeks a property value of a given concept, recognition seeks a concept that has some specified property values. The recognition problem may be described as follows: "Given a description consisting of a set of properties, find a concept that *best* matches this description". Notice that the properties of concepts are not necessarily available locally at the concept, and may have to be determined via inheritance. For this reason, recognition may be viewed as a very general form of *pattern matching*: one in which the target patterns, i.e., the set of patterns to which an input pattern is to be matched, are organized in a hierarchy, and where matching an input pattern A with a target pattern T_i involves matching properties that appear in A with properties local to T_i as well as to properties that T_i inherits from its ancestors.

Besides physical objects and their properties, inheritance and recognition may be defined with respect to hierarchically organized information about events and relations. For example, the notion of inheritance may be generalized to include reasoning about parts and temporal intervals [Fox 79][Allen 83][Fahlman

16

79][Schubert et al 83].

The stance taken in this work is that inheritance and recognition are important forms of *limited inference*. These two complementary forms of reasoning probably lie at the core of intelligent behavior and act as precursors to more complex and specialized reasoning processes. Figure 2.1 is intended to illustrate the role of inheritance and recognition.

The top of figure 2.1 represents the semantic memory component of an agent's knowledge. The bottom half depicts the two broad classes of queries that are posed to the semantic memory by other cognitive processes. Entry point α corresponds to recognition queries. A recognition query corresponds to a request for generalized pattern matching and is initiated whenever a mental process has a partial description of an unknown entity "X" and wants to ascertain the identity of "X" or the class to which "X" belongs. Here "X" may refer to a physical object, the precondition part of a production rule, a schema, an action etc. The central role of such a recognition or pattern matching step in cognitive processing is not a matter of debate.

Entry point β corresponds to inheritance queries. Here some internal process knows the identity or class of "X" but wants to ascertain the value of some property of "X". In addition to commonsense reasoning tasks, one can identify many other cognitive subtasks that would require inheritance as an intermediate step. Consider natural language understanding (NLU). Various steps in the NLU process such as word sense disambiguation and determination of case-fillers require answers to inheritance-like questions. For instance, one can use inheritance to enforce selectional restrictions during the process of determining case fillers. Given the restriction: *the filler of the* **instrument** *case for the verb* **to cut** *should have* **sharpness** *as one of its properties*, one can easily see how this restriction may be enforced by posing an inheritance query: "is sharpness a property of X" and accepting or rejecting "X" as a filler of the case *instrument* depending on whether the answer to the query is "yes" or "no".

In many cases the appropriate query is a combination of a recognition and an

Semantic Network (Memory)

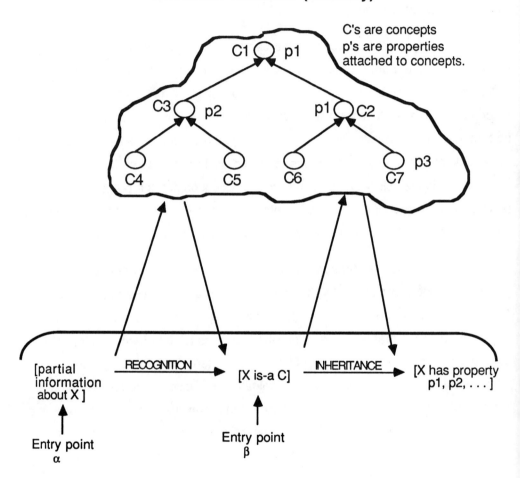

Figure 2.1: Significance of inheritance and recognition

inheritance query. In this situation some internal process has a partial description of an unknown entity and needs to determine the value of a property of this entity. In this case, first a recognition has to be performed to determine what "X" is, and once "X"'s identity or its class membership has been determined, an inheritance step has to be carried out to determine the value of the required property of "X". One can view such a query as a general form of *pattern completion*.

In addition to their ubiquity, inheritance and recognition are significant because in spite of operating with a large knowledge base, humans perform these inferences effortlessly and *extremely fast* - often in a few hundred milliseconds. This suggests that inheritance and recognition are perhaps *basic* and *unitary* components of symbolic reasoning - probably the smallest and simplest cognitive operations that i) produce *specific responses* and ii) can be initiated by complex and higher-level symbolic reasoning processes. The speed with which these operations are performed also suggests that they are performed fairly automatically, and typically do not require any conscious and attentional control[6].

Given the significance of inheritance and recognition, it appears worthwhile to seek a *computational account* of how these inferences may be drawn with the requisite efficiency. Such an exercise may provide insights into constraints that shape conceptual structures and inferential processes that operate on these structures. But it has been difficult to arrive at such a computational account because satisfactory formalization of semantic networks, inheritance and recognition has been lacking. Several formalizations have been proposed in the past, but each of these has certain limitations. The following section discusses some of these proposals.

---

[6]Examples of atypical situations are: queries referring to concepts that are not explicitly represented in the agent's conceptual structure and queries that lead to ambiguous answers. In such cases conscious intervention would probably occur.

2.2 Semantic networks are notational variants of first-order logic.

Attempts to explain semantic networks as notational variants of first-order predicate calculus (FOPC) date back to Cercone & Schubert [Cercone & Schubert 75]. They argued that semantic networks were simply a graphical notation for predicate calculus and even developed an elaborate graphical notation to represent all of FOPC. A formalization of semantic networks based on FOPC appears in [Hayes 79] and [Charniak 81].

The translation involves mapping Tokens to constants, Types to unary predicates, and properties to either binary or unary predicates. Thus an *IS-A* link between TWEETY and BIRD is expressed as: BIRD(TWEETY), while the *IS-A* link between BIRD and LIVING-THING is expressed as

$\forall$ (x) BIRD(x) => LIVING-THING(x)

If a property is mapped to a unary predicate then property specifications such as "Canaries are yellow" and "Birds fly" may be expressed as

$\forall$ (x) CANARY(x) => YELLOW(x)

$\forall$ (x) BIRD(x) => FLYER(x)

Alternately, if properties are treated as two place predicates, the above information may be expressed as

$\forall$ (x) CANARY(x) => HAS-COLOR(x, YELLOW)

$\forall$ (x) BIRD(x) => HAS-MODE-OF-TRANSPORT(x, FLYING)

In the translation described above, inheritance amounts to one or more applications of universal specialization and modus ponens. For example, starting with CANARY(TWEETY) one may deduce HAS-COLOR(TWEETY, YELLOW), by a single application of universal specialization and modus ponens. Similarly, one can infer HAS-MODE-OF-TRANSPORT(TWEETY, FLYING) by repeated applications of the same.

2.3 Limitations of FOPC based formalizations

Despite its elegance and simplicity, the direct translation of semantic networks into FOPC has several shortcomings.

- It obscures the *control* aspect of *IS-A* links because it treats *IS-A* links as any other implication in the knowledge base.
- It does not deal with critical aspects of world knowledge such as the presence of exceptions, multiple hierarchies, and conflicting information.
- It does not explain how the information encoded in a semantic network may be used to solve recognition problems.

A knowledge representation framework should not merely prescribe how small bits of information ought to be represented, but *it should also detail how the totality of information ought to be structured and organized so that information may be retrieved and relevant inferences may be drawn efficiently.* Semantic networks not only encode information about the world, but they also make certain commitments about which inferences are important, and provide mechanisms for facilitating these inferences. For example, inheritance in semantic networks reduces to a graph traversal problem. The translation to FOPC described above does not include the additional control information embedded in the network representation[7].

A more serious problem with the proposed translation, however, is the manner in which information about properties is translated. Needless to say, the above translation is clearly appropriate for dealing with certain kinds of world knowledge. For example, if we want to assert that "John is the father of Mary" or that "John is the manager of Tom" then clearly the translation into FOPC is perfect. The proposed translation is also appropriate for describing properties of entities that belong to formally defined domains such as geometry. For example,

$$\forall (x) \; \text{TRIANGLE}(x) => \text{HAS-NUMBER-OF-SIDES}(x, 3)$$

---

[7]Most implementations overcome this shortcoming by introducing special purpose *LISP* code to mark certain deductions as preferred. In a similar vein, Allen and Frisch [Allen & Frisch 82], introduce special predicates: TYPE and SUBTYPE together with specific axioms that describe the transitive nature of *IS-A* links, in order to capture the special role played by these links during inheritance.

would be a perfect rendering of "triangles have three sides".

In general, the FOPC translation is adequate as long as we restrict ourselves to *necessary* properties of concepts - properties that hold for *every* member of the class being described - but breaks down if we want to associate non-necessary (i.e., *default*) properties with concepts. Thus encoding "Birds fly"[8] as

$\forall(x)$ BIRD(x) => HAS-MODE-OF-TRANSPORT(x, FLYING)

would lead to serious problems because not *all* birds fly; penguins, and ostriches do not. We cannot simultaneously assert that

$\forall$ (x) BIRD(x) => HAS-MODE-OF-TRANSPORT(x, FLYING)

$\forall$ (x) PENGUIN(x) => BIRD(x)

$\forall$ (x) PENGUIN(x) => HAS-MODE-OF-TRANSPORT(x, ~FLYING)

The above assertions are simply inconsistent, and hence, useless.

One might think that the problem can be fixed by simply modifying the assertion about birds to be

$\forall$ (x) BIRD(x) & ~PENGUIN(x) & ~OSTRICH(x) => HAS-MODE-OF-TRANSPORT(x, FLYING)

The above translation, however, does not solve the problem because it does not permit the inference "Tweety flies" given that "Tweety is a bird" unless it is *explicitly* known that Tweety is neither a penguin nor an ostrich. Recall that our goal is to capture the intuition that an agent should be able to conclude "Tweety flies" in situations where all he knows about Tweety is that "Tweety is a bird".

The inability to encode and make use of default properties is a serious inadequacy because there is a preponderance of situations in which we associate a property with a class and use such information during property inheritance even though - strictly speaking, the property does not hold for all members of the class. Similarly, we often associate properties with a concept and use them to recognize instances of this

---

[8]Notice that in natural discourse we do say "Birds fly", even though what we actually mean is: "Most birds fly", or "Typically, birds fly".

concept, even though these properties are not unequivocally indicative of that concept.

2.4 Default properties lead to exceptions and multiple inheritance

Admitting default properties directly leads to two kinds of problematic situations that are referred to in the literature as cases of *exceptions* and *multiple inheritance*.

Exceptions

A property may apply to most members of a class A but it may not apply to most members of some subclass, B, of A. For example, while we may want to associate property P with concept A we may want to associate the property ~P with some offspring, B, of A. The situation concerning birds, penguins, and the ability to fly constitutes one such case of exceptions. So does the following example:

> Most Molluscs are shell-bearers.
> Cephalopods are Molluscs but most Cephalopods are not shell-bearers.
> Nautili are Molluscs but all Nautili are shell-bearers.

With reference to the nature of their outer covering, Cephalopods are exceptional with respect to Molluscs, while Nautili are exceptional with respect to Cephalopods.

Exceptions lead to non-monotonicity. Assume that an agent knows that "Molly is a Mollusc". It is likely that he would conclude that "Molly is a shell-bearer". If in *addition* to the above, he is now told that "Molly is a Cephalopod", he would probably *retract* his earlier conclusion - "Molly is a shell-bearer" - and conclude that "Molly is not a shell-bearer". Hence, non-monotonicity.

Multiple inheritance

Often there exist several alternate but equally useful ways of classifying objects in a domain. Consequently, it becomes more natural to organize concepts in the form of multiple hierarchies wherein a concept may have more than one parent, each belonging to a distinct hierarchy. This may lead to problems because the information inherited by a concept from its parents may be conflicting. For example, concept A may have two parents B and C, and while most B's may have the property P, most C's may have the property ~P. Such a situation is illustrated by the *quaker example*.

The agent may simultaneously believe that

Most Quakers are pacifists.	-- Q1
Most Republicans are non-pacifists.	-- Q2
Dick is a Quaker.	-- Q3
Dick is a Republican.	-- Q4

In this example, Dick has two parents in the conceptual hierarchy, one (Quaker) arose from classifying persons in terms of their religious beliefs, and the other (Republican) arose from classifying persons on the basis of their political beliefs. A translation into FOPC leads to inconsistency and renders the resulting theory unusable.

2.5 A closer look at exceptions and multiple inheritance

Exceptions and multiple inheritance are problematic because both involve dealing with conflicting information. The nature of conflict in these two cases, however, is quite different. This difference can be explicated if we view *IS-A* links as defining a *partial ordering*, <<, on concepts.

In the case of exceptions the concepts at which conflicting information is situated can be *totally ordered* under the partial ordering <<. Consequently, the conflict may be resolved by simply identifying the "nearest" (i.e the most relevant or most specific) concept and using the information available at it[9]. Thus in the case of exceptions the conflict can be resolved simply on the basis of the *location* of concepts in the conceptual hierarchy. Consider an example. Given that

---

[9]Notice that "nearness" or "distance" is being defined in terms of the partial ordering and NOT in terms of path lengths in a network.

Most Elephants are gray.   -- E1
Royal elephants are elephants.   -- E2
Most Royal elephants are not gray.   -- E3
Clyde is a Royal elephant.   -- E4

it is clear that with reference to "Clyde" the class "Royal elephant" is more specific than the class "Elephant" - both "Royal elephant" and "Elephant" are << "Clyde", but "Royal elephant" << "Elephant". Therefore, the information available at "Royal elephant" should take precedence over information available at "Elephant" and we should conclude that Clyde is probably not gray (because most "Royal elephants" are not gray).

Notice that the situation *does not change* even if the redundant assertion

      Clyde is an Elephant   -- E5

is added to the above set of assertions. The class "Royal elephant" continues to be more specific than "Elephant" and hence, Clyde continues to inherit its color value from "Royal elephant", superseding the information about "Elephant".

Multiple inheritance situations are more complex than exceptional situations. A multiple inheritance situation may arise if a concept A has two ancestors B and C such that, A << B and A << C, but neither B << C nor C << B. Multiple inheritance situations are clearly more complex because any conflict in the information available at concepts B and C *cannot be resolved on the basis of their location in the conceptual hierarchy.* Witness the Quaker example - there is no basis for claiming that the information available at "Quaker" is more relevant than the information available at "Republican" because neither "Quaker" << "Republican" nor "Republican" << "Quaker".

There are at least two distinct ways of dealing with multiple inheritance.

   i) Treat *all* multiple inheritance situations as cases of genuine *ambiguity* and therefore do not try to resolve the conflict but simply enumerate all the possible answers.

   ii) Extend the *expressive power* of the representation language to include *additional information* that may help in resolving such conflicts. A direct way of doing so would be to associate a "degree of belief" or "evidential strength" with default properties. If available, such information could be used to *prioritize* and *combine* default information to arrive at meaningful conclusions. To do so, however, requires that we provide a precise interpretation of what such evidential strengths mean and how do they interact.

Although the first approach may suffice in restricted situations it is inadequate for dealing with a broader range of situations in which a system is required to make *informed choices* based on available information. The first approach treats *all* cases of multiple inheritance as if they were truly ambiguous even though such may not be the case. Often we have additional information that enables us to make an informed choice. For example, an agent may believe that even though most Republicans are non-pacifists, one is quite likely to find a Republican with pacifist beliefs. The agent may also believe that relative to pacifist Republicans, non-pacifist Quakers are definitely uncommon. Given these beliefs the agent will probably prefer the conclusion "Dick is a pacifist" over the conclusion "Dick is a non-pacifist". An effective treatment of multiple inheritance should allow us to capture such distinctions between default properties - but to do so requires that we adopt the second approach.

We review below, two recent formalizations of inheritance: the Etherington and Reiter proposal based on default logic [Etherington and Reiter 83][Reiter 80] and the proposal by Touretzky [Touretzky 86] based on the *principle of inferential distance ordering*. These proposals deal with exceptions quite effectively, but they essentially adopt the first approach to the problem of multiple inheritance and treat all cases of multiple inheritance as cases of ambiguity. These proposals also do not deal with the problem of recognition.

Before we proceed we need to rule out a possible source of misunderstanding. Touretzky uses the term *multiple inheritance* very differently from the way it is used in this work. He defines multiple inheritance in terms of *paths* in the conceptual structure whereas we define it in terms of a partial ordering. Thus in Touretzky's formulation the assertions: A *IS-A* B, B *IS-A* C, and A *IS-A* C, lead to a multiple inheritance situation because A has a direct *path* to B as well as to C. According to our definition of multiple inheritance, however, the above assertions do not constitute a multiple inheritance situation because A, B, and C are *totally* ordered - A << B << C, and A has only one parent, B. (The assertion A *IS-A* C is redundant). The above situation may at most lead to a case of exception if the information at A, B, or C conflicts. As a second example consider the facts about elephants discussed earlier. In Touretzky's formulation, the assertions E1-E4 constitute a case of exceptions while the assertions E1-E5 constitute an example of multiple inheritance. In our formulation both E1-E4 and E1-E5 are examples of exceptions because in both these cases the ordering of the concepts "Elephant" and "Royal elephant" remains unchanged - "Royal elephant" << "Elephant".

It is important to recognize this difference because a solution to the problem of exceptions in our formulation subsumes solutions to the problems of exceptions as well as unambiguous cases of multiple inheritance in Touretzky's formalism. Additionally, when we say that we have solved the problem of multiple inheritance we mean that we have also solved what would be termed as ambiguous cases of multiple inheritance in Touretzky's formalism.

2.6 Semantic networks are equivalent to suitable theories of default logic.

Etherington and Reiter (henceforth E&R) formulate the problem of exceptions in terms of default logic. This involves encoding exceptional information using default rules. Under the E&R proposal, assertions E1-E5 would be translated as

$$\frac{ELEPHANT(x) : GRAY(x) \ \& \ \sim ROYAL\text{-}ELEPHANT(x)}{GRAY(x)} \qquad \text{-- dr-1}$$

$$\frac{ROYAL\text{-}ELEPHANT(x) : \sim GRAY(x)}{\sim GRAY(x)} \qquad \text{-- dr-2}$$

$$\forall(x) \ ROYAL\text{-}ELEPHANT(x) => ELEPHANT(x) \qquad \text{-- A1}$$

$$ROYAL\text{-}ELEPHANT(CLYDE) \qquad \text{-- A2}$$

$$ELEPHANT(CLYDE) \qquad \text{-- A3}$$

While E2, E4, and E5 translate into first order assertions A1, A2, and A3 respectively, E1 and E3 map to *default rules* dr-1 and dr-2. In a default rule, the formula to the left of the colon is called the *prerequisite* of the default, the formula to the right of the colon is called the *justification*, while the formula in the "denominator" is called the *consequent*. A default rule has the following interpretation: if the prerequisite is known to be true, and if the justification is consistent with what is known, then one may infer the consequent. In default logic, the set of conclusions that can be drawn starting with a set, W, of first-order assertions and a set, D, of default rules is called an an *extension*. Such an extension includes W and is closed under the defaults of D as well as first-order theoremhood. Informally, we can view an extension as a maximal set of consistent conclusions that can be drawn from the given facts and default rules.

It is easy to see that given the above encoding, one can infer "~GRAY(Clyde)" and one cannot infer "GRAY(CLYDE)". Moreover, the conclusions do not change even if we exclude E5 (i.e., A3) from the initial set of assertions. One can also verify that adding the assertion "ELEPHANT(FRED)" would lead to the inference "GRAY(FRED)" (but we will not be able to infer "~GRAY(FRED)"). Similarly, adding the assertion "ROYAL-ELEPHANT(PINTO)" would lead to the inference "~GRAY(PINTO)" (but we will not be able to infer "GRAY(PINTO)"). This is exactly the kind of behavior we would like to achieve when dealing with exceptions and indeed, the E&R proposal provides a way of formalizing such behavior.

The E&R characterization of inheritance, however, suffers from a few drawbacks. First, the formalization does not exploit the natural information *implicit* in the ordering imposed by the *IS-A* hierarchy. Notice how we had to *explicitly* encode that ROYAL-ELEPHANT constitutes an exception in the default rule dr-1 in spite of the fact that this information is already implicit in the information encoded in dr-2 and A1 - if Royal elephants are a subclass of Elephants and if Royal elephants are not gray while Elephants are, then it follows that Royal elephants are exceptional with respect to Elephants in the context of grayness. This aspect of the E&R formalization is unfortunate because by requiring that all the exceptions be listed explicitly the proposal fails to capture what is arguably the most significant property of inheritance hierarchies: the hierarchical organization of information in itself leads to effective inference. In the elephant example, if we were to modify dr-1 to read

$$\frac{\text{ELEPHANT}(x) : \text{GRAY}(x)}{\text{GRAY}(x)} \qquad \text{-- dr-1}$$

and leave the rest unchanged, the system would yield two extensions, one of these will contain "GRAY(CLYDE)" the other would include "~GRAY(CLYDE)" and it would be left to some external process to make a choice. This aspect of the proposal leads to another disadvantage in that one may have to rewrite many existing default rules whenever a new class is defined so as to reflect any exceptions that might have been introduced. As discussed below, Touretzky's proposal overcomes this limitation.

The second shortcoming of the E&R proposal is that it treats all cases of multiple inheritance as if they were truly ambiguous. Earlier we stated that such an approach is inadequate, and now we substantiate this with the help of the Quaker example. Let us examine how a system based on the E&R proposal would draw conclusions about Dick's pacifism - or the lack of it - on the basis of the information given by Q1 through Q4 (refer to the Quaker example). In default logic, Q1 through Q4 would be represented as shown below:

$$\frac{\text{QUAKER}(x) : \text{PACIFIST}(x)}{\text{PACIFIST}(x)} \qquad \text{-- dr-3}$$

$$\frac{\text{REPUBLICAN}(x) : \text{NON-PACIFIST}(x)}{\text{NON-PACIFIST}(x)} \qquad \text{-- dr-4}$$

$$\text{QUAKER(DICK)} \qquad \text{-- A4}$$

$$\text{REPUBLICAN(DICK)} \qquad \text{-- A5}$$

$$\forall (x) \text{ PACIFIST}(x) <=> \text{~NON-PACIFIST}(x) \qquad \text{-- A6}$$

Q1 and Q2 map to default rules dr-3 and dr-4 respectively, while Q3 and Q4 translate into simple first-order assertions given by A4 and A5. The knowledge encoded in *dr-3*, *dr-4*, A4, A5, and A6 leads to two extensions. One of the extensions includes PACIFIST(DICK), while the other includes NON-PACIFIST(DICK). Default logic prescribes that "any one of these extensions may be interpreted as an acceptable set of beliefs about the world", and hence, a system based on the E&R proposal would arbitrarily choose between one of these extensions and respond with an answer that lies in the chosen extension. The choice of extension would depend on which of the two default rules is selected first by the inference algorithm. For example, if the default rule *dr-4* happens to be selected first, the system would infer that "Dick is a non-pacifist". Once this inference is made, *dr-3* would no longer be justifiable with reference to Dick and hence would not play any role in drawing conclusions about Dick. The case where *dr-3* happens to be selected first is exactly analogous. In either case, the conclusions drawn would depend on only *one* of the two rules and in turn, on an *ad hoc* order of rule application[10].

Our intuitions about the knowledge in the Quaker example, however, suggest that in drawing conclusions about Dick, both the statements - "Most Quakers are pacifists", and "Most Republicans are non-pacifists" - are *relevant* and hence, both must *affect* the final conclusion. In general, the *final conclusion should reflect the combined effect of all the relevant information*. But given that default logic makes the implicit assumption that all default rules have the same "significance" or "import", it follows that if two or more rules have conflicting consequences then either the use of one rule should preclude the use of the other rules (as was the case in the Quaker example), or no conclusions should be drawn based on these rules (see [Reiter & Crisculo 81]).

The problem is rooted in the assumption that all default rules have the same import, an assumption that may be inappropriate in many situations. As discussed above, an agent may believe that the tendency of Quakers to be pacifists outweighs the tendency of Republicans to be non-pacifists. In this case it may be appropriate to infer that Dick is probably a pacifist. The need to combine relevant information and

---

[10]In default logic, the order of rule application would be considered an *implementation* issue, and hence, outside the scope of the logic.

weigh the relative import of available information becomes even more apparent if we consider the following: suppose we add to the agent's beliefs that "Dick took part in anti-war demonstrations". Now it seems even more appropriate to infer that Dick is probably a pacifist.

In order to deal with situations that involve conflicting information it is necessary to adopt an epistemologically richer representation that allows one to represent the relative import of rules. It is argued in section 2.8 that an evidential approach offers a possible solution.

It may be argued that in order to handle interactions between default rules one could just enumerate all the possible cases of interactions and specify the correct inferences that need be drawn in each case. But having a formal calculus for *computing* the effects of interactions between default rules in a *justifiable manner* is far more desirable than having to explicitly list the outcome of every possible interaction. Furthermore, knowledge acquisition would be problematic in a scheme that handles interactions between defaults by explicit enumeration of cases because adding new knowledge will require extensive modifications of existing default rules.

2.7 Touretzky's inferential distance ordering

Touretzky's work has its basis in earlier work by Fahlman on a parallel knowledge representation system called NETL [Fahlman 79]. NETL was probably the first representation language that explicitly dealt with property inheritance and recognition. Fahlman was also one of the first to stress the importance of looking for computationally effective solutions to problems in knowledge representation. NETL, however, lacked a precise semantics and its behavior was defined in terms of the behavior of a network. The source of this problem was the use of CANCEL links that were proposed to handle exceptions. For example, using the CANCEL link one could say: A *IS-A* B and B *IS-A* C, and at the same time have a CANCEL link from A to C. This CANCEL link was supposed to imply that A's are not C's. As can be expected, this leads to serious semantic difficulties: how can A's be B's and B's be

C's and yet A's not be C's? (Also refer to [Fahlman et al. 81][Etherington & Reiter 83] and [Brachman 85].) The behavior of NETL became even more questionable in the presence of multiple hierarchies; in such situations, the answers provided by the network depended on the outcome of race conditions in the parallel network. Finally, though NETL addressed the issue of recognition, it could not deal with "best match" or "partial match" situations because in NETL recognition amounted to finding a concept that possessed *all* of a specified set of properties.

Touretzky's proposal is a clear improvement over NETL as well as the E&R proposal. It provides a precise specification of what inferences should be drawn by an inheritance hierarchy in situations involving exceptions and at the same time it makes use of the information implicit in the hierarchical ordering of concepts. Touretzky's proposal may be summarized by quoting what he calls the principle of *inferential distance ordering* (PIDO). The principle states that: if A inherits P from B, and ~P from C, then "if A has an inheritance path via B to C and not vice versa, then conclude P; if A has an inheritance path via C to B and not vice versa, then conclude ~P; otherwise report an ambiguity" ([Touretzky 86]). PIDO defines distance (or nearness) in exactly the same way as would a partial ordering, and specifies that the most specific (nearest) answer be selected. This is exactly the solution to the problem of exceptions discussed in section 2.5. As would be expected, PIDO leads to a clean solution to the the problem of exceptions[11]. PIDO, however, only uses the *location* of concepts in the partial ordering to decide which piece of information is relevant and treats *all* information at the same inferential distance as having the same import. Consequently, under PIDO all multiple inheritance situations are treated as cases of genuine ambiguity and a system based on PIDO would report ambiguity in all such cases. For instance, such a system would report an ambiguity in the Quaker example. Thus Touretzky's formalization suffers from the same shortcoming as the E&R proposal in that it cannot combine conflicting information from disparate

---

[11]Although Touretzky's solution to inheritance is precisely specified and produces desired results, it uses *IS-NOT-A* links which also lead to semantically problematic situations such as those that arise from the use of CANCEL links. For example, in Touretzky's formalism one can say: A *IS-A* B, B *IS-A* C, and at the same time say: A *IS-NOT-A* C.

sources to arrive at the most plausible or likely interpretation. Furthermore, Touretzky's formulation does not address the problem of recognition.

2.8 Evidential nature of knowledge in semantic networks

It was pointed out in section 2.3 that often we associate a property with a concept even though the property may not hold for all members of the concept. Similarly, many of the properties that we use in recognizing instances of a concept are not unequivocally indicative of the concept.

Given that default properties cannot support *deductions* about objects and their properties, one may ask why an agent should maintain such information? The heuristic value of such information is quite evident. When dealing with the environment, an agent has to recognize objects and predict their properties based on whatever information is *available* at hand. Often the available information is insufficient to *deduce* the object's category or its property. But if the agent *has to* make a decision he must try and make the best use of available information and guess the object's *most likely* category or properties. From this it follows that a good strategy for the agent would be to record generalizations that suggest how *readily available* information may be exploited to guess the most likely category and properties of objects[12]. In the long run it would pay to use such generalizations to jump to conclusions of the sort: "Tweety flies because Tweety is a bird" - even though all birds do not fly, or to conclude that the person walking down the hallway is "Jack" - even though there is a distinct possibility that the person may just be a look-alike. It is obvious that some of the recognitions and predictions based on heuristic information will turn out to be wrong, *but this is a small price to pay for being most often right, especially when the alternative is inaction.*

Having admitted information of the kind "birds fly" or "Quakers are pacifists", we still need to specify a principled way of expressing and utilizing this information. One

---

[12]The weak generalizations mentioned above correspond to what are referred to as *identification procedures* by Smith and Medin [Smith & Medin 81].

possibility is to treat assertions such as "birds fly" as *evidential assertions*. Thus "birds fly" may be interpreted to mean that if "x is a bird" then there is some evidence α that "x flies", and also that "if x flies" then there is some evidence β that "x is a bird". In the general case, if we are told that an object is flying then we would have varying degrees of evidence that it is a bird, an airplane, a frisbee .... . Similarly, if we are told that an object is a bird, then we would have varying degrees of evidence that its preferred mode of transportation is flying, swimming, walking, etc.

2.9 An overview of the evidential formulation.

Within an evidential formulation, finding solutions to inheritance and recognition problems would amount to choosing the most likely alternative from among a set of alternatives; the computation of likelihood being carried out with respect to the knowledge encoded in the conceptual hierarchy. For example, an inheritance problem would not be posed as

"What is the mode of transportation of Tweety"

but rather as

"On the basis of available information, is the mode of transportation of Tweety most likely to be running, swimming, or flying".

In general, the evidential mode of reasoning may be viewed as *decision making* that involves *choosing* from among a set of mutually exclusive hypotheses. The important steps are:

i) combining evidence provided by relevant evidential assertions

ii) computing the likelihood of competing hypotheses based on the above, and

iii) *choosing* the most likely hypothesis.

The notion of likelihood is made more precise below:

Let $a_1, a_2, ... a_n$ be the n competing hypotheses and let K be the agent's knowledge. With each alternative, a_i, associate a measure of likelihood, l_i, given by the ratio of the number of interpretations of the world that are consistent with K and that also satisfy a_i, to the the number of interpretations of the world that are consistent with K. Thus an interpretation a_i is more likely than a_j if, and only if, from among the interpretations of the world that satisfy K, a greater fraction of interpretations satisfy a_i than a_j. Furthermore, the most likely hypothesis is the one that is consistent with the greatest fraction of interpretations that satisfy K.

What is significant about the evidential model of reasoning is that a conclusion is justified not on the grounds that it is true in *all* possible worlds that are consistent with the agent's knowledge (as is the case in deduction), but rather on the grounds that if we consider all the possible worlds that are consistent with the agent's knowledge, then there are "more" possible worlds in which the conclusion is true, than there are those in which *any one* of the competing conclusions is true.

At this point, two observations are pertinent:

- The evidential formulation does not suggest that all decisions should be based solely on the likelihoods of possible outcomes, the most likely outcome always being preferred. In many situations the agent may want to take into account the *utilities* of various outcomes, i.e., evaluate the cost and benefit of choosing a particular action. Then again, he may choose to take risks or be conservative, or he may adopt some other strategy. The contention is that any strategy (unless it simply involves making random choices) will perforce require the knowledge of, or at least an estimate of, the likelihoods of the possible outcomes.

- The evidential approach subsumes the deductive case. If only one of the hypotheses is provable and hence, the rest are provably false, then only the provable hypothesis will receive any evidence; all other hypotheses will receive zero evidence. This is exactly analogous to the result that would be obtained from applying deduction.

In order to accommodate evidential information we will extend the traditional semantic network representation to include evidential information in the form of certain *relative frequencies*. Chapters 3 and 4 describe exactly which relative frequencies are stored and how these are used in computing solutions to the inheritance and recognition problems. For now let us look at two examples that illustrate how such information may be used during inheritance.

The penguin example

Let us assume that an agent's knowledge consists of the beliefs that 80% of all birds fly, penguins and robins are subtypes of birds, and while none (0%) of the penguins fly, 95% of the robins do. Let us posit that there is a property has-mode-of-transport, one of whose values is FLY. For convenience let us gather all other values into a single value ~FLY.

Assume that the agent is told that "Tweety is a bird", and asked "does Tweety fly?" As the agent does not know whether Tweety can fly or not, he considers all possible configurations of the world that are consistent with his knowledge and computes the ratio of the number of feasible configurations in which Tweety can fly, to the number of feasible configurations in which Tweety cannot fly. As Tweety can be *any* bird (it can *even* be a penguin, a robin, and if there were any other subtypes such as ravens and ostriches, it could also be any one of these), the relevant ratio turns out to be 80 : 20 (i.e., 4 : 1). This suggests that it is four times more likely that Tweety flies than that Tweety does not fly. Hence if the agent *has to* make a choice he should choose "Tweety flies".

There are three points that need to be made here:

1. The agent is not certain that Tweety flies. He only believes that it is *more likely* that Tweety flies.
2. The above does not imply any fuzziness about birds that fly or about Tweety. It is not as if Tweety is a 0.8 flier and a 0.2 non-flier. Tweety either flies or it does not; it is only the likelihood of Tweety being either of these that is 4 : 1.
3. It is *not necessary to assume* that Tweety is *not a penguin*. The agent would have arrived at the same answer even if he had reasoned by cases: considering Tweety to be a penguin or not a penguin ... etc.

Now consider another situation. The agent has the same information as before about birds and penguins but this time he is told that Tweety is a penguin. (It does not matter whether he is told that Tweety is a bird, for it follows from the fact that

Tweety is a penguin and all penguins are birds.) Given that 0% penguins fly and 100% don't, the ratio of the number of feasible configurations of the world in which Tweety can fly, to the number of feasible configurations in which Tweety cannot fly is 0 : 100, i.e., 0 : 1. This result tells the agents that it is *impossible* that Tweety flies, and therefore, he will infer that "Tweety does not fly".

Using the same line of reasoning, one can see what will happen if the agent is told that "Tweety is a Robin". He will choose "Tweety flies"; the ratio being 95 : 5, i.e., 19 : 1. The agent's response is the same as it was when he was told that "Tweety is a bird", but this time he will be much more confident about his choice.

The above example demonstrates that in each of the three situations evidential reasoning gives a crisp meaning to what a rational agent should believe about Tweety. The likelihood of Tweety being a flier, or not being one, changed in each of the three cases because the agent had different information about Tweety. Each of these conclusions, however, were *mutually consistent* and were based on the same body of a priori knowledge. In each case the evidential framework offered a model-theoretic justification of the conclusions that were drawn because the choices made by the agent could be *justified* in terms of his beliefs about the possible configurations of the world. Notice that this was achieved without introducing "cancel" links, without *arbitrarily* selecting one of many extensions, and without introducing notions of non-monotonicity or fuzzy truth values.

The Quaker example

The Quaker example presents a multiple inheritance situation in which two conflicting pieces of evidence have to be resolved in order to arrive at a conclusion. As stated above, the evidential approach employs an extended representation that includes information about relative frequencies. Let us assume that underlying the agent's beliefs that

> "Most Quakers are pacifists" and
> "Most Republicans are non-pacifists",

is the following information:

> 70% of all Quakers are pacifists while 30% are non-pacifists, and 80% of all Republicans are non-pacifists while 20% are pacifists. In addition to the above, let us assume that in the agent's conceptual representation, "Person" is a superconcept of "Quaker" and "Republican", and the agent believes that 5% of all persons are Quakers, 40% of all persons are Republicans, 70% of all persons are non-pacifists, while 30% are pacifists[13].

> Let us also assume that the agent's conceptual representation includes a property (i.e., attribute) "has-belief" which is attached to the concept "Person". This property signifies that persons have the property that they "hold beliefs", some of the values of this property being "pacifist" and "non-pacifist".

Notice that the agent does not know what fraction of people, who are both Republicans and Quakers (Republican-Quakers for convenience), profess pacifism, and what fraction believe in non-pacifism. If this information were available, the issue of Dick's pacifism could have been resolved with ease: Dick is an instance of the class Republican-Quaker, and if more people in this class are pacifists then it is more likely that Dick is a pacifist, otherwise it is more likely that Dick is a non-pacifist. Thus the key problem is to use the available information to arrive at the most likely estimates of the fraction of Republican-Quakers that are pacifists and the fraction that are non-pacifists.

By following an approach outlined in chapter 4 it can be shown that it is possible to compute the most likely estimate of the fraction

$$\frac{\text{The number of Republican-Quakers who are pacifists}}{\text{The number of Republican-Quakers who are non-pacifists}}$$

As the agent only needs to compare the fraction of Republican-Quakers who are pacifists with the fraction of Republican-Quakers who are non-pacifist in order to determine the likelihood of Dick being a pacifist or a non-pacifist, the above information is sufficient to resolve the issue of Dick's pacifism. In particular, if the above ratio is greater than 1.0 then it follows that a Republican-Quaker, and hence,

---

[13]The set of relative frequencies assumed to be known to the agent may seem arbitrary at first glance, but this is not the case. There is a natural interpretation of what is known and what is not known. This is made precise in chapter 3 which discusses the representation language.

Dick, is more likely to be a pacifist than a non-pacifist. By a similar argument, if the ratio is less than 1.0 then Dick is more likely to be a non-pacifist.

The method for computing the estimates of unknown relative frequencies is based on the principle of maximum entropy, and can be summarized as follows: if the agent does not know a relative frequency, he may estimate it by ascertaining the *most likely state of the world* that is consistent with his knowledge, and use the frequency that holds in that world. By following this approach it can be shown that, with reference to the agent's knowledge in the Quaker example, the *most likely state of the world* is one in which 60% of all Republican-Quakers are pacifists and 40% are non-pacifists. Hence a rational agent would infer that Dick is more likely to be a pacifist. Of course, a different set of underlying beliefs would lead to a different conclusion.

The Quaker example shows how the evidential approach handles multiple inheritance situations involving conflicting information. The precise rules for handling exceptions and more general cases of multiple inheritance that involve combining information available at multiple concepts situated at different levels in the conceptual hierarchy are described in chapter 4.

3   Representation Language

The proposed evidential representation language lies between two extremes characterized by

| Traditional semantic networks with no probabilistic information. | ------------------> ------------------> ------------------> | Representations that encode all conjunctive conditional probabilities. |

In addition to supporting the specification of *necessary* properties, the language also allows one to associate *default* or *evidential* properties with concepts. This evidential information is encoded in terms of *relative frequencies* that specify how instances of certain concepts are distributed with respect to certain property values. Even such a limited amount of evidential information leads to a principled treatment of exceptions, multiple inheritance, and conflicting information during inheritance, and best-matches or partial-matches during recognition.   In certain respects, the representation language may be viewed as an evidential extension of a frame-based language such as KL-ONE. In some other respects, however, the language is more restricted than KL-ONE - for instance, it does not support structural dependency relations.   Before describing the language, let us briefly consider the underlying intuitions.

3.1 Structure of knowledge

A cognitive agent interprets the external world in terms of **conceptual attributes** and their associated **values**, and his factual knowledge is represented using these attributes and values.   In addition to the conceptual attributes such as "has-color" (with values: red, blue, purple, etc.), "has-texture", and "has-odor", knowledge structuring relations such as *IS-A* and *PART-OF* are also considered to be conceptual attributes (henceforth, simply attributes).

An [attribute, value] pair in our formulation corresponds to a "feature" in many psychological models. Thus what we refer to as [has-color, RED] would correspond to the feature RED in a feature-based model.

Attributes need not be unstructured entities, for instance, "has-color" may be defined in terms of "sub-attributes" such as "has-hue", "has-brightness", and "has-saturation". In the restricted representation language described here, it is assumed that all attributes are primitive.

Concepts are *labelled* collections of [attribute, value] pairs. For instance, a concept labelled FIDO may partially consist of the following [attribute, value] pairs:

> { [*IS-A*, DOG],   [*IS-A*, ANIMAL],
>   [has-coat-type, FURRY],   [has-body-part, TAIL],
>   [has-color, BROWN]   ...   }

The values of attributes are also concepts, and hence, concepts may be arbitrarily complex. This definition does not imply circularity because some concepts are grounded in perception while some others are assumed to be innate.

Attributes may be classified into two broad categories: **properties** and **structural links**.

Structural links provide the coupling between structure and inference. They reflect the epistemological belief that world knowledge is highly organized and that much of this structure can be factored out to provide general *domain independent* organizational strategies that in turn lead to efficient inference. Each structural link embodies one such organizational strategy. If we map knowledge onto a data structure (or a physical device) so that structural links get represented *explicitly* as arcs in the data structure (or interconnections in the physical device), then these arcs (or interconnections) provide hard-wired, and hence, efficient *inference paths*. The most representative structural link is the *IS-A* link[14] that is used for inheritance in

---

[14]Recall that we are using *IS-A* both in the sense of *is-a-subtype-of* - as in DOG *IS-A* MAMMAL, and in the sense of *is-an-instance-of* - as in FIDO *IS-A* DOG.

semantic networks. One can extend the notion of inheritance to include other structural links such as the *is-a-part-of*, and *occurs-during* links [Schubert et al. 83][Allen 83]. For example, *is-a-part-of* links may be used to infer values of attributes such as has-location, while *occurs-during* links may permit inferences pertaining to time. The work described here, however, only deals with IS-A links, but may be extended to include other structural links as well.

Properties relate to the intrinsic features of concepts and may vary from one domain to another. They correspond to the notion of "roles" in KL-ONE, "role nodes" in NETL and "slots" in FRL. But the interpretation of a property and its associated values is different from any of the above approaches because of the evidential information associated with property values.

We stated that a concept is a labelled collection of [attribute, value] pairs. As it stands, this statement is too undiscriminating and does not indicate which collections of [attribute, value] pairs ought to be labelled a concept. To answer this question we re-examine the notion of concepts.

Concepts may be classified into **Tokens** and **Types**.

An agent interprets the world as consisting of *instances*, and collections of [attribute, value] pairs that are perceived to correspond to an instance are represented as Tokens in the agent's conceptual structure.

In order to deal with a complex environment an agent must impose some structure on the external world. A way of achieving this is to record similarities between objects and to make suitable generalizations based on these. Once recorded these generalizations may be exploited to categorize novel objects and to make predictions about their properties. Types serve exactly this purpose. Types are *abstractions* defined over Tokens that capture *useful* generalizations about a number of Tokens. These generalizations are represented by appropriate [attribute, value] pairs. For example, the Type ELEPHANT may include the *value* GRAY for the property has-color to indicate that: "most elephants are gray", while the Type APPLE may include the values RED, GREEN, and YELLOW to indicate that: "apples may be red, green or yellow"[15].

Simply *associating* property values with Types, however, does not suffice. The agent may want to make finer distinctions such as: "An apple is more likely to be red than green" and "a red colored object is more likely to be an apple than a rose", and use such information to recognize things and predict their properties. One way of capturing these distinctions would be to store frequency distributions of concepts with respect to *certain* property values. Thus, instead of "Apples are red, green or yellow", an agent's conceptual representation may hold: "60% of all apples are red, 30% are green, and 10% are yellow". In this thesis we will pursue this possibility in depth. We will assume that all *evidential* relationships between concepts and their attribute values - in particular, the strength of such relationships - are derived from certain frequency distributions. This approach involves an obvious oversimplification, for clearly, there are situations in which an agent may have to encode an evidential relationship between a concept and an attribute value without the knowledge of any frequency distributions. Consider a situation in which an agent is told: "Most Quakers are pacifists". This statement certainly has an evidential import but it does not indicate what fraction of Quakers are pacifists? So how should the agent establish the strength of the evidential relationship between "Quakers" and "pacifism"? This is an extremely important problem and I intend to address it in future research. For now let us pursue a simpler approach - wherein we assume that the agent determines evidential strengths solely on the basis of its knowledge of certain frequency distributions of concepts with respect to their property values - and investigate how such information may be used to reformulate the inheritance and recognition problems in order to deal with conflicting and partial information.

The process of abstraction and differentiation applied to Types leads to a **hierarchical structure**. In general, *multiple* hierarchies may be defined over the

---

[15]This and other descriptive statements made in this thesis are meant to be illustrative and do not make claims about the exact nature of the real world.

same set of Tokens. For example, one may define a hierarchy over physical objects based on the function they perform and at the same time one may classify such objects according to their form (i.e., their appearance). The consequence of having multiple hierarchies is that a concept may have multiple ancestors in the conceptual structure.

3.2 Concepts and attribute values

An agent could represent the fact that certain objects are red in color by positing a concept RED-THING - which is completely described by { [has-color, RED] } - and making all red objects an instance of this concept. Alternately, he could just associate the [property, value] pair [has-color, RED] with concepts that represent red colored objects. The choice of designating any [property, value] pair(s) to be a concept is always available to an agent, but doing so involves a clear-cut trade-off: on the one hand, it requires a commitment of additional computational resources such as nodes, links, processing elements etc., but on the other hand, it makes it easier to draw certain inferences. For example, introducing the concept RED-THING would make it easier to record and retrieve general facts about red objects but embedding this concept in the conceptual structure would require additional links and nodes.

In the proposed representation the concepts RED and RED-THING may co-exist. If the concept RED is the value of the property has-color and the concept RED-THING is the concept { [has-color, RED]} then it is interesting to determine the relationship between these two concepts. If we seek a purely extensional interpretation then these two concepts refer to the same set of objects - the red objects in the domain. If, however, we seek an intensional interpretation then these two concepts are quite different. While RED-THING connotes all objects - real, imaginary, or dreamed of - that can be projected by the agent as being red in color, RED refers to the perceptual and projected memory of *redness* itself. While RED-THING records information about *things* red, RED records information about *red*.

3.3 A formal description of the representation language

Formally, an agent's a priori knowledge consists of the septuple

$$\Theta = \langle C, \Phi, \lambda, \Lambda, \#, \delta, << \rangle$$

where **C** is the set of *concepts*, Φ is the set of *properties*, λ is a mapping from **C** to the power set of Φ, Λ is a mapping from Φ to the power set of **C**, # is a mapping from **C** to the integers I, δ the *distribution* function is a mapping from **C** X Φ to the power set of **C** X I, and << is a partial ordering defined on **C**. The terms concepts and properties have already been described in the previous section, the remaining terms are discussed below.

For each C $\in$ **C**, λ(C) is the subset of Φ that consists of properties that are applicable to C. For example, λ(APPLE) may be {has-color, has-taste, has-shape}. λ captures the notion that different properties apply to different sorts of concepts.

For each P $\in$ Φ, Λ(P) is the subset of **C** that consists of all possible values of P. For example, Λ(has-color) may be {RED, GREEN, BLUE, YELLOW, BROWN}

For each C $\in$ **C**, if C is a Token then #C = 1, and if C is a Type then #C = the number of instances of C *observed by the agent.*

Recall that values are also concepts. If the only role played by a concept V is that it is a value of a specific property P, then #V is defined to be equal to the number of instances that possess this value. Thus #RED equals the number of red colored entities in the domain. The # assignment for a concept that is a value of more than one property is more involved. It is posited that such a concept has multiple *facets* - one for each property that it is a value of - and the # mapping assigns the appropriate integer to each of these facets. In general, if we restrict ourselves to simple perceptual properties such as has-color, has-taste, has-texture etc., then values of these properties belong to disjoint classes and these values are assigned a single integer by the # mapping.

The number mapping may be extended so that

$\#C[P_1,V_1][P_2,V_2] \ldots [P_n,V_n] =$
the number of instances of C observed to have the values V_1 for property P_1, V_2 for property P_2, ... and V_n for property P_n.

Thus #APPLE[has-color, RED] equals the number of red colored apples observed by the agent, while #APPLE[has-color, RED][has-taste, SWEET] refers to the number of red and sweet apples observed by the agent.

The distribution function $\delta(C,P)$, where $C \in \mathbf{C}$ and $P \in \lambda(C)$, specifies how instances of C are distributed with respect to the values of property P. Recall that a concept may have several values for the same property and hence, if C is a Type, then $\delta(C,P)$ corresponds to the summary information abstracted in C based on the observed instances of C. For example, if $\lambda(P) = \{$RED, GREEN$\}$ then, $\delta($APPLE, has-color$)$ may be expressed as:

{(RED 60), (GREEN 40)}

indicating that 60 apples are red and 40 are green. Alternately, $\delta(C,P)$ may be expressed in terms of #C[P,V]'s. Thus $\delta($APPLE, has-color$)$ may also be expressed as:

{ #APPLE[has-color, RED] = 60, #APPLE[has-color, GREEN] = 40}

The relation << structures the concepts in **C** into a partially ordered set and corresponds to the *IS-A* relation. In this formulation, << relates Types to other Types as well as to Tokens.

It is assumed that the applicability of properties is such that once associated with a concept, a property is applicable to all concepts that lie below in the conceptual hierarchy. In other words, if $P \in \lambda(A)$, then for all B such that B << A, $P \in \lambda(B)$. Notice that the above statement refers to properties and not to property values.

The ordering induced by << on **C** may be compactly represented in the form of an

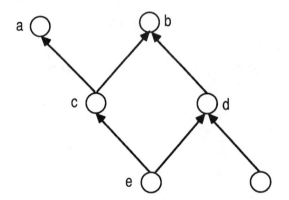

The partial ordering is:
{(c,a) (e,a) (c,b) (d,b)
(e,b) (f,b) (e,c) (e,d) (f,d)}

The directed graph on the left is the ordering graph for the
partial ordering defined on the right.

Figure 3.1: Ordering graph

ordering graph. Figure 3.1 depicts an ordering graph for a specified <<. Each node in the graph denotes a concept. A directed link connects a_i to every node a_j, $(a_i \neq a_j)$ such that $a_i << a_j$ and there exists no a_k - other than a_i and a_j - such that $a_i << a_k << a_j$. If there is a direct link from a_i to a_j then a_j is referred to as a *parent* of a_i.

Given a set of concepts S, where S = {s_1 s_2 ... s_n}, the *lowest common ancestor* of S, i.e., the *join* of S, is referred to as the **reference concept** for S. For instance, in figure 3.1, b is the reference concept for {c e f}.

An Example

An agent's knowledge about a hypothetical domain may comprise of (refer to figure 3.2):

C = {FRUIT, APPLE, GRAPE, A-5, A-9, G-8, COLOR, RED, GREEN, TASTE, SWEET, SOUR}

Φ = {has-taste, has-color}

λ(FRUIT), λ(APPLE), λ(GRAPE), λ(A-5), λ(A-9), λ(G-8) = {has-taste, has-color}

λ(COLOR), λ(TASTE), λ(RED), λ(GREEN), λ(SWEET), λ(SOUR) = φ

Λ(has-color) = {RED, GREEN}; Λ(has-taste) = {SWEET, SOUR}

#FRUIT = 150
    δ(FRUIT, has-color) = {(RED 65), (GREEN 85)}
    δ(FRUIT, has-taste) = {(SWEET 100), (SOUR 50)}
#APPLE = 100
    δ(APPLE, has-color) = {(RED 60), (GREEN 40)}
#GRAPE = 50
    δ(GRAPE, has-taste) = {(SWEET 30), (SOUR 20)}
#COLOR = 150; #RED = 65, #GREEN = 85; #TASTE = 150; #SWEET = 100; #SOUR = 50;

<< is given by:
    (APPLE << FRUIT), (GRAPE << FRUIT), (A-5 << APPLE),
    (A-9 << APPLE), (G-8 << GRAPE), (RED << COLOR),
    (GREEN << COLOR), (SWEET << TASTE), (SOUR << TASTE)

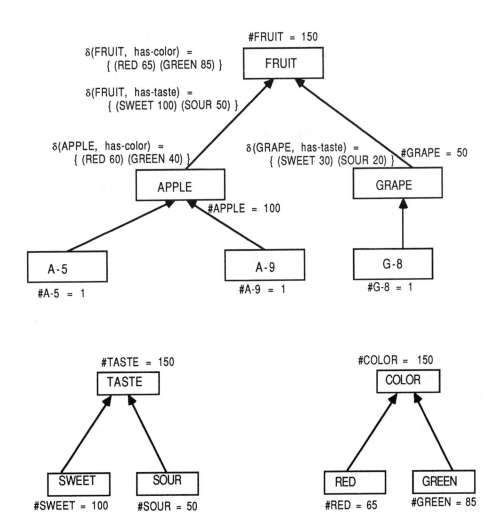

Figure 3.2: An example domain

3.4 Some salient features of the representation language

Selective (partial) nature of knowledge: Notice that the agent's knowledge is partial with respect to his experience; he *does not store all the information that he observes*. Although the agent has observed 100 apples and 50 grapes, only 2 apples and 1 grape are stored explicitly. The agent's knowledge of the distribution mapping δ is also *partial*. Specifically, the agent may not know (i.e., record) $\delta(C,P)$ even though P may belong to $\lambda(C)$. In the above example, the agent remembers $\delta(APPLE, has\text{-}color)$ but does not remember $\delta(APPLE, has\text{-}taste)$. This may happen either because this information is not significant to the agent, or because it may be inferred (inherited) from some other information recorded by him.

Probabilistic as well as exemplar representation: The language supports a *probabilistic* as well as an *exemplar* based description of concepts: $\delta(C,P)$'s encode probabilistic information about concepts whereas Tokens encode exemplars of their parent concepts. In the above example, $\delta(APPLE, has\text{-}color)$ encodes summary probabilistic information about apples, while A-5 and A-9 encode two exemplars of apples.

Associating properties as well as property values to concepts: The framework permits associating properties as well as property values with concepts and it is possible to specify the properties that apply to a concept without specifying any values. Once a property is associated with a Type it becomes associated with all Types or Tokens that occur below the Type in the concept hierarchy.

Multiple and default property values: For a concept C and a property P, $\delta(C,P)$ may specify *multiple* values for P, and additionally, the specification of $\delta(C,P)$ involves stating the quantities #C[P,V] for each $V \in \Lambda(P)$. This allows one to specify multiple values for the same property together with information that indicates the relative likelihood of occurrence of these values. In the example above, the agent believes that apples may be red or green in color, but the relative likelihood of an apple being red (as against green) is 3:2.

Only property values may be exceptional, but not *IS-A* **links:** A concept is either an instance of (or subtype of) another concept or it is not; the << relation specifies this unequivocally. The notion of exceptions applies only to property values, and even here exceptions do not entail "cancellation" or "blocking" of properties. This leads to a clear semantics of conceptual taxonomies. Problems arising from allowing exceptions to *IS-A* links are discussed in [Brachman 85].

Necessary properties are a special case of default ones: The evidential representation of property values suggested here subsumes the non-evidential case. It has been pointed out that properties correspond to roles or slots. Consequently, δ may be taken as a specification of role values or slot fillers in a frame based language with the distinction that the specification of $\delta(C,P)$ also includes the quantities $\#C[P,V]$ for each $V \in \Lambda(P)$. But if the domain is extremely well behaved and generalizations such as

$\forall\, x\, C(x) => P(x,V_1)$
{i.e. all instances of C have the value V_1 for property P.}

may be made, then δ reduces to a non-evidential specification of a property value and may be expressed as

$\{\#C[P,V_1] = \#C\}$

because $\#C[P,V_i] = 0$, for all V_i other than V_1. In turn, $\delta(C,P)$ may be expressed as

$\delta(C,P) = V_1$ or equivalently as $P(C,V_1)$

which is the FOPC version of property value specification (see section 2.2). The above discussion, however, glosses over the distinction between "necessary truths" and "contingent truths". This distinction is important and is dealt with in detail in the following section.

Only relative frequencies are required: Although we have used absolute numbers to specify the distributions and the size of concepts, sections 4.4 and 4.5 establish that *an agent need only deal with **ratios** of such frequencies.* These ratios lie in the interval [0,1] and appear as weights on links in a connectionist realization. What is significant is that these weights may be computed based on purely *local* interactions between nodes in the connectionist network using a Hebbian synaptic weight change rule.

3.5 Necessary properties versus contingent ones

In the previous section we suggested that *necessary* properties are simply special cases of evidential ones. In particular, we said that if all instances of Type C have the value V_i for property P then δ reduces to a "non-evidential" specification of property values and may be expressed as $\delta(C,P) = V_i$, or equivalently, as $P(C,V_i)$

The evidential formulation also allows the representation of *sufficient* property values of concepts. A property value [P, V_j] is a *sufficient* property value of C if

$$\forall \, x \, P(x,V_j) \Rightarrow C(x)$$

i.e., all instances that have the value V_j for property P are instances of Type C. In the evidential formulation the sufficiency condition amounts to:

$$\#C[P,V_j] = \#V_j, \text{ and for all D other than C, } \#D[P,V_j] = 0.$$

The above discussion may seem overly simplistic; it appears as though the notions of necessary and sufficient property values are being reduced to a mere matter of frequencies. In particular, no distinction is being made between "necessary" truths and truths that are "contingent" (i.e things just happen to be true). But surely there is a difference between these two kinds of truths: isn't there a difference in the nature of truth expressed by "all triangles have three sides" and "all students in the CSE121 class this fall are over 5' 4" tall"?

Indeed, there exists a fundamental difference between property values that are necessarily true and those that just happen to be true. This difference, however, is not manifest in the surface representation - where both cases are represented by associating equivalent frequency counts - but rather in the *learning/knowledge assimilation/classification procedure* (henceforth, learning procedure) that operates on the conceptual structure. The effect of this distinction manifests itself during the acquisition of new information and is best illustrated with the help of an example.

Suppose an agent has observed that: "*all* swans are white". It follows that in the frequency based representation, the property value [has-color, WHITE] would appear as a necessary property of SWAN:

$$\#SWAN[\text{has-color, WHITE}] = \#SWAN.$$

This, however, does not tell us whether the agent's conceptual structure treats "being white" as a "necessary" necessary property value of swans (all swans have to be white for some fundamental reason) or whether it treats this as a mere "contingent" necessary property value of swans (it just so happens that all the swans seen by the agent are white). Now imagine that the agent observes a novel entity. This entity clearly matches the concept BIRD - and is therefore, classified as one - but does not match any of the subconcepts of BIRD present in the agent's conceptual structure. On closer examination we find that *except for its color, which happens to be black, the entity satisfies all the requirements of being a swan*; it possesses all the necessary property values associated with SWAN, and it also matches all the evidential property values indicating that it could be a swan.

The manner in which the agent's learning procedure will classify the new entity will indicate whether he believes "being white" to be a "necessary" necessary property value of SWAN or just a "contingent" necessary one. Observe that the agent's learning procedure has the following choices open to it:

i) Posit a new subconcept of BIRD that is a sibling of SWAN and treat the new entity as an instance of this new concept. In this case, the necessary property value associated with SWAN remains unchanged.

ii) Posit a new concept that lies between the concepts BIRD and SWAN. This new concept is a generalization of the existing concept SWAN in that its instances may be white or black. The new entity is represented as an instance of this new concept. Notice that SWAN still retains [has-color,

WHITE] as a necessary property value.

iii) Decide that being white is not a necessary property value of SWAN, i.e. relegate the property value [has-color, WHITE] to an evidential status and note that swans are mostly white but may also be black (this in terms of frequency ratios). The new entity may now be represented as an instance of SWAN. Choosing this option does not involve creating any new concepts, rather it involves changing the "definition" of an existing concept by dropping one of its necessary property values.

The learning procedure will choose the first or the second option if the agent believes that [has-color, WHITE] is a "necessary" necessary property value of swans. On the other hand, it will choose the third option if the agent believes that [has-color, WHITE] is just a "contingent" necessary property value. In other words, if the agent believes that "all swans are white" is only a "contingent truth", the learning procedure will simply change the frequency ratios to update the agent's knowledge about the color of swans (option 3). But if the agent believes that being white is a "necessary truth" about swans then the learning procedure will have to do something more drastic such as introducing a new concept (options 1 and 2).

What is more interesting, however, is that there exists another possibility. Before seeing the novel instance the agent might have believed and acted as though "all swans are white" was a "necessary" truth about the world. But on seeing this novel instance the agent may wish to *revise his beliefs* - he may decide that "all swans are white" may not be a "necessary" truth after all! If this happens, the agent's learning procedure will once again choose the third option and modify the "definition" of the existing concept SWAN by relegating its property value [has-color, WHITE] to an evidential status. Such belief revisions are not farfetched if one is willing to step out of the domain of formally defined objects with a priori definitions. Such situations may arise when dealing with *natural concepts*, to wit, the platypus in the context of mammals.

3.6 Inheritance and recognition problems in terms of the representation language.

Recall that within the evidential formulation finding solutions to inheritance and recognition problems amounts to choosing the most likely alternative from among a set of alternatives. An inheritance problem that would traditionally be posed as: What is the color of an apple? would now be posed as: Is the color of an apple more likely to be red, green, blue, or yellow? Similarly, a recognition problem such as: What is red in color and sweet in taste? would be posed as: If something is red and sweet, is it more likely to be an apple, a grape, or a banana?

In terms of the representation language introduced above, the inheritance and recognition problems can be stated as follows:

Inheritance
Given: $\Theta = \langle \mathbf{C}, \Phi, \lambda, \Lambda, \#, \delta, << \rangle$,
             $C \in \mathbf{C}, P \in \lambda(C)$, and
             an enumeration of possible answers, i.e., a subset of $\Lambda(P)$
                    V-SET = $\{V_1, V_2, ... V_n\}$,

Find: $V^* \in$ V-SET, such that among members of V-SET, V^* is the *most likely value* of property P for concept C. In other words, find $V^* \in$ V-SET such that, for any $V_i \in$ V-SET, the best estimate of #C[P,V^*] ≥ the best estimate of #C[P,V_i]'s for all other $V_i \in$ V-SET.

In terms of the formal specification, the inheritance problem mentioned above would be stated as: C = APPLE, P = has-color, V-SET = {RED, BLUE, GREEN}.

The requirement that a set of possible answers be specified is not a restriction; by default one may always assume V-SET to be the set of all possible values of P. Also the relative measure of correctness is, in fact, a generalization of the standard measure of correctness; if a particular member of V-SET is the *only correct* answer - and all the other candidate answers are impossible - then this answer will be selected. However, if no *certain* answer exists, the proposed formulation will ascertain the most likely answer.

Recognition

Given: $\Theta = \langle \mathbf{C}, \Phi, \lambda, \Lambda, \#, \delta, <<, \rangle$,

an enumeration of possible answers, i.e., a set of concepts, C-SET = $\{C_1, C_2, ... C_n\}$, and

a description, DESCR, consisting of a set of property value pairs - $\{ [P_1,V_1], [P_2,V_2], ... [P_m,V_m] \}$ such that:

$$\forall [P_j,V_j] \in \text{DESCR},$$

$$V_j \in \Lambda(P_j) \text{ and } P_j \in \cap_{C \in \text{C-SET}} \lambda(C)$$

In other words, each property mentioned in the description should apply to every concept in C-SET, and the values specified for these properties should be appropriate.

Find: $C^* \in$ C-SET such that *relative* to the concepts specified in C-SET, C^* is the *most likely* concept described by DESCR.

Hence the recognition example mentioned above would be stated as: C-SET = {APPLE, GRAPE, BANANA}, DESCR = {[has-color, RED], [has-taste, SWEET]}.

Once again, a choice is made relative to a set of possibilities and the most likely answer is selected. As before, the requirement that a set of possible answers be specified is not a restriction - by default, one may always assume C-SET to be the set of all concepts in **C**. In the simple case - where only one of the answers matches the given description - the appropriate answer is selected, but if many possibilities exist or the description is only partial, the answer that best matches the given description is found.

4 Evidential Formalization of Inheritance and Recognition

In section 2.8 it was stated that reasoning within the evidential framework may be viewed as *decision making* that involves *choosing* the most likely hypothesis from among a set of hypotheses. The notion of likelihood was defined as follows:

Let $a_1, a_2, \ldots a_n$ be the n competing hypotheses and let K be the agent's knowledge. With each alternative, a_i, associate a measure of likelihood, l_i, given by the ratio of the number of interpretations of the world that are consistent with K and that also satisfy a_i, to the the number of interpretations of the world that are consistent with K. Thus an interpretation a_i is more likely than a_j if, and only if, from among the interpretations of the world that satisfy K, a greater fraction of interpretations satisfy a_i than a_j. Furthermore, the most likely hypothesis is the one that is consistent with the greatest fraction of interpretations that satisfy K.

Evidential reasoning justifies a conclusion not on the grounds that it is true in *all* possible worlds that are consistent with the agent's knowledge (as is the case in deduction), but rather on the grounds that if we consider all the possible worlds that are consistent with the agent's knowledge, then there are "more" possible worlds in which the conclusion is true, than there are those in which *any one* of the competing conclusions is true.

The above provides the model-theoretic justification for conclusions drawn using evidential reasoning. The reasoning *process*, however, is better expressed in the following "operational" manner.

i) Compute the likelihood of each hypothesis by:
    a. ascertaining the evidence provided to it by the various evidential assertions in the agent's body of knowledge and

    b. *combining* the individual pieces of evidence to compute the overall likelihood of the hypothesis

ii) *choose* the hypothesis with the highest likelihood

The rule for combining evidence should produce results that are in accordance with the model-theoretic justification detailed above. The following section outlines a solution to this problem based on the notion of maximum entropy, a notion that is fundamentally related to information theory and statistical mechanics (see [Jaynes 57], [Jaynes 79], and [Cheeseman 83]). Subsequent sections apply the solution to the problems of inheritance and recognition.

4.1 The problem of combining evidence

Consider a situation in which the agent has the following knowledge:

C = {APPLE, GRAPE, RED, GREEN, SWEET, SOUR}

Φ = {has-taste, has-color}

λ(APPLE), λ(GRAPE) = {has-taste, has-color}

λ(RED), λ(GREEN), λ(SWEET), λ(SOUR) = ϕ

Λ(has-color) = {RED, GREEN}; Λ(has-taste) = {SWEET, SOUR}

#APPLE = 100
      δ(APPLE, has-color) = {(RED 60), (GREEN 40)}
      δ(APPLE, has-taste) = {(SWEET 70), (SOUR 30)}
#GRAPE = 50
      δ(GRAPE, has-color) = {(RED 5), (GREEN 45)}
      δ(GRAPE, has-taste) = {(SWEET 30), (SOUR 20)}
#RED = 65, #GREEN = 85; #SWEET = 100; #SOUR = 50;

<< is given by: ϕ

Given the above knowledge, a rational agent would have no difficulty in guessing the most probable identity of an object given *one of its property values*. The following table lists the choices we expect him to make:

Description of object	most likely identity of object
has-color RED	APPLE (60 apples v/s 5 grapes)
has-color GREEN	GRAPE (45 grapes v/s 40 apples)
has-taste SWEET	APPLE (70 apples v/s 30 grapes)
has-taste SOUR	APPLE (30 apples v/s 20 grapes)

In each case the agent can make direct use of the available information to compute whether the object is more likely to be an apple or a grape. For example, there are 30 instances of sour apples as against 20 instances of sour grapes and hence, in the absence of any other information, a rational agent will predict that a sour object is more likely to be an apple than a grape and act accordingly.

But how should a rational agent decide the most probable identity of an object given a description such as "red and sweet"? The agent does not know how many apples are red and sweet and neither does he know how many grapes are red and sweet, and therefore, making a choice is no longer straightforward. This situation raises the central problem in evidential reasoning - the problem of combining evidence.

4.1.1 Problem formulation

The information about apples and grapes given above may be expressed in the form of matrices as shown in figure 4.1. The rows of the two matrices correspond to the different values of the property has-taste while the columns correspond to the different values of the property has-color. The numbers at the end of each row(column) represent the number of instances of the concept that have the appropriate value of taste(color).

In general, an agent's knowledge about a concept A may be represented as an n-dimensional matrix where $n = | \lambda(A) |$. Each dimension of the matrix corresponds to an applicable property and the marginals correspond to #A[P,V]'s - the number of instances of A having the value V for property P. The extent of a dimension is given by the number of distinct values the property may have. The internal matrix elements now denote the number of instances of the concept that have the appropriate combination of property values. For example, the top left element of the APPLE matrix in figure 4.1 indicates the number of apples that are both red and sweet.

The problem of guessing the identity of an object given its color as well as its taste would be trivial if the agent knew the internal matrix elements. For example, to decide

APPLE

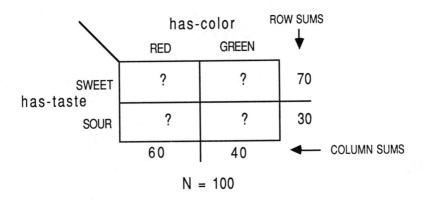

GRAPE

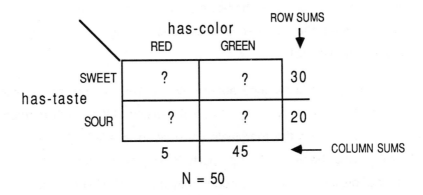

Figure 4.1: A matrix representation of Apples and Grapes

whether a red and sweet object is an apple or a grape, the agent could simply compare the top left elements of the two matrices in figure 4.1 and choose the concept that has the higher value.

But if the agent does not know the internal matrix elements he can do his best by finding the most probable estimates of these on the basis of the available information and using these estimates to reason about the world.

The following section proposes how to find such an estimate.

4.1.2 Computing the most probable configuration

The general 2-dimensional case, may be represented as shown in figure 4.2. The matrix represents the concept A, and

$$R_i = \#A[P_1, i^{th} \text{ value of } P_1];$$

$$C_j = \#A[P_2, j^{th} \text{ value of } P_2];$$

$$N = \#A = \sum_{i=1}^{n} R_i = \sum_{j=1}^{m} C_j$$

$$a_{ij} = \#A[P_1, i^{th} \text{ value of } P_1][P_2, j^{th} \text{ value of } P_2]$$

The a_{ij}'s are unknown and need to be determined on the basis of N, R_i's, and C_j's.

Let a **macro-configuration** be a specification of all the a_{ij}'s. Then our goal may be described as finding the *most probable* macro-configuration indicated by the following information:

$$\forall i \, (i = 1, n) \sum_{j=1}^{m} a_{ij} = R_i \, ;$$

$$\forall j \, (i = 1, m) \sum_{i=1}^{n} a_{ij} = C_j \, ;$$

$$\sum_{i=1}^{n} \sum_{j=1}^{m} a_{ij} = N$$

This problem may be recast as follows: Consider distributing N *distinct* objects into a 2-dimensional array of cells. One may now interpret a_{ij} as specifying the *number* of objects placed in the ij^{th} cell. A macro-configuration then specifies the

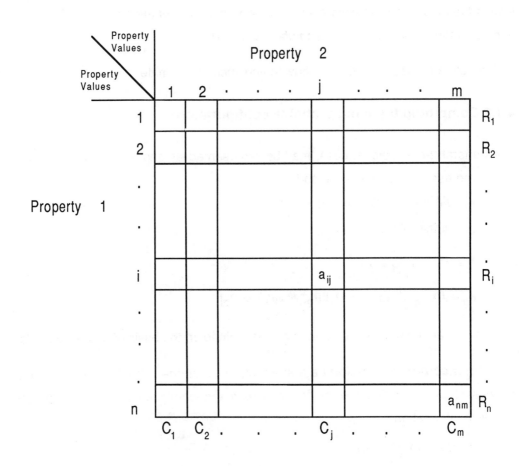

Figure 4.2: The general 2-dimensional case

number of objects placed in each of the $n \times m$ cells in the array.

Let a **micro-configuration** be the *complete* specification of the result of such a distribution. That is, a micro-configuration not only specifies the *number* of objects placed in each cell, but it also specifies the *identity* of these objects. Notice that there is a *many to one* mapping from the space of micro-configurations to the space of macro-configurations.

Let a micro-configuration be termed *feasible* if it satisfies the constraints imposed by row sums and column sums. One can now make the following observation:

> Given his knowledge, an agent has *no basis* for assuming that a particular feasible micro-configuration is more probable than some other feasible micro-configuration; the *only rational* assumption he can make is that all feasible micro-configurations are equally probable[16].

In view of the above assumption the *most probable macro-configuration* will be that which is supported by the *greatest number of feasible micro-configurations*.

If ω denotes the number of micro-configurations supporting a macro-configuration, then ω equals the number of ways of dividing N distinct objects into $n \times m$ groups of $a_{11}, a_{12} \ldots a_{nm}$ each. That is,

$$\omega = \frac{N!}{\prod_{i=1}^{n} \prod_{j=1}^{m} a_{ij}!}$$

In order to find the most probable macro-configuration we need to maximize ω subject to the constraints:

$$\forall\, i \ (i = 1, n) \ \sum_{j=1}^{m} a_{ij} = R_i \, ;$$

$$\forall\, j \ (i = 1, m) \ \sum_{i=1}^{n} a_{ij} = C_j \, ;$$

$$\sum_{i=1}^{n} \sum_{j=1}^{m} a_{ij} = N$$

---

[16]This is in essence the principle of indifference or the *principle of insufficient reason* first stated by Bernoulli in 1713.

The above problem is an example of a constrained maximization problem and can be solved using the technique of Lagrange multipliers. It can be shown that the solution given by

$$\forall\, i, j\,(i = 1, n;\, j = 1, m) \quad a_{ij} = \frac{R_i C_j}{N}$$

satisfies the condition of maximality.

In other words, if we consider all possible ways of distributing n distinct objects into a 2-dimensional array of cells, *subject to* the constraints imposed by row and column sums, R_i's and C_j's, then the distribution of objects - wherein each cell, a_{ij}, contains $R_i C_j / N$ objects - will occur *more often* than any other distribution.

Referring back to the example about apples and grapes (figure 4.1) - the above result implies that if we consider *all possible* ways of assigning color and taste to 100 apples and 50 grapes respectively, while honoring the constraints that 70 apples are sweet while 30 are sour, 60 apples are red while 40 are green, 30 grapes are sweet while twenty are sour, and 5 grapes are red while 45 are green, then the distribution of apples and grapes given in figure 4.3 will occur *more often than any other distribution*. Thus a rational agent would believe that on the basis of the available information, the most probable distribution of apples and grapes is as given in figure 4.3. Consequently, he will identify a "red and sweet" object to be an apple as most probably there are 42 apples that meet this description as against only 3 grapes.

A derivation of the most probable macro-configuration result follows.

Keeping in view the presence of product terms in ω we work with the natural logarithm of ω ($\ln \omega$) instead of ω, and use Stirling's approximation for factorials (if $n \gg 0$ then $\ln n! \approx n \ln n - n$). Thus we have,

$$\ln \omega = \ln N! - \sum_{i=1}^{n} \sum_{j=1}^{m} \ln a_{ij}! \qquad \text{; taking natural logarithm}$$

$$\ln \omega = N \ln N - N - \sum_{i=1}^{n} \sum_{j=1}^{m} (a_{ij} \ln a_{ij} - a_{ij}) \qquad \text{; Stirling's approximation}$$

APPLE

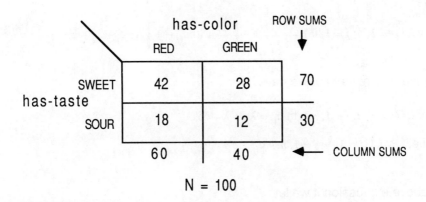

has-color

	RED	GREEN	ROW SUMS
SWEET	42	28	70
SOUR	18	12	30
	60	40	← COLUMN SUMS

has-taste

N = 100

GRAPE

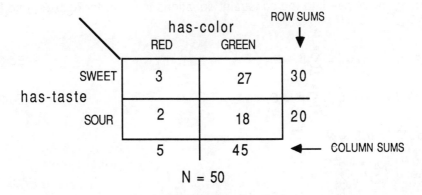

has-color

	RED	GREEN	ROW SUMS
SWEET	3	27	30
SOUR	2	18	20
	5	45	← COLUMN SUMS

has-taste

N = 50

Each matrix element = $\dfrac{\text{ROW SUM} \times \text{COLUMN SUM}}{N}$

Figure 4.3: The most likely distribution of Apples and Grapes

Differentiating the above and introducing Lagrange multipliers obtained by differentiating the constraint expression

$$\lambda_o((\sum_{i=1}^{n}\sum_{j=1}^{m} a_{ij})-N) + \sum_{i=1}^{n}\lambda_i((\sum_{j=1}^{m} a_{ij}) - R_i)) + \sum_{j=1}^{m}\delta_j((\sum_{i=1}^{n} a_{ij}) - C_i))$$

we have

$$\forall i,j \ (i = 1, n; j = 1, m) \ \frac{d\ln \omega}{d a_{ij}} = - \left[\frac{a_{ij}}{a_{ij}} + \ln a_{ij} - 1\right] + \lambda_o + \lambda_i + \delta_j$$

Setting the derivative to 0, we have

$$\forall i,j \ (i = 1, n; j = 1, m) \ \ln a_{ij} = \lambda_o + \lambda_i + \delta_j$$

i.e., $\forall i,j \ (i = 1, n; j = 1, m) \ a_{ij} = e^{\lambda_o + \lambda_i + \delta_j}$

In the above expression if we let

$e^{\lambda_o} = \alpha_o, \ \forall i \ (i = 1, n) \ e^{\lambda_i} = \alpha_i, \ \text{and} \ \forall j \ (j = 1, m) \ e^{\delta_j} = \beta_j$

We have, $\forall i,j \ (i = 1, n; j = 1, m) \ a_{ij} = \alpha_o \alpha_i \beta_j$

Substituting the above into the constraint equations to solve for α_o, α_i's, and β_j's, we have

$$\forall i \ (i = 1, n) \ \alpha_o \alpha_i \sum_{j=1}^{m} \beta_j = R_i \qquad \text{-- Eq-3.1}$$

$$\forall j \ (i = 1, m) \ \alpha_o \beta_j \sum_{i=1}^{n} \alpha_i = C_j \qquad \text{-- Eq-3.2}$$

$$\alpha_o \sum_{i=1}^{n}\sum_{j=1}^{m} \alpha_i \beta_j = N$$

i.e. $\alpha_o (\sum_{i=1}^{n} \alpha_i) \sum_{j=1}^{m} \beta_j = N \qquad \text{-- Eq-3.3}$

We now show that

$$\alpha_o = \frac{1}{abN} ; \ \forall i \ (i = 1, n) \ \alpha_i = aR_i ; \ \text{and} \ \forall j \ (j = 1, m) \ \beta_j = bC_j$$

where a and b are arbitrary constants, constitute a solution to Eq-3.1 through Eq-3.3. This may be shown by substituting the above values of α_o, α_i's, and β_j's into these equations.

Notice that $\sum_{j=1}^{m} \beta_j = b$, $\sum_{j=1}^{m} C_j = bN$, and $\sum_{i=1}^{n} \alpha_i = a \sum_{i=1}^{n} R_i = aN$

Hence, $\forall\, i\, (i = 1, n)\;\; \alpha_o \alpha_i \sum_{j=1}^{m} \beta_j = \dfrac{aR_i bN}{abN} = R_i$, as required by Eq-3.1.

Similarly, $\forall\, j\, (j = 1, m)\;\; \alpha_o \beta_j \sum_{i=1}^{n} \alpha_i = \dfrac{bC_j aN}{abN} = C_j$, as required by Eq-3.2.

Finally, $\alpha_o (\sum_{i=1}^{n} \alpha_i)(\sum_{j=1}^{m} \beta_j) = \dfrac{aNbN}{abN} = N$, as required by Eq-3.3.

The above shows that the suggested solutions of α_o, α_i's and β_j's are indeed correct.

Hence the values of a_{ij}'s are given by

$$\forall\, i, j\, (i = 1, n; j = 1, m)\quad a_{ij} = \alpha_o \alpha_i \delta_j = \dfrac{aR_i bC_j}{abN} = \dfrac{R_i C_j}{N}$$

The above result can be extended to higher dimensions and its more general form will be referred to as the **best estimate rule**. In terms of the representation language, this result may be stated as follows:

Based on the knowledge of #A[P_1, V_1], #A[P_2, V_2], ... and #A[P_n, V_n], the **best** (i.e., the most probable) estimate of #A[P_1, V_1][P_2, V_2]... [P_n, V_n] is given by

$$\dfrac{\prod_{i=1}^{n} \#A[P_i, V_i]}{\#A^{n-1}}$$

4.2 Maximum entropy and the Dempster-Shafer rule

The Dempster-Shafer (DS) evidence theory [Shafer 76] suggests an evidence combination rule. It can be shown that a straightforward application of the DS rule for evidence combination does not produce the correct results for the kinds of problems we wish to solve. It can also be shown that the DS result agrees with the best estimate rule if one assumes that the frequency (i.e., the prior probability) of all concepts is the same.

A simple example illustrates the point. Consider the information about apples and grapes as given in section 4.1.

If one wishes to use the DS rule to decide whether a green and sour object is an apple or a grape one would essentially proceed as follows:

Each property value would be treated as a source of evidence and the evidence provided by green and sour will be given by

$$E(Apple \mid green) = \frac{40}{85}; \quad E(Grape \mid green) = \frac{45}{80}$$

$$E(Apple \mid sour) = \frac{30}{50}; \quad E(Grape \mid sour) = \frac{20}{50}$$

Applying the DS rule evidence combination we get

$$E(Apple \mid green \ \& \ sour) = \frac{40 \times 30}{85 \times 50} \quad \text{and}$$

$$E(Grape \mid green \ \& \ sour) = \frac{45 \times 20}{85 \times 50}$$

The above is a simplified account of the actual steps using the DS theory. We have only focused on the essentials, in particular, we have not normalized the quantities because we are only interested in a relative measure.

Comparing the evidence for apples and grapes we have

E(Apple | green & sour) : E(Grape | green & sour) equals,

$$\frac{40 \times 30}{85 \times 50} : \frac{45 \times 20}{85 \times 50} = 4 : 3$$

and the decision is in favor of Apple.

However, on the basis of the given information, the best (most probable) estimate of the number of green and sour apples is 12 and that of green and sour grapes is 18. (See figure 4.3). Hence the appropriate ratio is

$12 : 18 = 2 : 3$

and the decision is in favor of Grape!

It is not difficult to pinpoint the reason for this discrepancy. Given that one is only interested in making comparisons, the ratio of the relative likelihood of two concepts A and B using the DS rule is given by

$$\prod_{i=1}^{n} \frac{\#A[P_i,V_i]}{\#B[P_i,V_i]} \qquad\qquad -- DS_{ratio}$$

However, the best estimate rule gives the ratio as:

$$\left(\frac{\#B}{\#A}\right)^{n-1} \times \prod_{i=1}^{n} \frac{\#A[P_i,V_i]}{\#B[P_i,V_i]}$$

which may be restated as: $DS_{ratio} \times (\#B/\#A)^{n-1}$

If one were to assume $\#A = \#B$, or in effect that *all concepts have the same prior probability*, then the DS rule and the best estimate rule become equivalent.

One might suggest that by including an additional source that provides evidence about the prior probabilities of apples and grapes, one might be able to correct the DS result. However, the problem is more complex. In order to make the DS_{ratio} the same as that obtained by the best estimate result it will have to be multiplied by the factor: $(\#B/\#A)^{n-1}$. But introducing an evidential source to account for the prior probability only introduces the factor $\#A/\#B$, which acts in the wrong direction.

.3 Maximum entropy and Bayes' rule

In this section we show that in case none of the internal entries in the concept map are known then conventional Bayesian inference used in conjunction with certain independence assumptions produces the same results as those obtained by the maximum entropy formulation. However, the maximum entropy formulation is more attractive because it offers a precise way of conceptualizing the problem of estimating unknown probabilities; independence assumptions do not appear as ad hoc assumptions but can be justified as the only meaningful assumptions one may make *given the state of one's knowledge*. If additional information suggesting dependence is available (i.e., if a few internal entries are known), the maximum entropy formulation exploits this information in a consistent manner.

One can pose the problem raised in section 4.1 about deciding whether an object is an apple or a grape, in terms of conditional probabilities. The decision task amounts to determining which of the two conditional probabilities is greater

Pr(Apple | red & sweet) or Pr(Grape | red & sweet)

Here Pr(A | B) denotes the conditional probability of A given B. "Apple" and "Grape" are to be read as "x is an apple" and "x is a grape" respectively, while "red" and "green" are to be read as "x has the value RED for property has-color" and "x has value SWEET for property has-taste" respectively.

The following are some of the probabilities known to the agent by virtue of the information given in section 4.1

$$\frac{Pr(Apple)}{Pr(Grape)} = \frac{\#APPLE}{\#GRAPE}$$

$$Pr(red \mid Apple) = \frac{\#APPLE[has\text{-}color,RED]}{\#APPLE}$$

$$Pr(red \mid Grape) = \frac{\#GRAPE[has\text{-}color,RED]}{\#GRAPE}$$

$$Pr(\text{sweet} \mid \text{Apple}) = \frac{\#APPLE[\text{has-taste},SWEET]}{\#APPLE}$$

$$Pr(\text{sweet} \mid \text{Grape}) = \frac{\#GRAPE[\text{has-taste},SWEET]}{\#GRAPE}$$

Using Bayes' rule of conditional probabilities,

$$Pr(\text{Apple} \mid \text{red \& sweet}) = \frac{Pr(\text{red \& sweet} \mid \text{Apple}) \times Pr(\text{Apple})}{Pr(\text{red \& sweet})}$$

and

$$Pr(\text{Grape} \mid \text{red \& sweet}) = \frac{Pr(\text{red \& sweet} \mid \text{Grape}) \times Pr(\text{Grape})}{Pr(\text{red \& sweet})}$$

Hence,

$$\frac{Pr(\text{Apple} \mid \text{red \& sweet})}{Pr(\text{Grape} \mid \text{red \& sweet})} = \frac{Pr(\text{red \& sweet} \mid \text{Apple}) \times Pr(\text{Apple})}{Pr(\text{red \& sweet} \mid \text{Grape}) \times Pr(\text{Grape})} \qquad \text{-- Eq-3.4}$$

If we make the following *independence assumption*:

$$Pr([P_i,V_i] \& [P_j,V_j] \mid C_k) = Pr([P_i,V_i] \mid C_k) \times Pr([P_j,V_j] \mid C_k) \qquad \text{-- IA-1}$$

We have

$$Pr(\text{red \& sweet} \mid \text{Apple}) = Pr(\text{red} \mid \text{Apple}) \times Pr(\text{sweet} \mid \text{Apple}), \text{ and}$$

$$Pr(\text{red \& sweet} \mid \text{Grape}) = Pr(\text{red} \mid \text{Grape}) \times Pr(\text{sweet} \mid \text{Grape})$$

Substituting these probabilities in Eq-3.4 we have

$$\frac{Pr(\text{Apple} \mid \text{red \& sweet})}{Pr(\text{Grape} \mid \text{red \& sweet})} = \frac{Pr(\text{red} \mid \text{Apple}) \times Pr(\text{sweet} \mid \text{Apple}) \times Pr(\text{Apple})}{Pr(\text{red} \mid \text{Grape}) \times Pr(\text{sweet} \mid \text{Grape}) \times Pr(\text{Grape})}$$

Expressing the probabilities in terms of $\#C[P_i, V_j]$'s and $\#C$'s,

73

$$\frac{\text{Pr(Apple | red \& sweet)}}{\text{Pr(Grape | red \& sweet)}} \text{ equals:}$$

$$\frac{\text{\#APPLE[has-color,RED]} \times \text{\#APPLE[has-taste,SWEET]} \times \text{\#GRAPE}}{\text{\#GRAPE[has-color,RED]} \times \text{\#GRAPE[has-taste,SWEET]} \times \text{\#APPLE}}$$

as would be computed using the best estimate rule.

Thus using Bayes' rule in conjunction with the independence assumption IA-I leads to the same result that would be obtained by the best estimate rule derived in section 4.1. But the use of the best estimate rule does not appear to involve any assumption such as IA-I. What then is the relation between IA-1 and the best estimate rule?

The independence assumption IA-1 is equivalent to the independence assumption of the form

$$\text{Pr}(e_i \text{ \& } e_j \mid H) = \text{Pr}(e_i \mid H) \times \text{Pr}(e_j \mid H)$$

where H is a hypothesis, and e_i, e_j are two pieces of evidence (or two symptoms). This form of independence is often assumed in reasoning systems based on Bayesian statistics [Hart & Duda 77], but its use is often criticized as being unreasonable and even unwarranted [Charniak 83]. The problem is that the independence assumption usually appears as an ad hoc assumption, unrelated to the rest of the agent's body of knowledge. Because it is not stated as to how the rest of the agent's knowledge affects the validity of this assumption, it remains unclear as to when the assumption is warranted and when it is not.

In the derivation of the best estimate result, the agent's knowledge consisted solely of terms of the form #A's and $\text{\#A}[P_i,V_i]$'s for different concepts A and property value pairs $[P_i,V_i]$'s; *none of the quantities* $\text{\#A}[P_i,V_i][P_j,V_j]$ *were known*. The best estimate result established that in this *specific situation*, the most probable estimate of the unknowns $\text{\#A}[P_i,V_i][P_j,V_j]$ equals

$$\frac{\text{\#A}[P_i,V_i] \times \text{\#A}[P_j,V_j]}{\text{\#A}}$$

It is only in this specific condition that the best estimate result matches the result obtained by using Bayes' rule in conjunction with the independence assumption. Indeed, *it is only under this condition* that the independence assumption IA-1 is justified.

The maximum entropy approach is equivalent to the basic probabilistic approach but offers a precise way of conceptualizing the problem of estimating unknown probabilities. Under the maximum entropy approach, each piece of information is viewed as a constraint. These constraints are used to determine the most probable macro-configuration of the domain[17] and all the unknown probabilities are computed with reference to this macro-configuration. If there is no dependence or correlation in the underlying information, the result obtained by the maximum entropy principle agrees with the result obtained by using Bayes' rule in conjunction with the independence assumption. But if additional information indicating dependence is available, it is incorporated as additional constraints and the result reflects this dependence. For example, if the agent knows one of the #A$[P_i, V_i][P_j, V_j]$'s (with respect to figure 4.2 this means that the agent knows one of the internal matrix elements) then the constraints used during the maximization of

$$\omega = \frac{N!}{\prod_{i=1}^{n} \prod_{j=1}^{n} a_{ij}}$$

would be augmented to include this additional information. Without loss of generality, let the agent know that $a_{11} = \alpha$. Then the constraints are:

$$\sum_{j=2}^{m} a_{1j} = R_1 - a \; ; \quad \sum_{i=2}^{n} a_{i1} = C_1 - a \; ;$$

$$\forall i (i=2,n) \sum_{j=1}^{m} a_{ij} = R_i \; ; \quad \forall j (j=2,m) \sum_{i=1}^{n} a_{ij} = C_j \; ; \text{ and } \sum_{i=1}^{n} \sum_{j=1}^{m} a_{ij} = N$$

---

[17]The most probable macro-configuration is the one that is supported by the largest number of feasible micro-configurations; recall that a micro-configuration is feasible if it satisfies all the constraints.

and the most probable configuration is given by

$$\forall j (j=1,m) \; a_{1j} = C_j \frac{(R_1 - \alpha)}{(N - C_1)}$$

$$\forall j \; (i=1,n) \; a_{i1} = R_i \frac{(C_1 - \alpha)}{(N - R_i)}$$

$$\forall \; i,j \; (i \neq 1 \; and \; j \neq 1) \; a_{ij} = R_i \, C_j \frac{(N + \alpha) - (R_i + C_j)}{(N - R_i)(N - C_j)}$$

As should be obvious, if many internal elements are known then the above computations get complex; the implications of this are discussed in section 6.1.

4.4 Evidential inheritance

Recall the definition of the inheritance problem given in section 3.6.

Given: $\Theta = \langle \mathbf{C}, \Phi, \lambda, \Lambda, \#, \delta, << \rangle$,
         $C \in \mathbf{C}, P \in \lambda(C)$, and
         V-SET $= \{V_1, V_2, \dots V_n\}$

Find: $V^* \in$ V-SET, such that among members of V-SET, V^* is the *most likely value* of property P for concept C. In other words, find $V^* \in$ V-SET such that the best estimate of $\#C[P,V^*] \geq$ the best estimate of $\#C[P,V_i]$'s for all other $V_i \in$ V-SET.

The solution to the above problem is trivial if the agent knows $\delta(C,P)$ - the agent simply has to compare the known $\#C[P,V_i]$'s and choose the V_i for which this is the maximum. But if the agent does not know $\delta(C,P)$ then he has to compute the most probable estimates of the $\#C[P,V_i]$'s based on knowledge available at other concepts in the conceptual structure. This section develops a solution to this problem based on the results derived in the preceding section. The solution applies to situations involving exceptions as well as multiple inheritance.

4.4.1 Direct inheritance

If an agent believes that 40% of the fruits are red, then in the absence of any other information except that apples are a subtype of fruits, the best estimate of the percentage of red apples is 40%. This intuitive result follows directly from the best estimate result. Formally,

Given two concepts C and B, and a property P such that

   i) C << B,
   ii) $\delta(C,P)$ is not known, but
   iii) $\delta(B,P)$ is known,

then - in *the absence of any other information*:

$$\text{the best estimate of } \#C[P,V] = \#B[P,V]) \times \frac{\#C}{\#B}$$

Direct inheritance is analogous to the notion of direct inference in statistical inference.

The applicability of the direct inheritance rule can be extended to include situations where B has other offsprings besides C if we make the following assumption about the well-formedness of the conceptual structure:

WFR-cs-1: The agent stores (or remembers) all distributions that are *important* to him *and* that *cannot be estimated accurately* on the basis of information available at concepts higher up in the conceptual structure.

This is a very natural requirement. Its analog in a traditional frame language would be: "if the value of a property is exceptional and if the ability to correctly predict this value is crucial for the agent then he must store (remember) this exception".

The following example illustrates the justification of this well-formedness rule:

Assume that there are 150 fruits, of which 100 are apples and 50 are grapes. Also assume that 40% of the fruits are red (i.e., 60 fruits are red). In the absence of any other information, the best estimate that one can make is that there are 40 red apples, and 20 red grapes (this follows from direct inheritance). However, if it is also known that 50% (i.e., 50) of the apples are red then it follows that only 20% (i.e., 10) of the grapes are red, and this differs significantly - the error being 100% - from the estimate obtained by direct inheritance. WFR-cs-1 says that *if it is important* for the agent to be able to predict the number of red grapes, then in the above situation he would store δ(has-color, GRAPE).

If we reverse the situation, so that instead of knowing that 50% of the apples are red, it is known that 50% (i.e., 25) of the grapes are red, then the correct estimate of the number of red apples is 35%. Now 35% may not be considered significantly different from 40% - the estimate obtainable by direct inheritance. In this case the error is only 12.5%, and therefore, the agent may not store δ(has-color, APPLE) even though it may be important for him to predict the number of red apples.

4.4.2 Principle of relevance

Given that 40% of the fruits are sweet and 70% of the apples are sweet, we would expect the likelihood of an apple, A1, being sweet to be 70%. In determining the likelihood of A1 being sweet, the more specific information about apples dominates the more general information about fruits. In our terminology, we would say that with respect to the property has-taste the concept apple is relevant to A1 whereas the concept fruit is not. This motivates the following definition:

Given a concept C and a property $P \in \lambda(C)$, a concept B is **relevant** to C with respect to P, if and only if

  i) $C << B$,
 ii) $\delta(B,P)$ is known, and
iii) there exists no concept A (distinct from C and B) such that $\delta(A,P)$ is known and $C << A << B$

We will often need to refer to the set of concepts that are relevant to C with respect to P, and this set will be referred to as $\Gamma(C,P)$. Figure 4.4 illustrates the above notions. Notice that it is possible for a concept to be relevant to itself; C is relevant to itself w.r.t. P if $\delta(C,P)$ is known. Furthermore, it follows that for such a

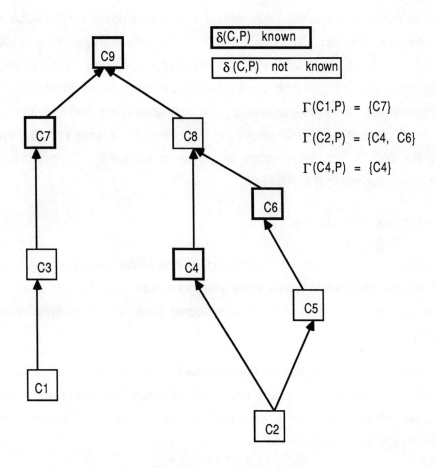

$\delta(C,P)$ known

$\delta(C,P)$ not known

$\Gamma(C1,P) = \{C7\}$

$\Gamma(C2,P) = \{C4,\ C6\}$

$\Gamma(C4,P) = \{C4\}$

Figure 4.4: Relevance

concept there are no other concepts relevant to it with respect to P.

The *principle of relevance* states that

> Given a concept A and a property P such that P ∈ λ(A) and δ(A,P) is not known, and if there *is only one* concept (say B) that is relevant to A with respect to property P, then the *best estimate* of δ(A,P) may be directly inherited from B and all other information may be ignored.

The principle of relevance captures the notion that specific information should dominate general information. This principle alone suffices to solve the problem of exceptions - i.e., merely by using this principle, one can correctly handle all situations wherein the *ordering* of concepts can be exploited to reconcile conflicting information. The principle of relevance appears as the reference class problem in statistical inference [Kyburg 83] and is analogous to the notion of inferential distance ordering [Touretzky 86]. In fact, the principle of relevance subsumes the mathematics of inheritance proposed in [Touretzky 86].

4.4.3 Multiple inheritance

In a multiple inheritance situation there exist multiple relevant concepts and a solution to the inheritance problem requires that evidence from these concepts be *combined*. This section presents a solution to a restricted class of the multiple inheritance problem.

We begin by observing that for the purpose of inheriting the values of property P of concept C, we need to consider only those concepts D_i that are above C in the conceptual hierarchy, and for which $\delta(D_i,P)$ is known. This is the motivation behind introducing the following definition:

Given a concept C and a property P ∈ λ(C),

C/C,P, the *projection* of C with respect to C and P, is defined as

$$C/C,P = \{ x \mid x \in C, \delta(x,P) \text{ is known and } C << x \}$$

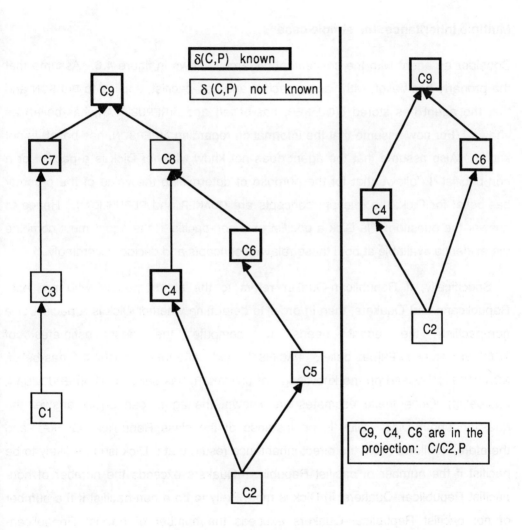

Figure 4.5: Projection

Figure 4.5 illustrates the above definition.

We now consider two cases of multiple inheritance. In the first case, all the relevant concepts must have a common parent. In the second, and more general, case, a common *parent* need not exist and the existence of a common *ancestor* suffices.

Multiple Inheritance: the simple case

Consider an agent with the conceptual hierarchy shown in figure 4.6. Assume that the property has-belief, with values pacifist and non-pacifist, applies to PERSON and that the agent has stored δ(QUAKER, has-belief) and δ(REPUBLICAN, has-belief) as shown. (For now assume that the information regarding δ(PERSON, has-belief) is not known.) Also assume that the agent does not know whether Dick is a pacifist or a non-pacifist. It follows that for the purpose of determining the value of the property has-belief for Dick, the relevant concepts are QUAKER and REPUBLICAN. Hence to answer the question: "Is Dick a pacifist or a non-pacifist?" the agent must combine the evidence available at both these relevant concepts and decide accordingly.

Specifically, if Republican-Quaker refers to the set of people who are both Republicans and Quakers, then in order to determine whether Dick is a pacifist or a non-pacifist, the agent needs to compute the best estimates of #REPUBLICAN-QUAKER[has-belief, PACIFIST] and #REPUBLICAN-QUAKER[has-belief, NON-PACIFIST] based on the knowledge of δ(QUAKER, has-belief) and δ(REPUBLICAN, has-belief). Once these estimates are known, the agent can easily answer the question about Dick: Dick is an instance of the class Republican-Quaker, and therefore, it follows (from the direct inheritance result) that i) Dick is more likely to be pacifist if the number of pacifist Republican-Quakers exceeds the number of non-pacifist Republican-Quakers, ii) Dick is more likely to be a non-pacifist if the number of non-pacifist Republican-Quakers exceeds the number of pacifist Republican-Quakers, and iii) Dick is equally likely to be pacifist or non-pacifist otherwise.

Computing the most likely estimate of #REPUBLICAN-QUAKER[has-belief, PACIFIST]

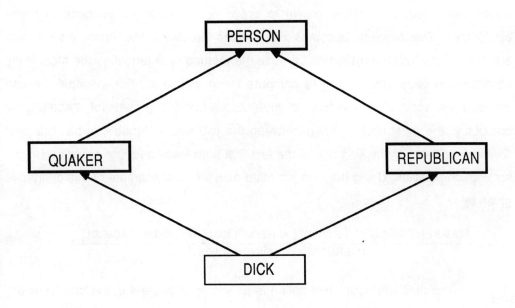

$$\delta(\text{QUAKER, has-belief}) \;=\; \{ \text{(PACIFIST 7) (NON-PAC 3)} \}$$

$$\delta(\text{REPUBLICAN, has-belief}) \;=\; \{ \text{(PACIFIST 16) (NON-PAC 64)} \}$$

$$\delta(\text{PERSON, has-belief}) \;=\; \{ \text{(PACIFIST 38) (NON-PAC 96)} \}$$

Figure 4.6: An example of multiple inheritance with a common parent

amounts to computing the most likely overlap between the two sets - Republican-pacifists and Quaker-pacifists. Similarly, computing the most likely estimate of #REPUBLICAN-QUAKER[has-belief, NON-PACIFIST] amounts to computing the most likely overlap between the two sets - Republican-non-pacifists and Quaker-non-pacifists. However, as stated thus far, the problem of computing these overlaps is grossly underconstrained; too little is known to arrive at a meaningful estimate of these quantities. The problem becomes much more precise if the agent also knows δ(PERSON, has-belief), for then he can use the method of determining the most likely configuration (vide section 4.1) to compute these estimates. For example, he can compute the most likely estimate of #REPUBLICAN-QUAKER[has-belief, PACIFIST] by computing the most likely overlap between the two sets - Republican-pacifists and Quaker-pacifists - by making use of the fact that both these sets are *contained* in the set Person-pacifists. Using the best estimate rule, the best estimate of this overlap is given by

$$\frac{\text{\#QUAKER[has-belief, PACIFIST]} \times \text{\#REPUBLICAN[has-belief, PACIFIST]}}{\text{\#PERSON[has-belief, PACIFIST]}}$$

If we assume that δ(PERSON, has-belief) is as shown in figure 4.6, the best estimate of #REPUBLICAN-QUAKER[has-belief, PACIFIST] turns out to be (7 × 16)/38, i.e., about 3. A similar argument applies to the computation of the most likely estimate of #REPUBLICAN-QUAKER[has-belief, NON-PACIFIST] and leads to an estimate of (3 × 64)/96, i.e., about 2. These estimates suggest that, given the information in figure 4.6, a rational agent would conclude that Dick is about 1.5 times more likely to be a pacifist than a non-pacifist.

The problem of inheritance is further simplified if we recognize that for the purpose of inheritance, it suffices to know the ratio of #REPUBLICAN-QUAKER[has-belief, PACIFIST] and #REPUBLICAN-QUAKER[has-belief, NON-PACIFIST] and the actual quantities need not be computed.

In the above example we had a situation wherein all the relevant concepts (i.e., QUAKER and REPUBLICAN) had a common parent (PERSON) for which δ(C,P) was

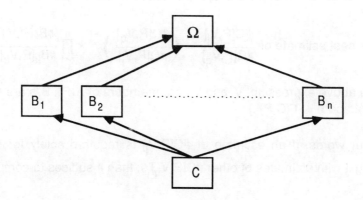

$B_1,\ B_2\ \cdots\ B_n$ are relevant to C w.r.t. P

Ω is the parent of all B_k's and $\delta(\Omega,P)$ is known

The best estimate of $\#C[P,V_j]\ /\ \#C[P,V_q]$ is given by:

$$\left[\frac{\#\Omega\,[P,\,V_q]}{\#\Omega\,[P,\,V_j]}\right]^{n-1} \times \prod_{k=1}^{n} \left[\frac{\#B_k\,[P,\,V_j]}{\#B_k\,[P,\,V_q]}\right]$$

Figure 4.7: Multiple inheritance with a common parent

known. What follows is a detailed specification of how this class of inheritance problems may be solved using the evidential approach.

Theorem-3.1: If the ordering induced on C/C,P by << is such that there exists a concept, Ω, such that it is a common parent of all members of $\Gamma(C,P)$ (recall that $\Gamma(C,P)$ is the set of concepts that are relevant to C with respect to P), then

$$\text{the best estimate of } \frac{\#C[P,V_j]}{\#C[P,V_q]} = \left(\frac{\#\Omega[P,V_q]}{\#\Omega[P,V_j]}\right)^{n-1} \times \prod_{k=1}^{n} \frac{\#B_k[P,V_j]}{\#B_k[P,V_q]}$$

{In the above expression, V_j and V_q are members of $\Lambda(P)$, B_i's are members of $\Gamma(C,P)$, and $n = |\Gamma(C,P)|$.}

In other words, if an estimate of $\#C[P,V_j]$ is required solely for the purpose of comparing it with estimates of other $\#C[P,V_q]$'s, then it suffices to compute

$$\frac{\prod_{k=1}^{n} \#B_k[P,V_j]}{\#\Omega[P,V_j]^{n-1}}$$

The result is summarized in figure 4.7. Notice that if there is only one relevant concept B, then Ω may be taken to be B itself, and the above result reduces to the direct inheritance result.

Proof of Theorem-3.1: We begin by establishing the following lemma:

Lemma-3.1: If S_1, S_2,... S_n are n subsets of a set V, and if W denotes $\cap_{k=1,n} S_k$, then the best estimate of $\#W$ based on this information is given by

$$\frac{\prod_{k=1}^{n} \#S_k}{\#V^{n-1}}$$

Proof: The problem of estimating $\#W$ is a special case of the problem of determining the most probable configuration. The correspondence is as follows: Each S_k may be treated as a 2-valued property applicable to V. For each $v \in V$, if $v \in S_k$ then the value of the property S_k for v equals 1 otherwise it equals 0. Hence finding the best estimate of #W is identical to finding the best estimate of the number of elements in V that have the value 1 for each of the properties S_1 through S_n. An application of the best estimate rule directly establishes the lemma. **Q.E.D.**

Lemma-3.2: If D be the set $\cap_{k=1,n} B_k$, then $\#D[P,V_j]$ is best estimated by

$$\#D[P,V_j] = \frac{\prod_{k=1}^{n} \#B_k[P,V_j]}{\#\Omega[P,V_j]^{n-1}}$$

Proof: The proof directly follows from Lemma-3.1 if we identify V in Lemma-3.1 with $\Omega[P,V_j]$ in Lemma-3.2 and each S_k in Lemma-3.1 with $B_k[P,V_j]$ in Lemma-3.2. **Q.E.D..**

Although the set D may not be explicitly defined as one of the concepts in the domain, it may be introduced for the purpose of this analysis[18].

Lemma-3.3: The best estimate of $\dfrac{\#C[P,V_j]}{\#C[P,V_q]}$ equals $\dfrac{\#D[P,V_j]}{\#D[P,V_q]}$

Proof: With reference to D,

The best estimate of $\#C[P,V_j] = \#D[P,V_j] \times \dfrac{\#C}{\#D}$ and

the best estimate of $\#C[P,V_q] = \#D[P,V_q] \times \dfrac{\#C}{\#D}$

Therefore, the best estimate of $\dfrac{\#C[P,V_j]}{\#C[P,V_q]}$ is given by

$$\frac{\#D[P,V_j] \times \#C}{\#D} \times \frac{\#D}{\#D[P,V_q] \times \#C} = \frac{\#D[P,V_j]}{\#D[P,V_q]}$$

This concludes the proof of Lemma-3.3. **Q.E.D..**

---

[18]Any arbitrary set may not be introduced in this manner. However, D is a well defined set in that it is the intersection of existing sets.

Theorem-3.1 directly follows from an application of Lemma-3.2 and Lemma-3.3. Q.E.D.

With reference to the derivation of Lemma-3.1 suppose it is known that there are a number of sets $V_1, V_2, ... V_m$ such that for each V_i, each $S_k \subseteq V_i$.

In this case there would be m different estimates of #W, one for each V_i given by

$$\frac{\prod_{k=1}^{n} \#S_k}{\#V_i^{n-1}}$$

Which of these is the best estimate of #W? In other words, which of the V_i's should be used as the reference set for finding the most likely intersection of S_k's. This is essentially the reference class problem mentioned in section 4.4.2.

If one of the V_i's - say V^*, is such that $V^* \subseteq V_i$, for each V_i $1 \le i \le m$, then the best estimate of #W is the one that is computed using V^* as the reference set. That is, the best estimate of #W is given by

$$\frac{\prod_{k=1}^{n} \#S_k}{(\#V^*)^{n-1}}$$

Notice that in the derivation of Theorem-3.1, the V referred to in Lemma-3.1 was identified with $\Omega[P,V_j]$ and each S_k with $B_k[P,V_j]$, where B_k's are the members of $\Gamma(C,P)$. This explains the motivation behind the requirement that Ω be a parent of all the members of $\Gamma(C,P)$.

Multiple inheritance: the more complex case

In more complex cases of multiple inheritance a common parent of the concepts in $\Gamma(C,P)$ does not exist. In this case evidence from relevant concepts is combined by progressively moving up the conceptual structure and repeatedly applying the result derived in the common parent situation. This is done until a common ancestor of all the relevant concepts is reached. It is shown that in doing so evidence from all relevant concepts gets assimilated.

Let us introduce the following notion of well-formedness:

WFR-inh-1: A conceptual structure is well formed with respect to an inheritance problem (or vice versa) if the graph induced by << on **C**/C,P includes a tree whose leaves are the members of Γ(C,P).

WFR-inh-1 entails that given any inheritance problem, there exists a unique reference concept, Ω, for Γ(C,P), such that Ω is the root of the above mentioned tree.

Theorem-3.2: If an inheritance problem is well-formed then for any pair of values V_j and V_q of P

$$\text{the best estimate of } \frac{\#C[P,V_j]}{\#C[P,V_q]} = \frac{\text{BEST-ESTIMATE}(\Omega, P, V_j)}{\text{BEST-ESTIMATE}(\Omega, P, V_q)}$$

{In the above expression, Ω is the common ancestor of Γ(C,P) and the function BEST-ESTIMATE - which operates on the graph induced by << on **C**/C,P - is as described below.}

Function BEST-ESTIMATE (ξ, ϕ, v) ; returns real

{ξ is a concept, ϕ is a property and v is a value}

If $\xi \in \Gamma(C,P)$ then BEST-ESTIMATE := $\#\xi[\phi,v]$

$$\text{else BEST-ESTIMATE} := \#\xi[\phi,v] \times \prod \frac{\text{BEST-ESTIMATE}(\xi_i, \phi, v)}{\#\xi[\phi,v]}$$

{The product is taken over all the sons, ξ_i's of ξ}

Explanation: The above algorithm combines evidence provided by each $B_i \in \Gamma(C,P)$ by repeated application of the result derived for the simple case of multiple inheritance until evidence provided by all the B_i's has been combined at Ω. The situation is illustrated in figure 4.8. Specifically, the result computed at each concept, ξ, that lies on a path from Ω to a B_i, combines the evidence provided by all the B_i's that lie below ξ. This ensures that the evidence provided by all the B_i's has been combined when the result is computed at Ω. The second and the third arguments of the function BEST-ESTIMATE (B.E. in brief), remain fixed during recursive invocations of the function. Hence in analyzing the computation performed by B.E. (Ω,P,V_j), we will refer to all recursive calls by specifying only the first argument. The first argument

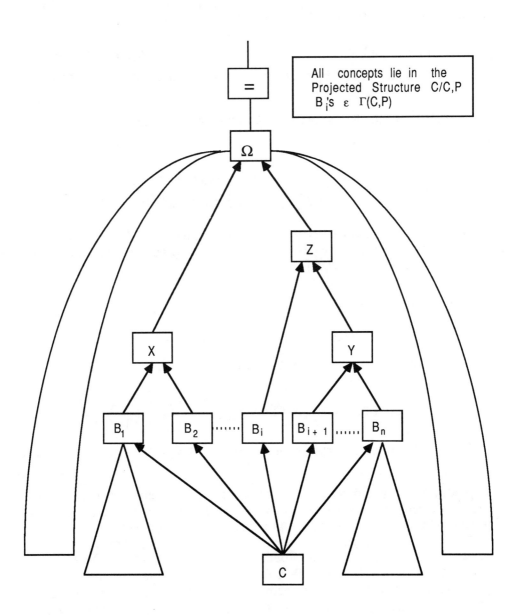

All concepts lie in the Projected Structure C/C,P
B_i's ε $\Gamma(C,P)$

Figure 4.8: Generalization of multiple inheritance

indicates the concept at which the function is currently being evaluated. The invocation trace of the function corresponds to a tree traversal, where the tree consists of the concept Ω, and all concepts that lie on paths from Ω to a B_i.

Proof of Theorem-3.2. As the first step of the proof we derive the following lemma:

Lemma-3.4: B.E. (Ω,P,V_j) computes the best estimate of $\#D[P,V_j]$, where D is the set $\cap_{i=1,n}B_i$, such that, for all i, $1 \leq i \leq r$, B_i's are the members of $\Gamma(C,P)$.

Proof (by induction):

Base case:

At the lowest level (level 0) of the ordering defined by $<<$ and $C/$ C,P, each concept ξ, is a member of $\Gamma(C,P)$. Hence the result computed by B.E.(ξ), where ξ is some $B_i \in \Gamma(C,P)$, is $\#\xi[P,V_j]$.

If ξ is a concept at level 1 then each of its offsprings will be a relevant concept. Let these be: B_1, B_2 ... B_r. Then it follows that B.E.(ξ) computes

$$\frac{\prod_{i=1}^{r} \#B_i[P,V_j]}{\#\xi[P,V_j]^{r-1}}$$

Therefore, the result computed by B.E.(ξ), for all concepts ξ at level 1 corresponds to the best estimate of $\#D[P,V_j]$ where D is the set $\cap_{i=1,r}B_i$ and B_1, B_2, ... B_r are *offsprings* of ξ. This establishes the base case (for level 1 nodes).

Induction step:

Inductive hypothesis: Assume that the result computed by B.E.(ξ), for each ξ at some intermediate level k, corresponds to the best estimate of $\#D[P,V_j]$, where D is the set $\cap_{i=1,r}B_i$ such that B_1, B_2, ... B_r are *descendants* of ξ.

We now show that the result computed by B.E.(ξ) for each ξ at level k+1, also corresponds to the best estimate of $\#D[P,V_j]$, where D is the set $\cap_{i=1,r}B_i$, such that, for all i, $1 \leq i \leq r$, B_i's are *descendants* of ξ.

Let ξ be a concept at level k+1, and let ξ_t, t =1, q, be its offsprings. As each offspring will be a concept at level k, it follows from the inductive hypothesis that

B.E.$(\xi_t) = \#D_t[P,V_j]$,

where D_t is the set $\cap_{i=at,bt}B_i$, such that, for all i, at $\leq i \leq$ bt, B_i's are *descendants* of ξ_t.

Then the result computed by B.E.(ξ), for some ξ at level k+1, is

$$\frac{\prod_{t=1}^{q} \#D_t[P,V_j]}{\#\xi \, [P,V_j]^{q-1}}$$

By virtue of Lemma-3.2, the above expression is the best estimate of $\#D[P,V_j]$ where D is given by

$$\cap_{t=1,q} \, (\cap_{i=at,bt}B_i)$$

which may be rewritten as

$$B_{a1} \cap B_{a1+1} \, ... \cap B_{b1} \cap B_{a2} \cap B_{a2+1} \, ... \cap B_{b2} \, ... \cap B_{aq} \cap B_{aq+1} \, ... \cap B_{bq}$$

which is the intersection of all B_i's that are descendants of ξ.

This concludes the inductive step.

But, by definition, Ω is the ancestor of all members of $\Gamma(C,P)$. Hence B.E. (Ω,P,V_j) computes the best estimate of $\#D[P,V_j]$, where D is the set $\cap_{i=1,n}B_i$, such that, for all i, $1 \leq i \leq r$, B_i's are the members of $\Gamma(C,P)$.

This concludes the inductive proof of Lemma-3.4. Q.E.D.

By virtue of Lemma-3.4 and Lemma-3.3

$$\frac{\text{B.E. } (\Omega,P,V_1)}{\text{B.E. } (\Omega,P,V_2)} = \frac{\#D[P,V_1]}{\#D[P,V_2]} = \text{the best estimate of } \frac{\#C[P,V_1]}{\#C[P,V_2]}$$

This concludes the proof of Theorem-3.2. Q.E.D.

4.4.4 Evidential inheritance: a summary

Problem statement:

Given: $\Theta = \langle \mathbf{C}, \Phi, \lambda, \Lambda, \#, \delta, << \rangle$,

$C \in \mathbf{C}, P \in \lambda(C)$, and

$\text{V-SET} = \{V_1, V_2, ... V_n\}$

Find: $V^* \in \text{V-SET}$, such that among members of V-SET, V^* is the *most likely value* of property P for concept C. In other words, find $V^* \in \text{V-SET}$ such that, for any $V_i \in \text{V-SET}$, the best estimate of $\#C[P,V^*] \geq$ the best estimate of $\#C[P,V_i]$'s.

Solution:

i) Find $\Gamma(C,P)$

ii) If the conceptual structure satisfies WFR-inh-1 (and therefore a unique reference concept Ω for $\Gamma(C,P)$ exists) then

$$\text{Find } V^* \text{ such that } \frac{\text{BEST-ESTIMATE } (\Omega,C,V^*)}{\text{BEST-ESTIMATE } (\Omega,C,V_i)} \geq 1$$

(Direct inheritance and the case where $\delta(C,P)$ is known are special cases of the above result)

The condition WFR-inh-1 is not unduly restrictive. The above condition does NOT require all concepts in **C** to be organized as a tree; if this were the case multiple inheritance situations would not even arise. The condition only requires that the ordering graph induced on **C**/C,P by << include a tree. In particular, the solution developed above applies to the Multiple Views Organization described in section 4.7. In fact, the Multiple Views conceptual structure is *more restricted* than what is required by WFR-inh-1.

Consider the concepts in figure 4.9. Assume that the property has-belief, with values pacifist and non-pacifist, applies to the concepts shown in the figure, and that

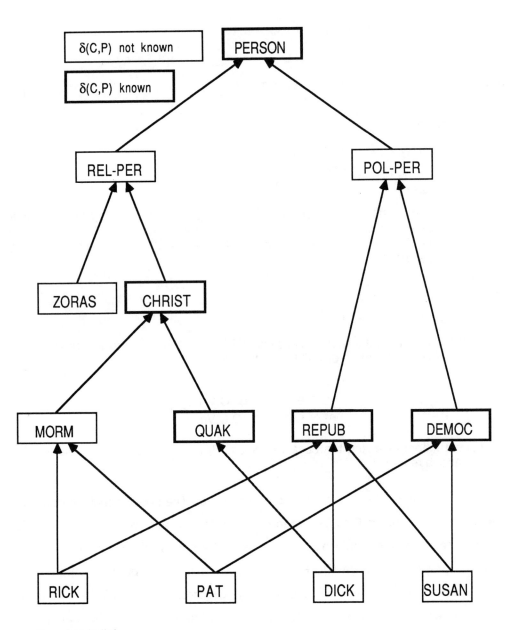

P = has-belief
Values: PACIFIST, NON-PACIFIST

Figure 4.9: An example of complex multiple inheritance

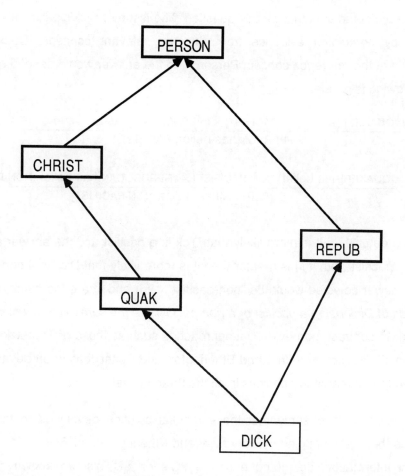

Figure 4.10: Projection with respect to DICK and has-belief

the agent has stored δ(C, has-belief) for all concepts C that are enclosed in a dark box. The concepts are embedded in a multilevel hierarchy and some of the concepts have multiple relevant concepts. Yet the most likely property-values of these concepts may be obtained via inheritance. In particular, the question: "Is Dick a pacifist or a non-pacifist", may be posed as an inheritance problem. Figure 4.10 shows the projected structure for this question. The issue of Dick's pacifism would be resolved by combining evidence from the two relevant concepts Quaker and Republican at the reference concept Person, and the answer would depend on which of the following is greater

i) $$\frac{\#QUAKER[\text{has-belief, PACIFIST}] \times \#REPUBLICAN[\text{has-belief, PACIFIST}]}{\#PERSON[\text{has-belief, PACIFIST}]}$$

ii) $$\frac{\#QUAKER[\text{has-belief, NON-PACIFIST}] \times \#REPUBLICAN[\text{has-belief, NON-PACIFIST}]}{\#PERSON[\text{has-belief, NON-PACIFIST}]}$$

If i) is greater then it is more likely that Dick is a pacifist and the answer selected would be "pacifist", but if ii) is greater then it is more likely that Dick is a non-pacifist, and the answer selected would be "non-pacifist". If i) and ii) are the same, then the *likelihoods of Dick being a pacifist or a non-pacifist are the same* and any choice may be made. In contrast, non-evidential approaches such as those of Touretzky (based on inferential distance ordering) and Etherington and Reiter (based on default logic). are forced to make arbitrary choices in all the three cases.

It is important to observe that the evidential solution developed in this thesis subsumes the cases handled by Touretzky and Etherington and Reiter. If there is no evidential information, i.e., if none of the #C's or δ(C,P)'s are known, then the formulation presented above is equivalent to those proposed by Touretzky and Etherington and Reiter. If evidential information is available, a system based on the evidential formulation will make use of it in a justifiable manner, whereas the other systems will not be able to use it at all.

4.5 Evidential recognition

Recall the definition of the recognition problem given in section 3.6.

Given: $\Theta = \langle \mathbf{C}, \Phi, \lambda, \Lambda, \#, \delta, << \rangle$,

an enumeration of possible answers, i.e., a set of concepts, C-SET = $\{C_1, C_2, \ldots C_n\}$, and

a description, DESCR, consisting of a set of property value pairs - { $[P_1,V_1]$, $[P_2,V_2]$, ... $[P_m,V_m]$ } such that

$$\forall \, [P_j,V_j] \in \text{DESCR},$$
$$V_j \in \Lambda(P_j)$$
$$\text{and } P_j \in \cap_{C \, \in \, \text{C-SET}} \, \lambda(C)$$

In other words, each property mentioned in the description should apply to every concept in C-SET, and the values specified for these properties should be appropriate.

Find: $C^* \in$ C-SET such that *relative* to the concepts specified in C-SET, C^* is the *most likely* concept described by DESCR.

In order to solve the recognition problem, we need to compute the most likely estimates of $\#C_i[P_1,V_1][P_2,V_2] \ldots [P_m,V_m]$ for each $C_i \in$ C-SET, and choose C^* such that the above estimate for C^* is greater than or equal to the estimates of all other members of C-SET.

By virtue of the best estimate result derived in section 4.1 the most likely estimate of $\#C_i[P_1,V_1][P_2,V_2] \ldots [P_m,V_m]$ based on the knowledge of $\#C_i[P_1,V_1]$, $\#C_i[P_2,V_2]$, ... $\#C_i[P_m,V_m]$ is

$$\frac{\prod_{j=1}^{m} \#C_i[P_j,V_j]}{\#C_i^{m-1}}$$

Hence the primary step in solving the recognition problem is the estimation of $\#C_i[P_j,V_j]$, for each C_i included in C-SET and each $[P_j,V_j]$ pair mentioned in DESCR.

The recognition problem is more complex than the inheritance problem because inheritance involves only a single concept and a single property whereas recognition involves multiple concepts and multiple properties. In this section we identify conditions under which the solution to the recognition problem remains computationally simple. We first consider the case where, for each C_i included in C-SET and each P_j mentioned in DESCR, there is only one concept relevant to C_i with respect to P_j. Following that, we solve a subclass of the more complex case involving multiple relevant concepts. It is shown that even the complex case can be handled with ease provided we make certain assumptions.

4.5.1 Unique relevant concepts

Theorem-3.3: A recognition problem such that, for each C_i included in C-SET and for each P_j mentioned in DESCR, there exists a unique concept, B_{ij}, relevant to C_i with respect to P_j, can be solved by computing the following for each C_i:

$$\#C_i \times \prod_{j=1}^{m} \frac{\#B_{ij}[P_j,V_j]}{\#B_{ij}}$$

Proof: If there exists a unique concept B_{ij} that is relevant to C_i with respect to P_j then by direct inheritance

$$\text{the best estimate of } \#C_i[P_j,V_j] = \#B_{ij}[P_j,V_j] \times \frac{\#C_i}{\#B_{ij}}$$

Therefore, the best estimate of $\#C_i[P_1,V_1][P_2,V_2] \dots [P_m,V_m]$ equals

$$\frac{1}{\#C_i^{m-1}} \times \prod_{j=1}^{m} \frac{\#B_{ij}[P_j,V_j] \times C_i}{\#B_{ij}} = \#C_i \times \prod_{j=1}^{m} \frac{\#B_{ij}[P_j,V_j]}{\#B_{ij}} \qquad \text{Q.E.D.}$$

Hence in the unique relevant concept situation the recognition problem may be solved as follows:

- For each $C_i \in$ C-SET

    a) For each P_j mentioned in DESCR, find B_{ij} that is relevant to C_i with respect to P_j.

b) Compute $\#C_i \times \prod\limits_{j=1}^{m} \dfrac{\#B_{ij}[P_j,V_j]}{\#B_{ij}}$

- Choose a C^* for which the quantity computed in b) has the highest magnitude.

4.5.2 Multiple relevant concepts

Theorem-3.4: A recognition problem where there exist multiple concepts, $B_{ij}{}^1$, $B_{ij}{}^2$, ... $B_{ij}{}^{qij}$, that are relevant to C_i with respect to P_j, can be solved by computing the following for each C_i in C-SET.

$$\#C_i \times \prod\limits_{j=1}^{m} \prod\limits_{k=1}^{q_{ij}} \dfrac{\#B_{ij}{}^k[P_j,V_j]}{\#B_{ij}{}^k}$$

The above result is, however, contingent on two assumptions that are stated in the body of the proof.

Proof: Consider the following well-formedness assumption about the conceptual structure:

WFR-rec-1: A conceptual structure is well-formed with respect to a recognition problem if for every C_i member of C-SET and every P_j mentioned in DESCR, the graph induced by $<<$ on $C/C_i,P_j$ is such that there exists a concept Ω_{ij} which is a reference concept of $\Gamma(C_i,P_j)$ as well as of every subset of $\Gamma(C_i,P_j)$.

If the conceptual structure satisfies WFR-rec-1 then the results of Lemma-3.2 apply and

$$\#\cap B_{ij}{}^k[P_j,V_j] = \dfrac{\prod\limits_{k=1}^{q_{ij}} \#B_{ij}{}^k[P_j,V_j]}{\Omega_{ij}[P_j,V_j]^{q_{ij}-1}} \qquad \text{-- Eq-3.5}$$

99

where $\cap B_{ij}{}^k$ refers to $\cap_{k=1,q_{ij}} B_{ij}{}^k$, the class obtained by intersecting $B_{ij}{}^k$'s, the members of $\Gamma(C_i,P_j)$. From Eq-3.5 it follows that

$$\text{the best estimate of } \#C_i[P_j,V_j] = \#\cap B_{ij}{}^k[P_j,V_j] \times \frac{\#C_i}{\#\cap B_{ij}{}^k} \qquad \text{-- Eq-3.6}$$

The expression for $\#C_i[P_j,V_j]$ in Eq-3.6 includes the factor $\#\cap B_{ij}{}^k$, the size of the set obtained by intersecting all $B_{ij}{}^k$'s. It is not possible to estimate $\#\cap B_{ij}{}^k$ without taking into account information about $\delta(B_{ij}{}^k, P_x)$ for all properties P_x that apply to $B_{ij}{}^k$'s - *even those that are not mentioned in* DESCR. However, if one makes the simplifying approximation that

$$\#\cap B_{ij}{}^k = \frac{\prod_{k=1}^{q_{ij}} \#B_{ij}{}^k}{\#\Omega_{ij}{}^{q_{ij}-1}} \qquad \text{-- APPROX-1}$$

then by substituting Eq-3.5 in Eq-3.6 and employing APPROX-1 we have

$$\#C_i[P_j,V_j] = \#C_i \times \left(\frac{\#\Omega_{ij}}{\#\Omega_{ij}[P_j,V_j]} \right)^{q_{ij}-1} \times \prod_{k=1}^{q_{ij}} \frac{\#B_{ij}{}^k[P_j,V_j]}{\#B_{ij}{}^k} \qquad \text{-- Eq-3.7}$$

The above expression depends only on the properties and property values mentioned in DESCR. Eq-3.7 may be further simplified by imposing the following conditions on the conceptual structure:

WFR-rec-2: For each P_j mentioned in DESCR, there exists a unique Ω_j such that for $1 \le i \le n$, $\Omega_{ij} = \Omega_j$. In other words, Ω_j is the common reference concept for the various $\Gamma(C_i,P_j)$'s corresponding to the different C_i's in C-SET.

WFR-rec-3: For each P_j mentioned in DESCR, the number of concepts relevant with respect to P_j is the same for all C_i in C-SET. In other words, $|\Gamma(C_1,P_j)| = |\Gamma(C_2, P_j)| \dots = |\Gamma(C_n,P_j)|$.

If the conceptual structure satisfies WFR-rec-2 and WFR-rec-3 then the term

$$\left(\frac{\#\Omega_{ij}}{\#\Omega_{ij}[P_j,V_j]} \right)^{q_{ij}-1}$$

in Eq-3.7 is identical for all $C_i \in$ C-SET. (WFR-rec-2 implies that all Ω_{ij}'s are equal to Ω_j and WFR-rec-3 entails that all q_{ij} are equal to some q_j).

Given that solving the recognition problem only requires a relative comparison of the magnitudes of $\#C_i[P_1,V_1][P_2,V_2] \dots [P_m, V_m]$ for different C_i's in C-SET, and given that $\#C_i[P_j,V_j]$'s only appear as multiplicative terms in the computation of $\#C_i[P_1,V_1][P_2,V_2] \dots [P_m, V_m]$, the common terms occurring in Eq-3.7 may be dropped. Consequently, it is only necessary to compute the following expression for each $C_i \in$ C-SET in order to solve the recognition problem:

$$\frac{1}{\#C_i^{m-1}} \times \prod_{j=1}^{m} \left(\#C_i \times \prod_{k=1}^{q_j} \frac{B_{ij}{}^k[P_j,V_j]}{\#B_{ij}{}^k} \right)$$

The above expression may be further simplified to

$$\#C_i \times \prod_{j=1}^{m} \prod_{k=1}^{q_j} \frac{\#B_{ij}{}^k[P_j,V_j]}{\#B_{ij}{}^k} \qquad \text{-- Eq-3.8}$$

Q.E.D.

To summarize, if the conceptual structure satisfies WFR-rec-1 through WFR-rec-3 then the recognition problem may be solved as follows:

- For each $C_i \in$ C-SET

    a) For each P_j mentioned in DESCR, find all the $B_{ij}{}^k$'s that are relevant to C_i with respect to P_j.

    b) Compute $\#C_i \times \prod_{j=1}^{m} \prod_{k=1}^{q_j} \frac{\#B_{ij}{}^k[P_j,V_j]}{\#B_{ij}{}^k}$

- Choose a C* for which the quantity computed in b) has the highest magnitude.

4.6 The role of numbers in the theory

The representation language specified in chapter 3 required the specification of absolute numbers. It was assumed that the agent knew the values of #C for each member of **C**. It was also assumed that he knew the values of #C[P,V], for C's and P's for which $\delta(C,P)$ was defined.

However, an important characteristic of the solution to the problems of inheritance and recognition developed above is that none of the calculations require the knowledge of absolute numbers. All the necessary numeric information is embodied in the following ratios each of which lies in the interval [0,1]:

- For all C and P such that $\delta(C,P)$ is known, ratios of the form:

$$\frac{\#C[P,V_i]}{\#D[P,V_i]}, \frac{\#C[P,V_i]}{\#V_i} \text{ and } \frac{\#C[P,V_i]}{\#C}$$

   where, D is a parent of C in the ordering induced by << on **C**/C,P, and V_i's are possible values of P.

- For all pairs of concepts C and D such that D is a parent of C in the ordering induced by << on **C**, the ratios:

$$\frac{\#C}{\#D}$$

4.7 Well-formedness constraints and a proposal for structuring concepts

In this section we suggest a particular conceptual organization, namely, the Multiple Views Organization. This organization obeys certain structural restrictions that simplify the evidence combination process during inheritance and recognition. We also discuss the translation of the well-formedness constraints introduced in the previous sections with respect to this organization.

4.7.1 The Multiple Views Organization

In the proposed scheme, concepts are organized in a three tier structure as shown in figure 4.11. The topmost tier consists of a pure taxonomy and is called the *ontological tree*. This tree classifies the universe of concepts into several distinct *ontological types*, where any two ontological types represent fundamentally different sorts of things. These may correspond to *categories* of Aristotle or the *ontological categories* suggested by Jackendoff [Jackendoff 83]. Keil [Keil 79][Sommers 65] has argued extensively in support of a hierarchical structure composed of ontological categories such as: Thing, Physical object, Solid, Aggregate, Event, Functional artifact, Animal, Plant, Human, etc., As our primary interest is in suggesting a way of *structuring* and organizing concepts, and not in the compilation of human knowledge, we will not argue for or against a specific set of ontological Types.

Ontological categories are derived using the principle of *predicability*, according to which, different sorts of things have different sorts of predicates[19] applicable to them, and things may be classified according to the predicates that apply to them. Predicates may be attached to categories at various levels in the ontological tree, and once a predicate is attached to a category it applies to all categories that are dominated by this concept. This agrees with our notion of property applicability described in chapter 3. Based on earlier work by Sommers, Keil proposes two constraints on the conceptual structure - the M-*constraint* and the W-*constraint*. These constraints require that ontological categories form a strict taxonomy. Figure 4.12 gives an example of an ontological tree based on [Keil 79].

In the Multiple Views Organization it is envisaged that the leaves of the ontological tree are Types such as: Animal, Human, Furniture, Instrument, Liquid, Color, Shape, Taste etc. These concepts correspond roughly to the superordinate categories of Rosch [Rosch 75] which appear to have the right level of complexity to be the leaves of the ontological tree.

---

[19]Predicates correspond to properties in our terminology.

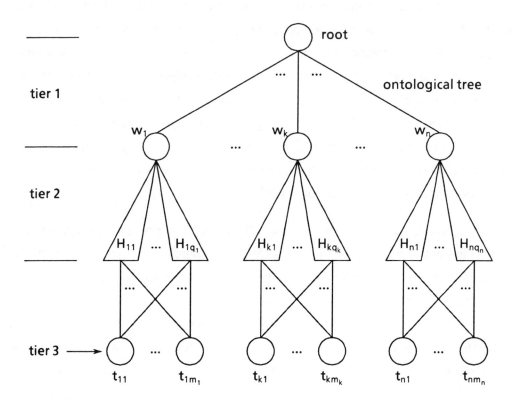

tier 1

tier 2

tier 3 →

$t_{11} ..., t_{nm_n}$ are tokens.

A token may have multiple parents but at most one parent per view.

$w_1, ..., w_n$ are leaves of the ontological tree.

$H_{i1}, ..., H_{iq_i}$ are q_i views defined over tokens of ontological type w_i.

Figure 4.11: The Multiple Views Organization

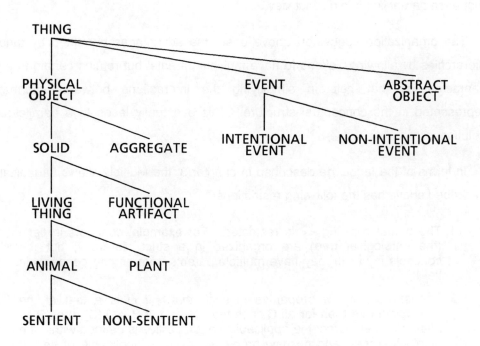

Figure 4.12: Ontological categories

The third, or the lowest tier of the conceptual structure consists of Tokens.

The second tier consists of a number of taxonomies called *views* where each view may be taken to be a distinct classification of the underlying Tokens. The root of a view is a leaf of the ontological tree while the leaves of a view are Tokens. There may be multiple views that have the same leaf of the ontological tree as their root and consequently, there may be multiple views that have the same Token as one of their leaves. The latter implies that Tokens may have multiple parents. Notice, however, that each parent lies in a distinct view.

The organization suggested above offers the advantages permitted by tangled hierarchies by allowing Tokens to have multiple parents, but retains certain tree like characteristics that help in simplifying the interactions between information represented in the conceptual structure. This eventually leads to a parallelizable solution.

In terms of the language described in chapter 3, the Multiple Views Organization described above has the following restrictions:

1. The partial ordering << is restricted. For example, concepts in tier I (the ontological tree) are organized in a strict hierarchy, but the concepts in tier III may have multiple parents from among concepts in tier II.

2. The applicability of properties is such that: if ω is a leaf of the ontological tree then for all C such that $C << \omega$, if $P \in \lambda(C)$, then $P \in \lambda(\omega)$. In other words, the applicability of properties is defined within the ontological tree, and no new properties become applicable at tiers II and III. Note that this restriction applies to *properties* and NOT to *property values*,

4.7.2 Inheritance in the Multiple Views Organization

In section 4.4.3 we introduced the following constraint on the conceptual structure in order to arrive at a computationally effective solution to inheritance.

WFR-inh-1: A conceptual structure is well formed with respect to an inheritance problem (or vice versa) if the graph induced by << on C/C,P includes a tree whose leaves are the members of Γ(C,P).

We now show that WFR-inh-1 is easily satisfied by the Multiple Views Organization if we make the following well-formedness assumption:

WFR-mv-1: If ω is a leaf of the ontological tree and $P_j \in \lambda(\omega)$, then $\delta(\omega, P_j)$ is known.

To see this consider two cases: one in which C_i is a Type and the other in which C_i is a Token.

C_i is a Type

In the Multiple Views Organization all Types are organized into a strict taxonomy. Therefore, C_i may have *at most* one concept relevant to it with respect to a property P_j. The existence of *at least* one relevant concept is guaranteed by WFR-mv-1. Hence a Type C_i has exactly one concept relevant to it with respect to any $P_j \in \lambda(C_i)$. This directly satisfies WFR-inh-1.

C_i is a Token

Since C_i is a Token it may have multiple relevant concepts with respect to a property P_j. But because C_i can have at most one parent per view, it follows that in any given view, C_i can have at most one relevant concept with respect to P_j. In other words, there may be multiple concepts relevant to C_i with respect to P_j - but at most one per view defined over C_i. Consequently, each relevant concept must lie in a different view, and hence, Ω_{ij}, the reference concept of $\Gamma(C_i, P_j)$ in the ordering defined by $<<$ on $C/C_i, P_j$, cannot lie within any of these views but must lie at or above ω - the ontological type to which C_i belongs. However, by virtue of WFR-mv-1 $\delta(\omega, P_j)$ is known, and hence, ω itself must be the reference concept in question. Furthermore, because ω is a leaf of the ontological tree and all members of $\Gamma(C_i, P_j)$ lie in different views - each of which is a strict taxonomy, the structure induced by $<<$ on concepts between ω and $\Gamma(C_i, P_j)$ must be a tree. This directly satisfies WFR-inh-1.

4.7.3 Recognition in the Multiple Views Organization

In section 4.5 we showed that there is a fairly straightforward solution to the recognition problem in case, for each C_i included in C-SET and each P_j mentioned in DESCR, there is a *single* concept relevant to C_i with respect to P_j. We then showed that there also exist tractable solutions to the recognition problem with multiple relevant concepts provided the following constraints are satisfied.

WFR-rec-1: A conceptual structure is well-formed with respect to a recognition problem if for every C_i member of C-SET and every P_j mentioned in DESCR, the graph induced by $<<$ on $C/C_i,P_j$ is such that there exists a concept Ω_{ij} which is a reference concept of $\Gamma(C_i,P_j)$ as well as of every subset of $\Gamma(C_i,P_j)$[20].

WFR-rec-2: For each P_j mentioned in DESCR, there exists a unique Ω_j such that for $1 \le i \le n$, $\Omega_{ij} = \Omega_j$. In other words, Ω_j is the common reference concept for the various $\Gamma(C_i,P_j)$'s corresponding to the different C_i's in C-SET.

WFR-rec-3: For each P_j mentioned in DESCR, the number of concepts relevant with respect to P_j is the same for all C_i in C-SET. In other words, $|\Gamma(C_1,P_j)| = |\Gamma(C_2, P_j)| \ldots = |\Gamma(C_n,P_j)|$.

We show below that WFR-mv-1 also satisfies WFR-rec-1. Furthermore, WFR-rec-2 and WFR-rec-3 can also be satisfied by imposing relatively simple and meaningful restrictions on the Multiple Views Organization. To see how the constraints WFR-rec-1 through WFR-rec-3 translate with reference to the Multiple Views Organization we will consider two distinct cases of recognition: one in which all concepts in C-SET are Types (Type recognition), and the other in which they are all Tokens (Token recognition).

Type Recognition

In the Multiple Views organization, all Types are organized into a strict taxonomy.

---

[20]Notice that WFR-rec-1 subsumes WFR-inh-1; WFR-inh-1 requires that the structure induced by $<<$ on $C/C,P$ include a tree, but WFR-rec-1 restricts the structure even further and requires that all nodes in the above tree, except the root, have an outdegree of at most one.

Therefore, each C_i may have *at most* one concept relevant to it with respect to a property P_j. The existence of *at least* one relevant concept is guaranteed by WFR-mv-1. Hence each Type C_i has exactly one concept relevant to it with respect to any $P_j \in \lambda(C_i)$. This means that Type recognition corresponds to the "Unique relevant concept" situation discussed in section 4.5.1, and hence, is easily solved.

Token Recognition

In this case each C_i may have multiple relevant concepts with respect to a property P_j, and hence, Token recognition amounts to the "multiple relevant concepts" situation discussed in section 4.5.2. Below we identify conditions under which WFR-rec-1 through WFR-rec-3 are satisfied by the Multiple Views Organization.

Each C_i can have at most one parent per view. Therefore, in any given view C_i can have at most one relevant concept with respect to P_j. In other words, there may be multiple concepts relevant to C_i with respect to P_j - but at most one per view defined over C_i. Consequently, each relevant concept must lie in a different view, and hence, Ω_{ij}, the reference concept of $\Gamma(C_i,P_j)$ in the ordering defined by $<<$ on $C/C_i,P_j$, cannot lie within any of these views but must lie at or above ω - the ontological type to which C_i belongs. However, by virtue of WFR-mv-1 $\delta(\omega,P_j)$ is known and hence ω itself must be the reference concept in question. Furthermore, because ω is a leaf of the ontological tree, no two concepts (Types) in tier II may have a common ancestor that lies below ω. This satisfies WFR-rec-1.

If we also impose the following constraint on the Multiple Views Organization we can show that WFR-rec-2 can also be satisfied.

WFR-mv-2: When posing a recognition problem, C-SET should be such that all its members are descendants of the *same* leaf of the ontological tree.

The above well-formedness rule requires that all members of C-SET should belong to the same ontological type. This condition is not unduly restrictive although it does rule out queries such as: "Is <*DESCR*}> a cat, water, a story, or red?

WFR-mv-2 entails that there exists a ω such that ω is a leaf of the ontological tree and for all $C_i \in$ C-SET, $C_i \ll \omega$. Let $H_1, H_2, \ldots H_q$ be q views defined with ω as their root. Now each C_i may have at most one parent in each view H_k, and therefore, there can be at most one concept that is relevant to C_i with respect to P_j and lies in H_k. Thus each relevant concept lies in a different view, and hence, Ω_{ij}, the reference concept for $\Gamma(C_i, P_j)$ in the ordering defined by $\ll$ on $C/C_i, P_j$ can be none other than ω. As all C_i's, members of C-SET, belong to the same ontological type, each of the $\Gamma(C_i, P_j)$'s corresponding to these C_i's will have ω as their reference concept. This satisfies WFR-rec-2.

Finally, it can be shown that WFR-rec-3 can be satisfied by imposing the following restriction on the Multiple Views Organization.

WFR-mv-3: If for some Token C_i, there exists a concept in H_k that is relevant to C_i with respect to P_j, then for *every* Token C_i that lies below H_k, there exists a concept in H_k that is relevant to C_i with respect to P_j.

The above well-formedness rule requires that if the distributions for property P_j are stored at concepts in some view H_k, then such distributions should be stored at enough concepts in H_k so that for every Token C_i that is under H_k, there exists at least one concept B_{ij} within H_k, for which $\delta(B_{ij}, P_j)$ is known (stored).

If the conceptual structure satisfies WFR-mv-3 then for a given property P_j and a given view H_k, either each $C_i \in$ C-SET has exactly one concept relevant to it with respect to P_j in view H_k, or each $C_i \in$ C-SET has no concept relevant to it with respect to P_j in view H_k. It follows that every $C_i \in$ C-SET will have the same number of relevant concepts with respect to any property P_j mentioned in DESCR. This satisfies WFR-rec-3.

In view of the above condition, namely - for a given property P_j and a given view H_k, either each $C_i \in$ C-SET has exactly one concept relevant to it with respect to P_j in view H_k, or each $C_i \in$ C-SET has no concept relevant to it with respect to P_j in view H_k - and recognizing that in case of Token recognition, $\#C = 1$, for all $C_i \in$ C-SET, Eq-3.8 (section 4.5.2) may be rewritten as

$$\prod_{j=1}^{m} \prod_{k=1}^{q} \beta_{ij}^{k}$$

where P_j, $1 \leq j \leq m$, are the properties mentioned in DESCR, q refers to the number of views defined below ω - the ontological Type to which the C_i's belong, and

$$\beta_{ij}^{k} = \frac{\#B_{ij}^{k}[P_j, V_j]}{\#B_{ij}^{k}} \quad \text{; if there exists a concept } B_{ij}^{k} \text{ in view } H_k \text{ that is}$$

relevant to C_i with respect to P_j

$$1 \qquad \qquad \text{; otherwise.}$$

Notice that the meaning of the index "k" in the above expression is different from what it was in Eq-3.8. "k" now ranges from 1 to q, where q refers to the number of views defined below ω, H_k refers to the kth view below ω, and B_{ij}^{k} refers to the concept in H_k that is relevant to C_i with respect to P_j. B_{ij}^{k} has no meaning for those "k" for which such a concept does not exist.

5 A Connectionist Realization of the Memory Network

In this chapter we describe how an agent's conceptual knowledge may be encoded as a *connectionist* network. It can be shown that if this knowledge satisfies the constraints listed in section 5.7 then the network computes solutions to the inheritance and recognition problems in accordance with the results developed in chapter 4. The time required to perform these operations is only $O(d)$, where d is the maximum depth of the conceptual hierarchy (i.e., the longest path in the ordering graph defined by **C** and $<<$).

The view that the Memory Network is a subsystem embodying an organized and structured body of knowledge and capable of supporting retrieval as well as inference, goes beyond the relatively simpler conception of memory as being an associative or content addressable store. Although considerable work has been done in the area of connectionist models of associative and content addressable memories [Willshaw 81][Kohonen et al. 81] [Hopfield 82], only limited progress has been made in the past towards the design of connectionist models of memories that are capable of representing structured knowledge and supporting retrieval and inference. In fact, a common criticism levelled against connectionism is that although it may be appropriate for modeling "low level" cognitive activities and "approximate" effects such as semantic priming and associative recall, it is unsuitable for dealing with "high level" problems related to representation and reasoning. Given the central role of knowledge representation and inference in AI, this criticism appears to be a serious one. The work described in this section partially answers this criticism.

Before discussing the encoding in detail, we will describe the connectionist model of computation and examine the reasons behind the growing interest in these models. We shall do so both in general terms as well as with specific reference to the problem of knowledge representation and limited inference. We shall also review some related work on massively parallel encoding of semantic networks.

5.1 Need for parallelism

We observed in section 1.1 that parallelism may be essential for achieving computational effectiveness. It was pointed out that many cognitive tasks, and certainly all of the perceptual ones, that humans can perform in a few hundred milliseconds require millions of instructions on a serial (von Neumann) computer and it is fairly obvious that even a serial computer made up of ultra fast devices will be unable to perform these tasks in acceptable time frames.

A possible solution to the above problem suggests itself if one examines the architecture of a traditional von Neumann computer. In such a computer the processing power - i.e., the computational and inferential power - is concentrated in a *single* processing unit, while the information on which computations have to be performed is stored in the computer's memory. This memory simply acts as an *inert* repository of the system's knowledge. As a result of the single processor design, only one processing step can be executed at any point in time, and during each processing step the CPU can only access a minuscule fraction of the memory. Therefore, at any given instant, only an insignificant portion of the system's knowledge participates in the processing. On the other hand, intelligent behavior requires dense interactions between many pieces of information, and any computational architecture for intelligent information processing must be capable of supporting such dense interactions. It would therefore seem appropriate to treat each memory cell - not as a mere repository of information, but rather as an *active* processing element capable of *interacting* with other such elements. This would result in a massively parallel computer made up of an extremely large number of simple processing elements - as many as there are memory cells in a traditional computer. The processing capability of such a computer would be *distributed* across its memory, and consequently, such a computer would permit numerous interactions between various pieces of information to occur simultaneously.

Adopting such a massively parallel architecture would greatly increase the computing power of a computer; such a computer would be capable of executing hundreds of billions of instructions per second because potentially millions of processors may compute simultaneously[21]. But a phenomenal increase in raw computing power is not the only advantage that accrues from adopting a massively parallel approach. Massive parallelism offers other significant advantages that have a fundamental impact on the way we formulate problems in artificial intelligence.

First, the massively parallel approach provides a distinct *scientific language* for expressing solutions to problems in AI and cognitive science [Feldman & Ballard 82]. This language complements traditional paradigms such as production systems and theorem proving, and offers a promising new way of looking at problems that have for long proved elusive. Computations in a massively parallel network proceed via interactions between a large number of highly interconnected but relatively simple processing elements. The elements communicate with their neighbors by propagating a level of activation and compute their own level of activity by integrating the activation arriving from their neighbors[22]. Consequently, the computations performed by such a network are best viewed as *knowledge aggregation* or *knowledge integration* where interactions among individual chunks of information are emphasized. This approach offers a natural computational model for encoding a number of interesting information processing paradigms such as constraint satisfaction, evidential reasoning[23], energy minimization, and entropy maximization. The use of this scientific language has already paid dividends in diverse areas of research in AI and cognitive science such as low and intermediate level vision, word perception, associative memory, word sense disambiguation, modeling of context

---

[21]For example, the Connection Machine a commercially available computer built along these lines has 64K processors. According to benchmark data supplied by the manufacturers, it executes about 1000 MIPS to 7000 MIPS. The actual throughput depends on the application. For a detailed description of the Connection Machine architecture see [Hillis 85].

[22]The precise rules governing the computation of activation and its propagation vary from model to model.

[23]This is discussed later in section 5.2.3.

effects in natural language understanding, speech production, and learning [Feldman 85][McClelland & Rumelhart 86][Rumelhart & McClelland 86].

Second, massive parallelism provides a point of contact between artificial intelligence and neuroscience. Both these fields stand to gain from such a marriage, for the brain is a working example of an "intelligent" information processor, and one suspects that artificial intelligence would profit from understanding the organization of information in the brain and the nature of computation performed on this information. Similarly, research on artificial intelligence using massively parallel networks results in the development of specific computational models of intelligent behavior and leads to a better understanding of the computational properties of such networks. This provides critical clues to neuroscientists who are trying to unravel the working of the animal brain. Such a symbiosis of artificial intelligence and neuroscience has already occurred, specially in the case of vision.

We said earlier that understanding neural architecture has had an impact on the development of massively parallel models of computation. In fact, there has been a succession of neurally inspired models that date back to work by McCullough and Pitts [McCullough and Pitts 43] and Rosenblatt [Rosenblatt 62]. In recent years, interest in such models has grown considerably within the artificial intelligence circles, and increasingly sophisticated models are being investigated and applied to a diverse set of problems. Some of the reasons for this heightened interest and the increased level of sophistication are: the realization that real-time performance requires parallelism, an improved understanding of neural behavior, and the availability of adequate computing power to support extensive simulations of massively parallel networks. The last of these factors is particularly important since to a great extent, the field is experimental in its character and relies heavily on simulations to evaluate new techniques and to gain deeper insights.

5.2 The Connectionist Model

The massively parallel model employed in this work is a variation of the *connectionist* model proposed in [Feldman & Ballard 82]. The Feldman and Ballard proposal offers a very general model of massively parallel computation and many other models referred to as "connectionist models", "parallel distributed processing models", or "neural networks" can be expressed as specializations of this model.

As this model is directly inspired by the computational properties of the animal brain, we digress to enumerate some of the more relevant of these properties. What follows is clearly a greatly oversimplified account.

5.2.1 A brief overview of the brain

The brain is a massively parallel information processor. The human brain consists of about 10^{10} to 10^{12} nerve cells. These cells, called neurons, are the basic information processing elements of the brain. They form an intricate and highly interconnected network; a typical neuron makes around 1000 - 10,000 connections (synapses) with other neurons, resulting in a total of around 10^{14} connections. A neuron receives incoming signals from other neurons, integrates them, and propagates the result to the set of neurons to which it is connected. The output of neurons is in the form of a train of electrical impulses, the frequency of which encodes the strength of the neuronal output. The switching time of a neuron is a few milliseconds, which makes it rather slow compared to switching elements used in modern day computers whose switching times may be in the nanosecond range. Furthermore, the nature of information transmitted from one neuron to another is severely constrained; the firing frequency of a neuron may vary from about 1 cps to a few hundred cps. This suggests that neurons communicate by transmitting only a few bits of information. Thus the biological computer is made up of relatively slow computing elements that exchange only a few bits of information per second.

An important aspect of neural computation is that inputs differ in their ability to affect the response of a neuron; some inputs are excitatory while some others are inhibitory. Additionally, there is a strength or "synaptic weight" associated with each synapse that encodes the degree to which inputs along a synapse affect the target neuron. It appears that - in large part - the information in the brain resides in the connections: in the pattern of connectivity and in the strengths of these connections.

5.2.2 Details of the connectionist model

A connectionist network consists of a large number of simple computing elements called **units** connected via weighted links. Units are computational entities defined by:

$\{q\}$:   a small set of states, (fewer than ten)
p: a continuous value called potential, often restricted to [0, 1]
v: an output value, often restricted to a small number of distinct values
i: a vector of inputs $i_1, i_2 \dots i_n$
         (this is elaborated below)

together with functions that define the values of potential, state and output at time $t+1$, based on the values at time t:

$$p_{t+1} \quad \longleftarrow \quad \mathbf{P}(i_t, p_t, q_t)$$

$$q_{t+1} \quad \longleftarrow \quad \mathbf{Q}(i_t, p_t, q_t)$$

$$v_{t+1} \quad \longleftarrow \quad \mathbf{V}(i_t, p_t, q_t)$$

A unit communicates with the rest of the network by transmitting the output (a single number) to all units to which it is connected. The output value is closely related to the unit's *potential* which may be viewed as the unit's *level of activation*. The potential is in turn supposed to be a monotonic function of the activation received by the unit from its neighboring units. A unit does not treat all inputs uniformly. Units receive inputs via weighted links. Each link contributes an input whose magnitude equals the output of the node at the source of the link times the weight on the link. A unit may have multiple *input sites* and incoming links are connected to specific sites. Each site has an associated site-function. These functions carry out local

118

computations based on the input values at the site, and it is the result of this computation that is processed by the functions **P, Q**, and **V**. The notion of sites is useful in defining interesting behavior. For example, some inputs may be treated as "enabling" inputs whose presence or absence determines whether the unit attends to the remaining inputs or ignores them. The functions **P**, **Q**, and **V** are arbitrary but in keeping with the underlying philosophy of these models, they are assumed to be simple.

The model described above is fairly general: it allows units in the network to have some local memory in the form of their states and potentials, and it admits a variety of nonlinear behavior. The latter may be encoded in the site-functions, potential-functions, and output-functions of units. Restrictions of the above definition result in some well known variations of the connectionist model. For example, if we equate the state and the potential of a unit and restrict these to be either ON or OFF, define **P** (or **Q**) to be such that the unit is ON if the weighted sum of inputs exceeds a prescribed threshold, and restrict the output to be 1 if the unit is ON and 0 otherwise, we have a classic binary threshold element. If in the above specification of a binary threshold element, we modify **P** to be a probabilistic function of the weighted sum of inputs, and assume that all links are symmetric - i.e., for all pairs of units i and j, the weight on the link from unit i to unit j equals the weight on the link from unit j to unit i - we get networks that are compatible with Hopfield's associative memory [Hopfield 82]. Finally, if we let the potential function **P** of the above units be a probabilistic function of the weighted sum of inputs, we have units that correspond to elements of a Boltzmann machine [Ackley et al. 85].

5.2.3 Why a connectionist model of massive parallelism?

There are three reasons for choosing a connectionist massively parallel model for encoding the Memory Network.

- It offers fine grained parallelism.
- It provides a natural encoding of evidential reasoning.

- The *relatively* sophisticated nature of its computing elements permits the encoding of a *variety* of computational and control functions.

Importance of fine-grained parallelism

The fine grain of parallelism supported by connectionism permits one to assign *a single processing element to each unit of information*. This has the following interesting consequence. Assume that besides enumerating facts about the world, we also identify the important *inferential connections* between these facts. Now if we encode each piece of information as a connectionist node (henceforth, node) and an inferential interconnection between pieces of information as an explicit link between the appropriate nodes, then we can view inference as spreading of activation in a connectionist network. The above metaphor has tremendous appeal because it suggests extremely efficient parallel implementations. This is not a new metaphor and dates back at least to Quillian's work on semantic memory wherein he used the propagation of discrete *activation tags* in a network to find common properties of concepts.

When knowledge is encoded in connectionist networks the traditional distinction between the representation and the inference engine (interpreter) gets blurred: the links, weights on links, and the computational characteristics of nodes encode not just the knowledge but also how the various constituents of knowledge interact during computation. In a connectionist network, the physical structure of the network directly determines what information is relevant for the computation. This strong coupling between the structure of knowledge and inference is a desirable state of affairs (see chapter 6).

Ease of encoding evidential computations

The connectionist framework provides the necessary primitives for capturing notions like "weighted evidence" and "evidence combination". This makes it ideal for performing evidential reasoning, and differentiates *value passing* connectionist models from marker passing schemes like NETL (see section 5.3). A node may be interpreted as representing a hypothesis, the inputs to the node may be viewed as evidence provided to it by the rest of the network, and a node's potential may be viewed as the result of combining all the evidence impinging on the node using the evidence combination rule encoded by the site-functions and the potential-functions.

Sophisticated processing elements

The presence of multiple sites, multiple states, and distinct potential functions make it possible to encode relatively sophisticated behavior in connectionist networks. The network described in this paper uses controlled spreading activation to draw precise and well specified inferences and does so without the benefit of a central controller or *interpreter*. The ability to operate without an interpreter is significant from the point of view of computational effectiveness.

5.3 Related work on massively parallel semantic memory

The use of spreading activation as a computational primitive in memory models dates back at least to Quillian's work on semantic nets. Since then, numerous models of memory based on some form of spreading activation or marker passing have been proposed in the psychological and cognitive science literature (e.g., [Collins & Loftus 1975][Anderson 1983][Charniak 1983a]). The two models that are most closely related to this work, however, are those of Fahlman [Fahlman 1979] and Hinton [Hinton 1981].

Fahlman's NETL was the first attempt at encoding semantic networks as a massively parallel network of simple processing elements. The NETL system design consisted of a central (serial) computer connected to a large number of node and link elements, each of which was a hardware element. A concept was represented as a node while a relation between concepts was encoded by a link that connected appropriate concept nodes. A node could communicate with other nodes by propagating a small number of simple messages called *markers* along its links. NETL used marker passing to perform simple inferences based on set *intersection* and *transitive closure* operations. The intersection operation located items that shared a set of properties (i.e., recognition) whereas the transitive closure operation handled *inheritance* as well as closures of relations like *part-of.* These operations were performed in parallel and allowed the system to conduct a very fast search.

A limitation of marker passing systems was that the communication between network elements was via a small number of *discrete* markers that were essentially boolean conditions and a network element could only detect the presence or absence of a marker in the input. This all or none nature of the system made it incapable of supporting "best match" or "partial match" operations. For example, in NETL recognition amounted to finding a concept that possessed *all* of a specified set of properties. Furthermore, NETL's solution to the inheritance problem suffered from serious drawbacks: the answers were sensitive to race conditions, specially in the presence of exceptions and multiple hierarchies. These limitations of marker passing systems are discussed at length in [Fahlman 82] and [Fahlman et al. 81][24]. The other limitation of NETL was that the communication between nodes in the parallel network critically depended on instructions issued by the central (serial) controller and only minimal control mechanisms were built into the parallel network. This lead to an underutilization of the potential parallelism.

Hinton proposed a "distributed" encoding of semantic networks using parallel hardware. Instead of representing a concept in the semantic network by an element in the parallel network, he suggested that a concept be encoded as a pattern of activity in a large assembly of elements. The information encoded in a semantic network was interpreted as consisting of a set of triples of the form: [relation, role1, role2]. The basic mode of operation of the parallel network was pattern completion: given two components of a triple, the network could produce the third tuple.

The proposed system had several interesting properties. For instance, it could be programmed using the perceptron convergence rule and it demonstrated that simple

---

[24]Subsequent work by Touretzky has remedied certain problems with inheritance. The use of discrete markers, however, still precludes partial match and best match operations.

property inheritance could be performed naturally by such a system. It however, lacked sufficient structure and control to handle general cases of inheritance, especially if these occurred in a complex, multilevel, semantic network that included exceptional and conflicting information. Hinton's paper did present a simple example of how an exception would be handled, but even in that extremely simple situation the results tended to be unstable. In the absence of any precise characterization of the network behavior it was also not possible to predict how the network would deal with partial matches during recognition.

More recently, Derthick [Derthick 86] is attempting an implementation of a variant of KL-ONE using the Boltzman machine formulation [Ackley et al. 1985].

Work on Bayesian networks by Pearl [Pearl 85] also deals with evidential reasoning in a parallel network. Pearl's results, however, apply only to singly-connected networks (networks in which there is only one underlying path between any pair of nodes), and more complex networks have to be *conditioned* to render them singly-connected. This is in part due to the unstructured form of the underlying representation language employed by Pearl. The language does not make distinctions such as "concept", "property", "property-value" that we make, and hence, its ability to exploit parallellism is limited.

5.4 Details of the connectionist encoding

In developing a connectionist encoding of the Memory Network two technical problems were solved:

Control of spreading activation: The proposed network had to perform specific inferences in accordance with the evidential formulation and it had to do so without the intervention of a central controller; once a query was posed the network was expected to function autonomously. This required that local mechanisms for controlling the spread of activation be encoded in each node, while honoring the constraint that each node be a simple processing element. The design involves introducing explicit control nodes - namely, binder nodes and relay nodes - that

123

provide *foci* for controlling the spread of activation.

Convergence: It had to be established that the network will converge to a stable solution state and would do so within an acceptable time frame. It can be shown that the network does converge in time proportional to the depth of the conceptual hierarchy - provided the conceptual structure satisfies certain constraints discussed in section 5.7.

The following sections describe how the above objectives were realized.

5.4.1 Connectivity and node types

The encoding of the Memory Network employs six distinct node types:

1. *enable* nodes: these provide a mechanism for distinguishing between recognition and inheritance queries.
2. ξ-nodes: these represent *concepts*
3. ϕ-nodes: these represent *properties*
4. δ_{inh}-nodes: these are *binder* nodes that bind a *<concept, property>* pair to a *value*
5. δ_{rec}-nodes: these are also *binder* nodes, but each such node binds a *<property, value>* pair to a *concept*
6. *relay* nodes: these encode *IS-A* links and control the directionality of the spreading activation in the conceptual hierarchy.

We now describe the rules that govern the connectivity of the above nodes. While reading the following description the reader is encouraged to make forward references to figures 5.7 and 5.8. With reference to these figures, all solid boxes denote ξ-nodes, all triangular nodes denote δ-nodes, and dashed boxes denote ϕ-nodes. Relay nodes and enable nodes are not shown in these figures. A point of clarification: for convenience, links are drawn emanating from various points on the node, but recall that a node transmits the same output value to all its neighbors.

There are exactly two enable nodes: INHERIT and RECOGNIZE. These nodes have one input site: QUERY, at which they receive an external input.

There exists a ξ-node for each concept in the conceptual structure. A ξ-node has six sites: **QUERY, RELAY, CP, HCP, PV** and **INV**. If concept B is a *parent* of concept A in the conceptual structure then there is a ↑ (bottom up) link from the ξ-node A to the ξ-node B and a ↓ (top down) link from the ξ-node B to the ξ-node A. Both these links are incident at the site **RELAY**, and the weights on these links equal #A / #B. The weight on the ↑ links has no special significance, but for convenience it is set equal to the weight of the corresponding ↓ link. Figure 5.1 illustrates this situation. As the ↑ and ↓ links always occur in pairs, they will be represented by a single undirected arc. Arcs between DICK and QUAKER and QUAKER and PERSON in figure 5.7 are examples of such connections.

φ-nodes represent properties and have one input site: **QUERY**.

Property values (remember, these are also concepts) are associated to concepts using binder nodes as follows: If $\delta(A,P)$ is known, then for every value V_i of P, there exists a pair of binder nodes [A,P -> V_i] and [P,V_i -> A] that are connected to the nodes A, P, and V_i as shown in figures 5.2 and 5.3 respectively.

A binder node such as [A,P -> V_i] is called a δ_{inh}-node and has two sites: **ENABLE** and **EC**. A δ_{inh}-node receives exactly three inputs at site **ENABLE**: one from a ξ-node, another from a φ-node, and a third from the *enable* node INHERIT, and each of these links has a weight of 1.0. For example, [A,P -> V_i] receives inputs from the ξ-node A, the φ-node P, and from INHERIT at site **ENABLE**; the weights along these links equal 1.0. For a δ_{inh}-node to become active it is essential that all three inputs incident at site **ENABLE** become active. The role of site **EC** is explained later.

The link from [A,P -> V_i] to the ξ-node V_i is incident at site **CP** and the weight on this link is given by #A[P,V_i] / #V_i. It is at the site **CP** that a ξ-node (in the role of a value) receives inputs from the appropriate *concept* and *property* nodes via a δ_{inh}-node. Refer to the triangular node connecting QUAKER, PACIFIST, and has-belief in figure 5.7 for an example of a δ_{inh}-node and its interconnections.

A binder node such as the node [P,V_i -> A] is called a δ_{rec}-node. Such a node

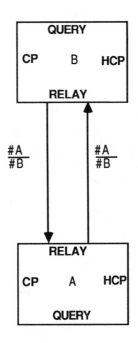

Figure 5.1: Encoding of *IS-A* links

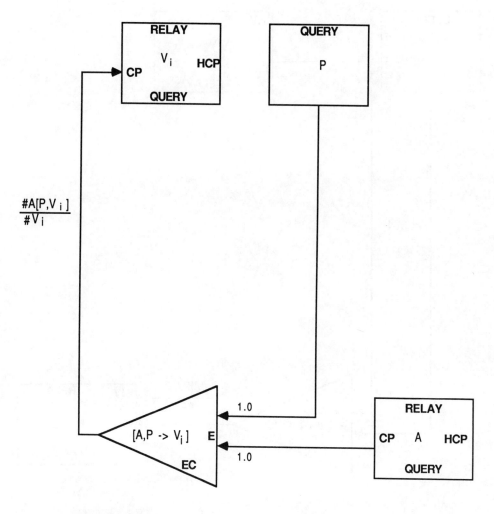

$\delta(A,P)$ is known

All δ_{inh}-nodes receive an input
from the INHERIT node at site **E**

E : ENABLE site

Figure 5.2: Encoding of δ_{inh}-nodes - I

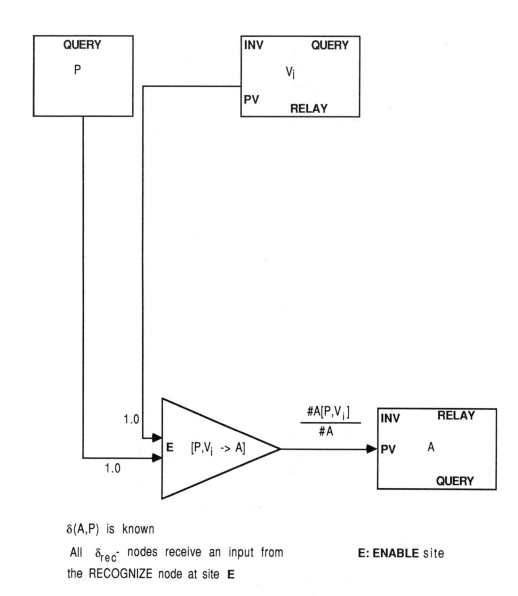

$\delta(A,P)$ is known

All δ_{rec}- nodes receive an input from
the RECOGNIZE node at site **E**

E: ENABLE site

Figure 5.3: Encoding of δ_{rec}-nodes - I

has one site ENABLE where it receives three inputs, one from the ξ-node P, another from the ξ-node V_i, and a third from the *enable* node RECOGNIZE. The weights on all these links are 1.0. As is the case with δ_{inh}-nodes, all three inputs incident at site ENABLE must be active for a δ_{rec}-node to become active.

The output from [P,V_i -> A] is incident at the site PV of the ξ-node A, and the weight on this link is given by #A[P,V_i] / #A. It is at the site PV that a ξ-node (in the role of a concept) receives inputs from the property value pairs associated with it. The triangular node connecting RED, has-color, and BEET in figure 5.8 is an example of a δ_{rec}-node.

If B is an ancestor of A such that δ(B,P) is known, and there is no concept, C, between B and A for which δ(C,P) is known, then there is a link from [A,P -> V_i] to [B,P -> V_i], incident at site EC with a weight of #A[P,V_i] / #B[P,V_i] (refer to figure 5.4). Similarly, there is a link from [P,V_i -> B] to the ξ-node A incident at site INV with a weight of #B[P,V_i] / #B (refer to figure 5.5). Finally, if B is such that it is the *highest* node for which δ(B,P) is known, then the link from [B,P -> V_i] to the ξ-node V_i is incident at site HCP, instead of site CP (refer to figure 5.6).

The site EC acts as an *evidence combination* site for combining evidence from underlying δ_{inh}-nodes. Such an interconnection is required to handle multiple inheritance situations. For example, the inputs from [QUAKER, has-belief -> PACIFIST] and [REPUBLICAN, has-belief -> PACIFIST] nodes combine at the EC site of [PERSON, has-belief -> PACIFIST] node. The site INV (for *inverse*) receives inputs to compensate for extraneous activation incident along $\downarrow$ links. This is required to ensure that non-local information about property values does not affect the computation when local information is available.

Besides the interconnections described above, all nodes representing concepts, properties, and values (ξ-nodes and ϕ-nodes) have an external input incident at the site QUERY, with a weight of 1.0.

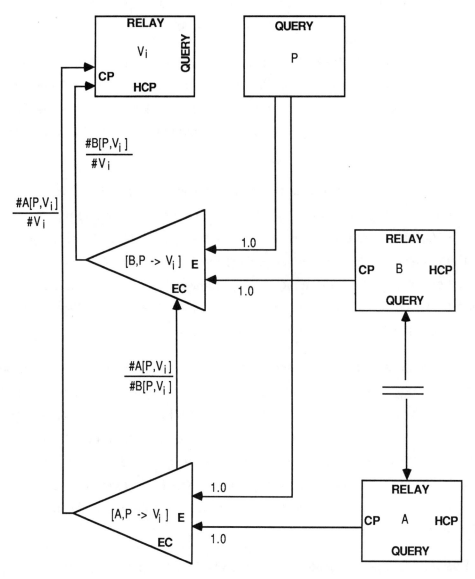

δ(A,P) and δ(B,P) are known, and there exists no C such that
A ≪ C ≪ B and δ(C,P) is known.

Figure 5.4: Encoding of δ_{inh}-nodes - II

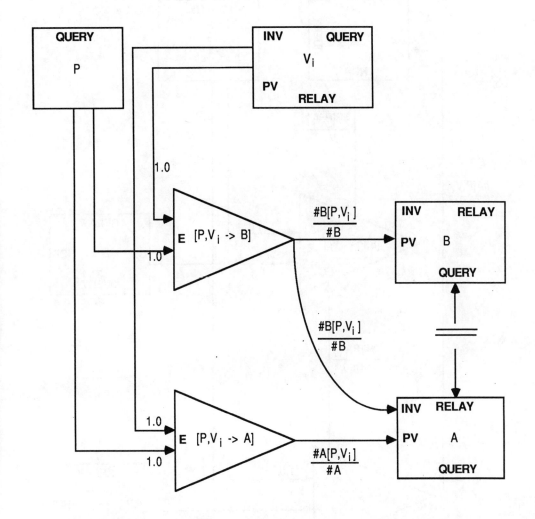

$\delta(A,P)$ and $\delta(B,P)$ are known, and there exists no C such that
$A \ll C \ll B$ and $\delta(C,P)$ is known.

Figure 5.5: Encoding of δ_{rec}-nodes - II

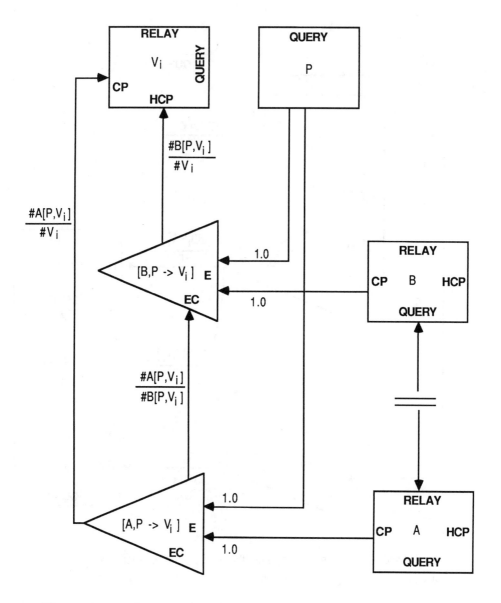

There exists no C such that $\delta(C,P)$ is known and $B \ll C$.

Figure 5.6: Encoding of δ_{inh}-nodes - III

5.4.2 Computational properties of nodes

Each node in the network can be in one of two states: **active** or **inert**. The quiescent state of each node is **inert**. A node switches to the **active** state under conditions specified below, and in this state, transmits an output equal to its potential. There is a distinction between a node transmitting no output (a nil output) and a node transmitting an output of magnitude 0. The computational characteristics of various node types are as described below:

ξ-nodes:

State: Node is in **active** state if it receives one or more inputs.

Potential: If no inputs at site **HCP** then

potential = the product of inputs at sites **QUERY, RELAY, CP,** and **PV** divided by the product of inputs at site **INV.**
else

potential = the product of inputs at sites **QUERY, RELAY, HCP**

δ_{inh}-nodes:

State: Node switches to **active** state if and only if it receives all three inputs at site **ENABLE**.

Potential: If state = **active** then

potential = 1.0 * the product of inputs at sites **EC**

else potential = NIL

δ_{rec}-nodes:

State: Node switches to **active** state if and only if it receives all three inputs at site **ENABLE**. Once **active**, the node remains in this state - even if the input from RECOGNIZE is withdrawn - as long as it continues to receive inputs from the property and value nodes.

Potential: If state = **active** then potential = 1.0 else potential = NIL

ϕ-nodes, INHERIT node, and RECOGNIZE node switch to **active** state if they receive input at site **QUERY**, and in this state their potential always equals 1.0.

The networks have the additional property that unlike other links that always transmit the output of their source node, the ↑ and ↓ links normally remain disabled and transmit activity only when they are enabled. This control is affected via *relay* nodes that are associated with ξ-nodes. Relay nodes make it possible to enable all ↑ or ↓ links emanating from a ξ-node. The enabling of ↑ and ↓ links has a chain effect: if the ↑ (↓) links emanating from node A are enabled, then the ↑ (↓) links emanating from all nodes that are reachable from A via ↑ (↓) links, also get enabled. This control machinery is described in section 5.6.

5.4.3 Posing queries and computing solutions

In the context of the network encoding, the inheritance and recognition problems are posed as follows:

Inheritance

Given: a concept C and a property P such that $P \in \lambda(C)$, (in other words, P should apply to C),

a set of possible answers V-SET, i.e., V-SET = $\{V_1, V_2, ...V_n\}$, such that each element of V-SET is also a member of $\Lambda(P)$ - the set of possible values of P, and

a reference concept REF for V-SET such that for all V_i, $1 \le i \le n$, there exists a unique path from V_i to REF in the ordering graph defined by **C** and <<. (Typically, REF is a parent of V_i's. For example, if V_i's are RED, GREEN, BLUE ... then REF could be COLOR).

Find: $V^* \in$ V-SET such that relative to the values specified in V-SET, V^* is the most likely value of property P for concept C.

Notice that the connectionist solution requires that we specify REF, an ancestor of values specified in V-SET. Specification of such a concept was not required for the evidential formalization.

The inheritance query is posed to the network as follows:

1. The nodes C, P, and INHERIT are activated by setting the external inputs, i.e., the inputs to the site **QUERY**, of these nodes to 1.0.

2. If one or more members of V-SET reach an **active** state within two time

steps, REF is activated by setting its external input to 1.0 and the ↓ links leaving REF are enabled.

3. If none of the members of V-SET receive any activation then not only is REF activated and the ↓ links leaving REF enabled, but the ↑ links leaving C are also enabled.

After $d + 4$ time steps - where d is the longest path in the ordering graph defined by C and << - the potentials of nodes will be such that for any two nodes V_i and $V_j \in$ V-SET, the following holds:

$$\frac{\text{potential of } V_i}{\text{potential of } V_j} = \text{the best estimate of } \frac{\#C[P, V_i]}{\#C[P, V_j]}$$

It follows that the node $V^* \in$ V-SET with the highest potential will correspond to the value that is the solution to the inheritance problem.

In the above specification, a time step corresponds to the time taken by a node to map its inputs to its output. There is no requirement that the operation of nodes be synchronized by a global clock. For simplicity one can take a unit of time to be the time taken by the "slowest" node and interpret "$d+4$ time steps" with reference to such a unit of time.

Recognition

Given: a set of concepts, C-SET = $\{C_1, C_2, ... C_n\}$, such that concepts in C-SET are either all Types or all Tokens,

a concept, REF, that is an ancestor of all concepts in C-SET and

a description consisting of a set of property value pairs, i.e., a set DESCR = $\{ [P_1, V_1], [P_2, V_2], ... [P_m, V_m] \}$, such that each P_j mentioned in DESCR applies to all the concepts in C-SET.

Find: $C^* \in$ C-SET such that relative to the concepts specified in C-SET, C^* is the most likely concept described by DESCR.

Notice that for the purpose of the connectionist encoding, we require that concepts in any C-SET are either all Types or all Tokens. This requirement stems from the assumption that the underlying conceptual structure adheres to the Multiple Views Organization described in section 4.7.1. We are making this assumption because - as discussed in section 4.7.3 - the Multiple Views Organization provides a natural interpretation of constraints required to arrive at a tractable evidential solution of the recognition problem.

The recognition query is posed as follows:

1. The nodes P_j and V_j corresponding to each $[P_j, V_j]$ mentioned in DESCR are activated together with the node RECOGNIZE. This is done by applying an external input to the site **QUERY** of these nodes.
2. After a single time step, the node RECOGNIZE is disabled, node REF is activated, and $\downarrow$ links emanating from REF are enabled.

After $d + 2$ time steps, the potential of the nodes in the network will be such that for any two nodes C_i and $C_j \in$ C-SET, the following holds:

$$\frac{\text{potential of } C_i}{\text{potential of } C_j} = \text{the best estimate of } \frac{\#C_i[P_1,V_1][P_2,V_2] \ldots [P_m,V_m]}{\#C_j[P_1,V_1][P_2,V_2] \ldots [P_m,V_m]}$$

It follows that the node $C^* \in$ C-SET with the highest potential corresponds to the solution of the recognition problem.

The queries to the Memory Network are posed by network fragments called routines. The requisite nodes in the Memory Network are activated by *query* nodes within a routine. Other nodes in the answer network component of the routines receive the ensuing potentials of the nodes in V-SET (for inheritance queries) or C-SET (for recognition queries). As described earlier, answer networks are designed to be winner-take-all gadgets and choose the answer with the highest potential. The design of routines is discussed in (Shastri & Feldman, 86) and applies to the present work with some minor modifications.

5.5 Examples of network encoding

This section presents three examples to illustrate the encoding and the functioning of the network. To keep the exposition simple, the first two examples focus on inheritance and suppress all details pertaining to recognition, while the third example focuses on recognition and ignores all interconnections related to inheritance. We also do not show any relay nodes and ignore the links from INHERIT and RECOGNIZE that are incident at the **ENABLE** sites of δ_{inh}-nodes and δ_{rec}-nodes respectively.

The Quaker examples

The first two examples are based on the following information:

> Quakers tend to be pacifists
> Republicans tend to be non-pacifists, and
> Dick is a Quaker and a Republican.

Figure 5.7 depicts how the above information is encoded in network form. We have interpreted the above information as follows:

> has-bel is a property, and pacifism and non-pacifism are two values of this property. The nodes PACIFIST and NON-PAC denote the concepts pacifism and non-pacifism respectively. The node BELIEF is purported to represent a concept comprising of all beliefs - pacifism, non-pacifism, liberalism, nationalism ..... The node PERSON denotes a concept that is a common ancestor of the concepts QUAKER and REPUBLICAN. It is assumed that the distribution of Quakers, Republicans, and Persons with respect to their beliefs is known.

As our first example, consider the query: Are Quakers more likely to be pacifists or non-pacifists? I.e., C = QUAKER, P = has-bel, V-SET = {PAC, NON-PAC} and REF = BELIEF.

To solve this query, the Memory Network is initialized by setting the external inputs of INHERIT, QUAKER, and has-bel to 1.0. The resulting potentials of the nodes are as follows: (QUAKER and PACIFIST have been abbreviated to QUAK and PAC respectively.)

QUAK, INHERIT, has-belief: 1.0

[QUAK, has-bel -> PAC] and [QUAK, has-bel -> NON-PAC]

> These nodes are in the **active** state because they receive inputs from QUAK, has-bel, and INHERIT nodes. Furthermore, they receive no inputs at site **EC**, therefore their potential equals 1.0

PERSON, REPUB, DICK, and δ_{inh}-nodes associated with REPUB and PERSON

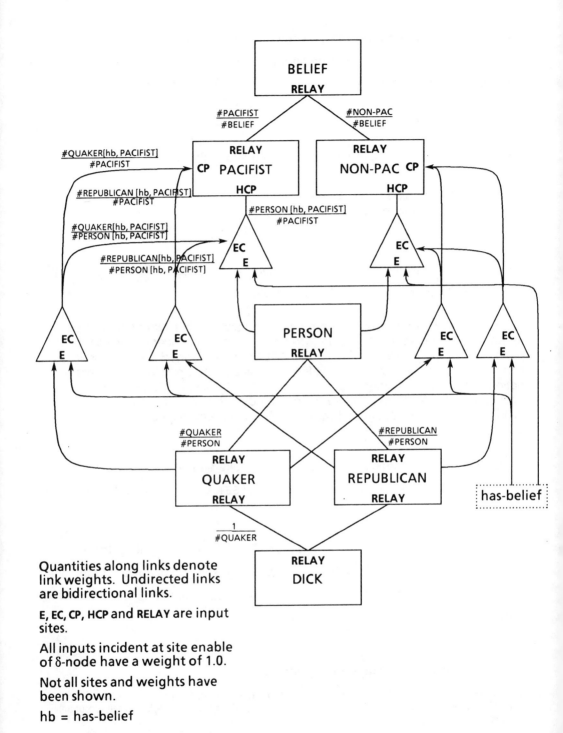

Quantities along links denote
link weights. Undirected links
are bidirectional links.

E, EC, CP, HCP and RELAY are input
sites.

All inputs incident at site enable
of δ-node have a weight of 1.0.

Not all sites and weights have
been shown.

hb = has-belief

Figure 5.7: An example network for inheritance

As the ↑ or ↓ links are not enabled these concepts do not receive any activation and remain **inert**. Consequently, the binder nodes associated with REPUB and PERSON also remain **inert**.

PAC and NON-PAC

These nodes receive a single input at site **CP** from δ_{inh}-nodes [QUAK, has-bel -> PAC] and [QUAK, has-bel -> NON-PAC] respectively. Hence their respective potentials are

$$\text{PAC: output of [QUAK, has-bel -> PAC]} \times \frac{\#QUAK[\text{has-bel},PAC]}{\#PAC} = \frac{\#QUAK[\text{has-bel},PAC]}{\#PAC}$$

$$\text{NON-PAC: } \frac{\#QUAK[\text{has-bel},NON\text{-}PAC]}{\#NON\text{-}PAC}; \quad \text{this is analogous to the potential of PAC.}$$

Thus within two time steps the potentials of nodes PAC and NON-PAC become nonzero and consequently, the ↑ and ↓ links emanating from QUAK remain disabled but the external input to BELIEF is set to 1.0 and its ↓ links are enabled. The potential of BELIEF now becomes 1.0 and this provides additional input to PAC and NON-PAC at site **RELAY**. The resulting potentials of these nodes are respectively:

$$\text{PAC: output of [QUAK, has-bel -> PAC]} \times \frac{\#QUAK[\text{has-bel},PAC]}{\#PAC} \times \text{output of BELIEF} \times \frac{\#PAC}{\#BELIEF}$$

$$= 1.0 \times \frac{\#QUAK[\text{has-bel},PAC]}{\#PAC} \times 1.0 \times \frac{\#PAC}{\#BELIEF} = \frac{\#QUAK[\text{has-bel},PAC]}{\#BELIEF}$$

$$\text{NON-PAC: } \frac{\#QUAK[\text{has-bel},NON\text{-}PAC]}{\#BELIEF}$$

Ignoring the common divisor, #BELIEF, in the potentials of the nodes PAC and NON-PAC, the potential of the node PAC equals the number of Quakers that subscribe to pacifism while the potential of the node NON-PAC equals the number of Quakers that subscribe to non-pacifism. Hence a comparison of the two potentials will give the most likely answer to the question: Are Quakers more likely to be pacifists or non-pacifists.

As a second query consider the more complex multiple inheritance problem: Is Dick a pacifist or a non-pacifist? I.e., C = DICK, P = has-bel, V-SET = {PAC, NON-PAC} and REF = BELIEF.

In order to solve this query, the Memory Network is initialized by setting the external inputs of INHERIT, DICK, and has-bel to 1.0. Because δ[DICK, has-bel] is not known, there will be no inputs reaching PAC or NON-PAC nodes. Hence, after two time steps, the external input to the node BELIEF will be set to 1.0, and the ↑ links originating from DICK and the ↓ links originating from BELIEF will be enabled. The resulting potentials of some relevant nodes are as follows:

DICK, INHERIT, has-belief: 1.0

QUAK: output of DICK $\times \dfrac{1}{\#QUAK} = 1.0 \times \dfrac{1}{\#QUAK} = \dfrac{1}{\#QUAK}$

REPUB: output of DICK $\times \dfrac{1}{\#REPUB} = 1.0 \times \dfrac{1}{\#REPUB} = \dfrac{1}{\#REPUB}$

PERSON: output of QUAK $\times \dfrac{\#QUAK}{\#PERSON} \times$ output of QUAK $\times \dfrac{\#REPUB}{\#PERSON} = \dfrac{1}{(\#PERSON)^2}$

[REPUB, has-bel -> PAC] and [REPUB, has-bel -> NON-PAC]: 1.0

> These nodes are in the **active** state because they receive inputs from REPUB, has-bel, and INHERIT nodes. As these nodes receive no inputs at site **EC**, their potential equals 1.0

[QUAK, has-bel -> PAC] and [QUAK, has-bel -> NON-PAC] nodes: 1.0

> These nodes are also in the **active** state because they receive inputs from QUAK, has-bel, and INHERIT nodes. As these nodes receive no inputs at site **EC**, their potential equals 1.0

[PERSON, has-bel -> PAC]

> This node also reaches the **active** state because it receives inputs from PERSON, has-bel, and INHERIT nodes. As this node also receives inputs at site **EC** from [QUAK, has-bel -> PAC] and [REPUB, has-bel -> PAC], its potential equals

$$1.0 \times \frac{1}{\#QUAK} \times \frac{\#QUAK[has\text{-}bel, PAC]}{\#PERSON[has\text{-}bel, PAC]} \times \frac{1}{\#REPUB} \times \frac{\#REPUB[has\text{-}bel, PAC]}{\#PERSON[has\text{-}bel, PAC]}$$

$$= \frac{\#QUAK[has\text{-}bel, PAC] \times \#REPUB[has\text{-}bel, PAC]}{(\#PERSON[has\text{-}bel, PAC])^2}$$

By symmetry (replacing PAC by NON-PAC),

[PERSON, has-bel -> NON-PAC]: $\dfrac{\#QUAK[has\text{-}bel, NON\text{-}PAC] \times \#REPUB[has\text{-}bel, NON\text{-}PAC]}{(\#PERSON[has\text{-}bel, NON\text{-}PAC])^2}$

PAC and NON-PAC

These nodes receive an input from BELIEF at site **RELAY**, an input from [PERSON, has-bel -> PAC] at site **HCP**, and inputs from [QUAK, has-bel -> PAC] and [REPUB, has-bel -> PAC] at site **CP**. However, because site **HCP** receives an input, the inputs at site **CP** are ignored. Therefore their potentials are:

$$\text{PAC: output of [PERSON,has-bel -> PAC]} \times \frac{\#\text{PERSON[has-bel,PAC]}}{\#\text{PAC}} \times \text{output of BELIEF} \times \frac{\#\text{PAC}}{\#\text{BELIEF}}$$

$$= \frac{\#\text{QUAK[has-bel,PAC]} \times \#\text{REPUB[has-bel,PAC]}}{\#\text{BELIEF} \times \#\text{PERSON[has-bel,PAC]}}$$

$$\text{NON-PAC:} \quad \frac{\#\text{QUAK[has-bel,NON-PAC]} \times \#\text{REPUB[has-bel,NON-PAC]}}{\#\text{BELIEF} \times \#\text{PERSON[has-bel,NON-PAC]}} \text{; analogous to PAC.}$$

Ignoring the common divisor, #BELIEF, in the potentials of the nodes PAC and NON-PAC, the potential of the node PAC corresponds to the best estimate of the number of people that are both Quakers and Republicans but subscribe to pacifism while the potential of the node NON-PAC corresponds to the best estimate of the number of people that are both Quakers and Republicans but subscribe to non-pacifism. Hence a comparison of the two potentials will give the most likely answer to the question: Is Dick a pacifist or a non-pacifist?

The fruit example

We illustrate how the network computes a solution to the recognition problem with reference to the network in figure 5.8. The network is intended to depict the following information:

Fruits and vegetables are kinds of edible things. Grapes and apples are kinds of fruits. Root-vegetables are a kind of vegetable, and Beet is a root-vegetable. Red and green are two values of has-color, while sweet and sour are two values of has-taste. Edible things have the property has-color and has-taste associated with them. The distribution for the property has-taste is known for fruits, grapes, and vegetables, while the distribution with respect to the property has-color is known for fruits, and beets.

The network encodes the above information except that the δ_{rec}-nodes and links associating SOUR and GREEN nodes to appropriate nodes in the hierarchy have been omitted as they do not play a role in the this example and if included, would make the diagram hopelessly complicated.

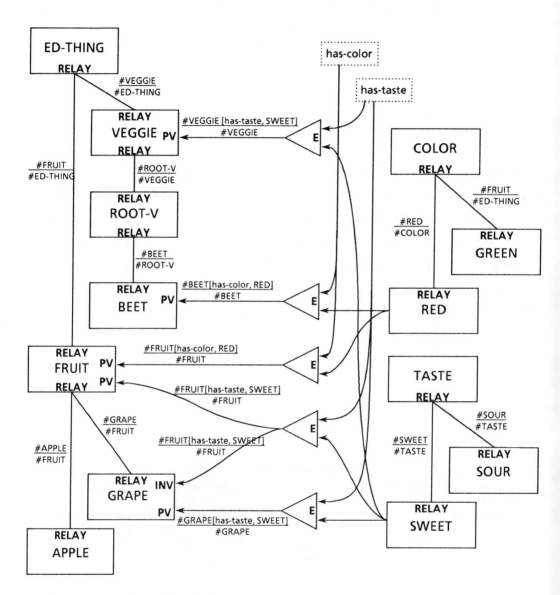

RELAY, PV, INV and E are input sites.

Not all sites have been marked.

Figure 5.8: An example network for recognition

Consider the recognition problem: Is a red sweet object an apple, grape or a beet? I.e., C-SET = {APPLE, GRAPE, BEET}, REF = ED-THING, DESCR = { [has-color, RED], [has-taste, SWEET]}

Notice that this recognition problem involves local as well as inherited information. For example, information about the color of GRAPE has to be inherited from FRUIT but specific information about the taste of GRAPE is available locally and must override the more general information available at FRUIT. For APPLE, information about color as well as taste has to be inherited from FRUIT. For BEET, the information about color is available locally, but the information about taste has to be inherited from VEGGIE which is two levels away in the conceptual hierarchy.

To solve the above problem, the network is initialized by setting the external inputs of RECOGNIZE, has-taste, has-color, RED, and SWEET to 1.0. After one step the external input to RECOGNIZE is withdrawn, but the external input to ED-THING is set to 1.0 and the $\downarrow$ links at ED-THING are enabled. The potentials of some of the relevant nodes after $d + 2$ time steps are given below. The explanations are analogous to those offered in the Quaker examples above. Recall that a δ_{rec}-node must receive all three of its inputs at site **ENABLE** in order to become active.

ED-THING: 1.0

All δ_{nodes} shown in figure 5.8 will be active and their potential will be 1.0.

FRUIT

$$= \text{potential of ED-THING} \times \frac{\#FRUIT}{\#ED\text{-}THING} \times \frac{\#FRUIT[has\text{-}color,RED]}{\#FRUIT} \times \frac{\#FRUIT[has\text{-}taste,SWEET]}{\#FRUIT}$$

$$= \frac{\#FRUIT[has\text{-}color,RED] \times \#FRUIT[has\text{-}taste,SWEET]}{\#FRUIT \times \#ED\text{-}THING}$$

VEGGIE

$$= \text{potential of ED-THING} \times \frac{\#VEGGIE}{\#ED\text{-}THING} \times \frac{\#VEGGIE[has\text{-}taste,SWEET]}{\#VEGGIE}$$

$$= \frac{\#VEGGIE[has\text{-}taste,SWEET]}{\#ED\text{-}THING}$$

GRAPE

$$= \text{potential of FRUIT} \times \frac{\#GRAPE}{\#FRUIT} \times \frac{\#GRAPE[\text{has-taste,SWEET}]}{\#GRAPE} \times \frac{\#FRUIT}{\#FRUIT[\text{has-taste,SWEET}]}$$

$$= \frac{\#FRUIT[\text{has-color,RED}] \times \#GRAPE[\text{has-taste,SWEET}]}{\#FRUIT \times \#ED\text{-}THING}$$

APPLE

$$= \text{potential of FRUIT} \times \frac{\#APPLE}{\#FRUIT}$$

$$= \frac{\#FRUIT[\text{has-color,RED}] \times \#FRUIT[\text{has-taste,SWEET}] \times \#APPLE}{(\#FRUIT)^2 \times \#ED\text{-}THING}$$

ROOTV

$$= \text{potential of VEGGIE} \times \frac{\#ROOTV}{\#VEGGIE}$$

$$= \frac{\#VEGGIE[\text{has-taste,SWEET}] \times \#ROOTV}{\#VEGGIE \times \#ED\text{-}THING}$$

BEET

$$= \text{potential of ROOTV} \times \frac{\#BEET}{\#ROOTV} \times \frac{\#BEET[\text{has-color,RED}]}{\#BEET}$$

$$= \frac{\#VEGGIE[\text{has-taste,SWEET}] \times \#BEET[\text{has-color,RED}]}{\#VEGGIE \times \#ED\text{-}THING}$$

Ignoring the common divisor, #ED-THING, in the potentials of nodes GRAPE, APPLE, and BEET, the potential of the node GRAPE corresponds to the best estimate of the number of red and sweet grapes, the potential of node APPLE corresponds to the best estimate of the number of red and sweet apples, while the potential of the node BEET corresponds to the best estimate of the number of red and sweet beets. Hence a comparison of the three potentials will give the correct answer to the question: Is a red and sweet edible thing an apple, a grape, or a beet?

In order to understand the significance of the potentials of the nodes GRAPE, APPLE, and BEET, we elaborate on the potential of GRAPE.

The best estimate of the number of red grapes is

$$\#FRUIT[\text{has-color,RED}] \times \frac{\#GRAPE}{\#FRUIT} \text{ ; } \textit{via direct inheritance}$$

The number of sweet grapes is

#GRAPE[has-taste,SWEET] ; as δ(GRAPE,has-taste) *is known*

Therefore, by the result derived in section 4.1, the best estimate of the number of red and sweet grapes is

$$\text{\#FRUIT[has-color,RED]} \times \frac{\text{\#GRAPE}}{\text{\#FRUIT}} \times \frac{\text{\#GRAPE[has-taste,SWEET]}}{\text{\#GRAPE}}$$

which may be simplified to yield

$$\frac{\text{\#FRUIT[has-color,RED]} \times \text{\#GRAPE[has-taste,SWEET]}}{\text{\#FRUIT}}$$

which is exactly the potential of the node GRAPE if we ignore the common denominator #ED-THING.

A similar analysis of the potentials of nodes APPLE, and BEET leads to similar result.

5.6 Implementation of ↑ and ↓ links

It was mentioned in section 5.4 that unlike other links that always transmit the output of their source node, the ↑ and ↓ links normally remain disabled and transmit activity only when they are enabled. It was also stated that the effect of enabling the ↑ (↓) links at a ξ-node has a chain effect; if the ↑ (↓) links emanating at a ξ-node C are enabled, then, the ↑ (↓) links at all nodes that are reachable from **C** via ↑ (↓) links also get enabled. We now describe how this is implemented.

A ↑ or ↓ link is not encoded as a simple link between two nodes, instead, it is encoded via *relay* nodes. Figures 5.9 and 5.10 illustrate the encoding: figure 5.10 shows the actual implementation of the ↑ and ↓ links for the network described in figure 5.9.

Each ξ-node, C, has two *relay* nodes: C-↓ and C-↑, associated with it; C-↓ for

145

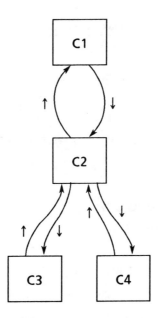

Figure 5.9: Encoding of relay nodes - I

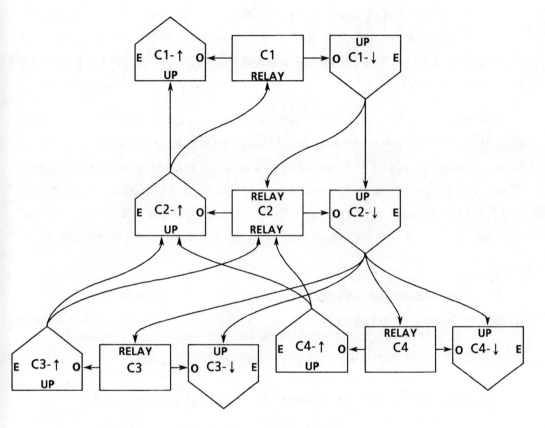

O: OWNER
UP: UPSTREAM

The site RELAY in node C2 has been duplicated for ease of illustration.

Figure 5.10: Encoding of relay nodes - II

encoding the ↓ links, and C-↑ for encoding the ↑ links.

A *relay* node, such as C-↑, receives an external input at site **ENABLE**, an input from the ξ-node C at site **OWNER**, and inputs from all *relay* nodes X-↑ such that C is a parent of X in the ordering graph defined by **C** and <<. All these inputs have a weight of 1.0. The output of C-↑ goes to the site **RELAY** of *all* ξ-nodes Y and to the site **UPSTREAM** of *all relay* nodes Y-↑, such that, Y is a parent of C in the ordering graph defined over **C** by <<. The weight of the link to Y-↑ nodes is 1.0, while the weight of the link to Y is #C/#Y.

The interconnections of a node such as C-↓ are analogous to that of the node C-↑. Thus C-↓ receives an external input at site **ENABLE**, an input at site **OWNER** from C, and inputs from nodes X-↓, such that X is a parent of C in the ordering defined by **C** and <<. The output of C-↓ goes to the site **RELAY** of all ξ-nodes Y and the site **UPSTREAM** of all *relay* nodes Y-↓ such that, C is a parent of Y in the ordering graph defined by << on **C**. The weight on the link to Y-↓ is 1.0, while the weight on the link to Y is #Y/#C.

The state function and potential functions of *relay* nodes are as follows:

State: Node is in **active** state if it receives input at site **ENABLE**, or if it receives one or more inputs at site **UPSTREAM**. Otherwise it is in **inert** state.

Potential: Potential equals the input at site **OWNER**.

5.7 Network behavior: an outline of a proof of correctness

In Appendix A we prove that the network described in section 5.4 computes solutions to inheritance and recognition problems in time proportional to the depth of the conceptual hierarchy and in accordance with the evidential theory developed in chapter 4. In this section we outline the basic strategy underlying the proof and list the additional constraints that need to be imposed on the conceptual structure to arrive at a connectionist solution.

The proof is based on establishing that if one focuses only on concept nodes (the ξ-nodes), then the structure of the network is such that with reference to any query, the network can be partitioned into two subparts. In each subpart, activation spreads in a single direction - top to bottom or bottom to top - the directions being defined with reference to the partial ordering <<. The two subparts interact via binder nodes (i.e., δ_{inh}-nodes and δ_{rec}-nodes). This interaction, however, is also strictly unidirectional: activation flows from one of the subparts to the other, but not vice versa. Consequently, there are no cycles and the potentials of nodes stabilize at the appropriate value in time proportional to the depth of the conceptual hierarchy. The potentials of nodes in the first subpart stabilize first and become available to nodes in the second subpart which then compute their potentials. Although the potentials of nodes in the second subpart can stabilize only after the potentials of nodes in the first subpart have done so, *no explicit synchronization is required*. The only requirement is that one wait long enough to let the activation sweep across the network before extracting answers from the Memory Network.

Additional conditions need to be imposed on the conceptual structure in order to establish convergence of the connectionist solution. The first set of conditions places restrictions on properties and their values. These conditions are:

WFR-parallel-1: A property should not be applicable to its own values or to the descendents of its values. In other words, property values, and the concepts they apply to, should belong to *distinct* ontological Types.

WFR-parallel-2: Properties that apply to the same concept should have distinct values.

WFR-parallel-3: All values of a property should be at a similar level of abstraction. For example, if PRUSSIAN-BLUE happens to be a sub-concept of BLUE, then this condition rules out the possibility of simultaneously treating both of them as values of has-color.

Of these, WFR-parallel-3 is not very critical and may be handled by a more elaborate connectionist encoding. The other two conditions are quite reasonable if we restrict ourselves to perceptual properties and concepts that correspond to natural kinds. Consider the values of properties such as has-taste, has-shape, has-color on the one hand and the concepts they apply to on the other. It is easy to convince oneself that the values of has-taste (SWEET, SOUR..), has-shape (ROUND, SQUARE ..), and has-color (RED, GREEN ...) fall into distinct classes and furthermore, the values of these properties are not subconcepts or superconcepts of objects that these properties apply to. Conditions WFR-parallel-1 and WFR-parallel-2, however, become restrictive if we wish to consider properties such as has-father or has-uncle, because the concepts these properties apply to (the sons and nephews) as well as the values of these properties (the fathers and the uncles) belong to the same ontological Type. In general, this problem will arise whenever we wish to represent relations that have overlapping domains.

Another constraint that must be satisfied is

WFR-parallel-4: The ordering graph defined by $\mathbf{C}/C,P$ and $<<$ should be a tree.

This condition is only a slightly stronger version of WFR-inh-1 (section 4.5), wherein only the portion of the ordering graph *below* the reference concept Ω of $\Gamma(C,P)$ was required to be a tree. Recall that even this condition trivially holds for the Multiple Views Organization (vide section 4.7.3.) As before, this condition does not require the conceptual structure to be a tree - this is a restriction on the projection $\mathbf{C}/C,P$, and not on the conceptual structure itself.

One final condition is required to solve the inheritance problem correctly. This condition requires that

WFR-parallel-5: REF should be such that C is not $<<$ REF.

Recall that REF is the reference concept of the members of V-SET. The above condition simply states that REF should not be so general as to be above C in the conceptual hierarchy. Given that members of V-SET and C belong to different ontological Types, this condition can always be satisfied by simply choosing REF to be the ontological Type to which members of V-SET belong. For example, if V-SET consists of color values, REF may be chosen to be COLOR

One final condition is also required to solve the recognition problem correctly. This condition refers to the Multiple Views Organization. Recall that REF is the reference concept of the members of C-SET and that the connectionist solution for recognition assumes that the conceptual structure adheres to this organization.

> **WFR-parallel-6:** Let ω be the leaf of the ontological tree that is the ancestor of all members of C-SET. Then if all the relevant information in the conceptual structure is to be utilized, REF should be such that $\omega \ll$ REF.

The above condition has the following interpretation. Only information available at concepts below REF affects the outcome of a recognition query. Therefore, REF must be sufficiently general to ensure that *all* the relevant information is utilized. The significance of this condition is discussed at length in section 6.2.

5.8 Simulation results

We have specified the design of a connectionist Memory network that can solve the inheritance and recognition problems in time proportional to the depth of the conceptual hierarchy. A proof of correctness of the suggested design is provided in Appendix A. In this section we present results of several simulations that were carried out to explicate the behavior of these networks and demonstrate the nature of inferences drawn by them. The simulated networks encode examples that are often cited in the knowledge representation literature as being problematic. The results of simulations demonstrate how the approach developed in this thesis deals with inheritance and recognition in an uniform manner, and solves some of the classic problems related to inheritance in the presence of exceptions and conflicting information.

The simulation involves three stages that are depicted in figure 5.11. During the first stage, a high level description of the information to be encoded in the network is processed by a compiler (SNAIL) and translated into a set of commands to a general purpose connectionist network builder (SPIDER).The high level input to SNAIL does not depend on any aspect of the connectionist realization. During the second stage, SPIDER constructs a network in accordance with the commands generated by SNAIL. Finally, in the third stage, the activity of the network constructed by SPIDER is

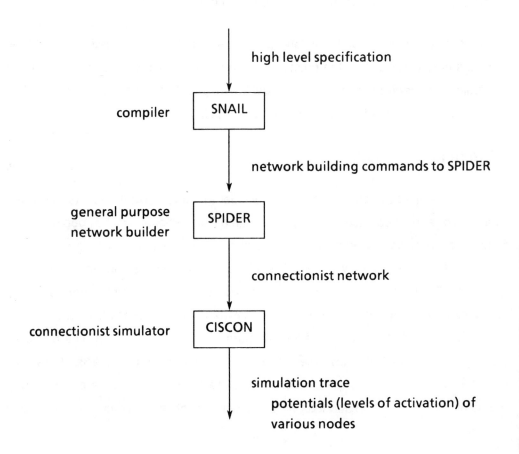

Figure 5.11: An overview of simulation

simulated using CISCON - a connectionist network simulator.

SNAIL and SPIDER are written in LISP, while CISCON is written in C. SPIDER and the current version of CISCON have been coded by Mark Fanty and are described in [Fanty 85a][Fanty 85b].

The first example is an extension of the Quaker example. It demonstrates how the network performs inheritance in the presence of conflicting evidence. Figure 5.12 depicts the information to be encoded. There are two properties, has-bel (has-belief) with values PAC (pacifist) and NON-PAC (non-pacifist), and has-eth-org (ethnic-origin) with values AFRIC (african) and EURO (european). In broad terms, the information encoded is as follows:

> Most Persons are non-pacifists.
> Most Quakers are pacifists.
> Most Republicans are non-pacifists.
> Most Persons are of european descent.
> Most Republicans are of european descent.
> Most Persons of african descent are Democrats.

The input to SNAIL consists of four lists:

- A list of concepts.

- A list of properties and their associated values.

- A list specifying the partial ordering << over concepts. Each element in this list is a triplet of the form (A B #A/#B), where concepts A and B are such that B is a parent of A in the ordering induced by << on **C**.

- A list specifying the distributions $\delta(C,P)$'s known to the agent. Each element in this list is a quintuple of the form

    (C P V #C[P,V]/#V #C[P,V]/#C)

Thus the input to SNAIL based on the information depicted in figure 5.12 is as follows:

```
(NB-concept '( PERSON POL-PER POL-PER DEMOC REPUB CHRIST ZORAS QUAK MORM
               BELIEFS PAC NON-PAC
               ETH-ORG AFRIC EURO
               DICK RICK SUSAN PAT))

(NB-property '( (has-bel PAC)          (has-eth-org AFRIC EURO))
```

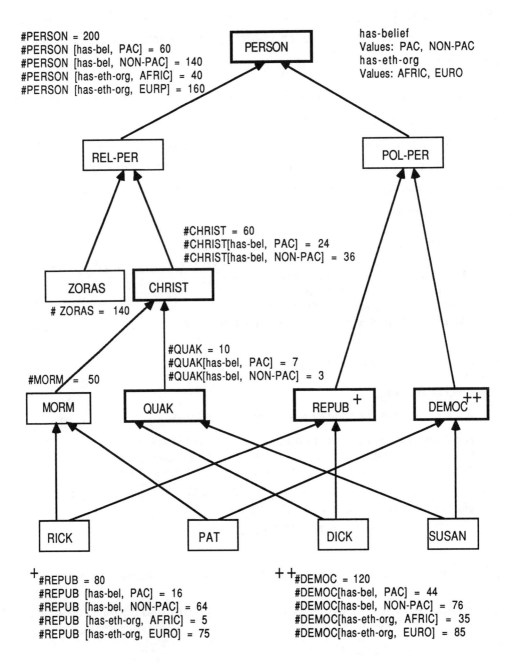

#PERSON = 200
#PERSON [has-bel, PAC] = 60
#PERSON [has-bel, NON-PAC] = 140
#PERSON [has-eth-org, AFRIC] = 40
#PERSON [has-eth-org, EURP] = 160

has-belief
Values: PAC, NON-PAC
has-eth-org
Values: AFRIC, EURO

PERSON

REL-PER

POL-PER

#CHRIST = 60
#CHRIST[has-bel, PAC] = 24
#CHRIST[has-bel, NON-PAC] = 36

ZORAS   CHRIST

ZORAS = 140

#QUAK = 10
#QUAK[has-bel, PAC] = 7
#QUAK[has-bel, NON-PAC] = 3

#MORM = 50

MORM   QUAK   REPUB +   DEMOC ++

RICK   PAT   DICK   SUSAN

+#REPUB = 80
#REPUB [has-bel, PAC] = 16
#REPUB [has-bel, NON-PAC] = 64
#REPUB [has-eth-org, AFRIC] = 5
#REPUB [has-eth-org, EURO] = 75

++#DEMOC = 120
#DEMOC[has-bel, PAC] = 44
#DEMOC[has-bel, NON-PAC] = 76
#DEMOC[has-eth-org, AFRIC] = 35
#DEMOC[has-eth-org, EURO] = 85

Figure 5.12: The Quaker world

```
(NB-is-a '(    (REL-PER PERSON 1.0)       (POL-PER PERSON 1.0)
               (ZORAS REL-PER 0.7)        (CHRIST PERSON 0.3)
               (QUAK CHRIST 0.1667)       (MORM CHRIST 0.8333)
               (REPUB POL-PER 0.04)       (DEMOC PL-PER 0.06)
               (DICK QUAK 0.1)            (DICK REPUB 0.0125)
               (RICK MORM 0.02)           (RICK REPUB 0.0125)
               (SUSAN QUAK 0.1)           (SUSAN DEMOC 0.0083)
               (PAT MORM 0.02)            (PAT DEMOC 0.0083)
               (PAC BELIEFS 0.3)          (NON-PAC BELIEFS 0.7)
               (AFRIC ETH-ORG 0.2)        (EURO ETH-ORG 0.8)))

(NB-delta '(   (PERSON has-bel PAC 1.0 0.3)
               (PERSON has-bel NON-PAC 1.0 0.7)

               (CHRIST has-bel PAC 0.4 0.4)
               (CHRIST has-bel NON-PAC 0.26 0.6)

               (QUAK has-bel PAC 0.12 0.7)
               (QUAK has-bel NON-PAC 0.02 0.3)

               (REPUB has-bel PAC 0.27 0.2)
               (REPUB has-bel NON-PAC 0.46 0.8)

               (DEMOC has-bel PAC 0.73 0.37)
               (DEMOC has-bel NON-PAC 0.54 0.63)

               (PERSON has-eth-org AFRIC 1.0 0.2)
               (PERSON has-eth-org EURO 1.0 0.8)

               (REPUB has-eth-org AFRIC 0.125 0.0625)
               (REPUB has-eth-org EURO 0.47 0.9375)

               (DEMOC has-eth-org AFRIC 0.875 0.29)
               (DEMOC has-eth-org EURO 0.53 0.71)))
```

On the basis of its input, SNAIL generates commands to SPIDER to create the required ξ-nodes, ϕ-nodes, δ_{inh}-nodes, δ_{rec}-nodes, and *relay* nodes; and to connect various nodes in accordance with the interconnection rules described in section 5.4.

As our first query, consider the inheritance question: Is Dick a pacifist or a non-pacifist?

This query is posed by activating (turning ON) INHERIT, DICK, and has-bel. The activity of PAC and NON-PAC is observed for five time steps[25]. Both PAC and NON-PAC remain **inert** and consequently, the nodes DICK-↑, BELIEF, and BELIEF-↓ are activated.

---

[25]In section 5.4 it was specified that we need to wait for two time steps. A uniform extra delay of three steps is introduced by the query posing mechanism.

The potentials of PAC and NON-PAC remain unchanged after the 15th step[26], and the final raw and normalized potentials of PAC and NON-PAC are[27]

Value	Raw potentials	Normalized potentials
PAC	0.00972	1.00
NON-PAC	0.00644	0.66

The above results indicate that the ratio of the likelihoods of Dick being a pacifist and Dick being a non-pacifist is about 3:2. Hence, on the basis of available information, Dick, who is a Republican and a Quaker, is more likely to be a pacifist.

Similar simulations for RICK, PAT, and SUSAN lead to the following results:

- Rick who is a Mormon Republican is more likely to be a non-pacifist. The ratio of pacifist v/s non-pacifist for Rick being 0.39 v/s 1.00.

- Pat who is a Mormon Democrat is also more likely to be a non-pacifist, but only marginally so. The ratio being 0.89 v/s 1.00.

- Finally, Susan who is a Quaker Democrat is very likely to be a pacifist, the ratio being 1.00 v/s 0.29.

As an example of recognition, consider the queries:

"Among the following persons, who is most likely to be a pacifist of african descent: DICK, RICK, SUSAN, or PAT?

" . . . who is most likely to be a non-pacifist of european descent"

The first query is posed by activating (turning ON) the nodes RECOGNIZE, PERSON-↓, PERSON, has-bel, has-eth-org, PAC, and AFRIC. The second query is posed in a similar manner but with NON-PAC and EURO being activated in place of PAC and AFRIC respectively.

The network computes the solution in 12 steps and the query leads to the

---

[26]In the current implementation it takes *two* time steps for the activation to propagate across a relay link. The depth of the conceptual hierarchy in this example is 4, and therefore, $d + 4$ translates into $2 \times 4 + 4$, i.e., 12. As stated before, the query posing mechanism takes an additional 3 steps, giving a total of 15.

[27]The potentials are normalized by setting the highest potential equal to 1.00.

following final potentials, shown here after normalization:

[has-bel, PAC][has-eth-org, AFRIC]   [has-bel, NON-PAC][has-eth-org, EURO]

Person	Potential	Person	Potential
SUSAN	1.00	RICK	1.00
PAT	0.57	PAT	0.59
DICK	0.11	DICK	0.50
RICK	0.05	SUSAN	0.30

As would be expected, Susan who is a Quaker and a Democrat best matches the description "Person of african descent with pacifist beliefs", while the person least likely to match this description turns out to be Rick. The latter also appears intuitively correct: Democrats correlate well with african origin and Quakers correlate well with pacifism, but Rick is neither a Democrat nor a Quaker. Rick, however, turns out to be the most likely "Person of european descent with non-pacifist beliefs". This appears to agree with Rick's being a Republican and a Mormon (i.e., a non-Quaker).

A query for finding the most likely person who is a pacifist leads to the following potentials:

[has-bel, PAC]

Name	Normalized potentials
DICK	0.54
RICK	0.31
SUSAN	1.00
PAT	0.57

As a second example, the information depicted in figure 5.13 was encoded in a network. This example corresponds to a situation that is often cited in the knowledge representation literature as being a particularly difficult case of inheritance [Etherington & Reiter 83]. The relevant information may be paraphrased as follows:

> Most Molluscs are shell-bearers.
> All Cephalopods are Molluscs, but most Cephalopods are not shell-bearers.
> All Nautili are Cephalopods and all nautili are shell-bearers.

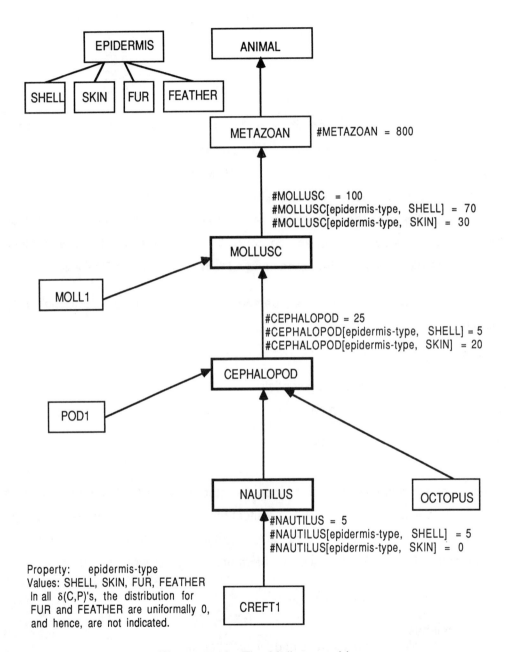

Figure 5.13: The Mollusc world

In addition to the concepts: MOLLUSC, CEPHALOPOD, and NAUTILI, a property "epidermis-type" with values: SHELL, SKIN, FUR, and FEATHER was used to encode the above example.

The normalized final potentials of the nodes SHELL and SKIN as a result of the inheritance of the property epidermis-type for MOLLUSC (or MOLL1), CEPHALOPOD (or POD1), and NAUTILUS (or CREFT1) are given below (the potentials of FUR and FEATHER were consistently 0.0 in each case):

VALUE	MOLLUSC	CEPHAL	NAUTILUS
SHELL	1.00	0.25	1.00
SKIN	0.43	1.00	0.00

Thus, a Mollusc is more likely to be a shell-bearer, a Cephalopod is not likely to be a shell-bearer, and a Nautilus is *definitely* a shell-bearer. Notice that the likelihood of a Nautilus having an epidermis-type other than shell computes to 0.00, which is exactly what should be expected given that *ALL* Nautili are shell-bearers.

Finally, a large network was constructed that included the two smaller network described above as sub networks. The large network had 75 concepts, 5 properties, and 30 $\delta(C,P)$'s. The depth of the network was 11. A total of 632 nodes and 1591 links were required to encode this network. The time taken to construct this network was approximately 40 minutes and the time taken to perform a single step of simulation was just under a second (all times are elapsed times). A description of the conceptual hierarchy underlying this example is given in figures 5.14, 5.15, and 5.16, while the known distributions are specified in figures 5.17a through 5.17e.

When any of the queries posed to the "Quaker network" and the "Mollusc network", were posed to the large network, the answers obtained were the same as those that were obtained by posing the query to the smaller networks.

When the following query was posed to the network:

Which of the following animal is most likely to have epidermis type SKIN and habitat LAND: MOLLUSC, REPTILE, BIRD, ELEPHANT, or PERSON?

the resulting potentials were as follows:

[epidermis-type, SKIN][has-habitat, LAND]

Name	Normalized potentials
MOLLUSC	0.02
REPTILE	0.21
BIRD	0.08
ELEPHANT	0.06
PERSON	1.00

Thus a land dweller with epidermis type skin is most likely to be a Person.

When the query sought the answer for epidermis type SKIN and habitat WATER, the following results were obtained:

[epidermis-type, SKIN][has-habitat, WATER]

Name	Normalized potentials
MOLLUSC	1.00
REPTILE	0.21
BIRD	0.13
ELEPHANT	0.02
PERSON	0.00

Thus a water dweller with epidermis-type skin is most likely to be a Mollusc.

In evaluating these answers we must bear in mind that they are based on the information encoded in the network, and if the information does not capture the reader's intuitions, then neither will the answers computed by the network.

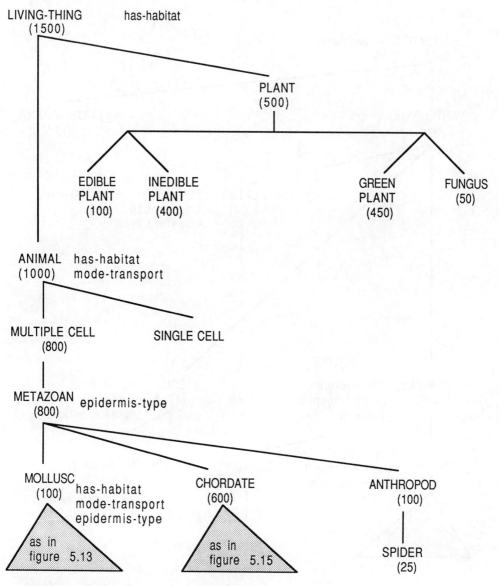

Properties listed with concepts are those for which the distribiutions are known.

Numbers listed with concepts specify #C.

Figure 5.14: The organism hierarchy - I

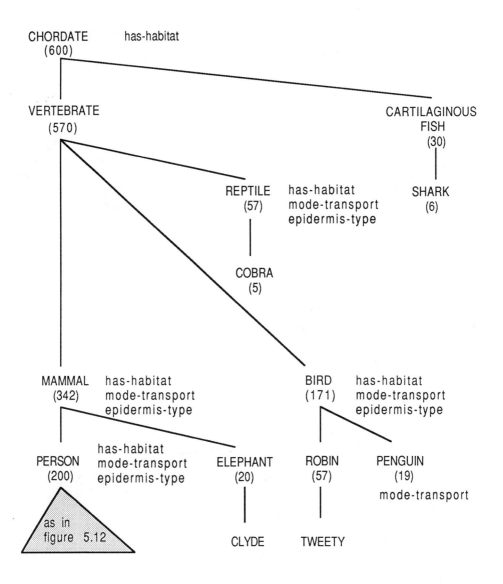

Properties listed with concepts are those for which the distribiutions are known.

Numbers listed with concepts specify #C.

Figure 5.15: The organism hierarchy - II

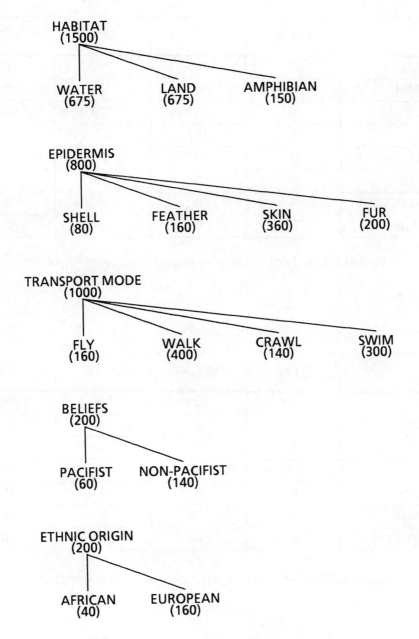

Figure 5.16: The organism hierarchy - III

163

	SHELL	FEATHER	SKIN	FUR
METAZOAN	80	160	360	200
MAMMAL	0	0	240	102
PERSON	0	0	200	0
BIRD	0	150	21	0
REPTILE	0	0	57	0
MOLLUSC	70	0	30	0
CEPHALOPOD	5	0	20	0
NAUTILUS	5	0	0	0

Figure 5.17a: Distribution with respect to epidermis type

	FLY	WALK	CRAWL	SWIM
ANIMAL	160	400	140	300
MOLLUSC	0	0	15	85
REPTILE	5	17	25	10
BIRD	140	16	0	15
PENGUIN	0	9	0	10
MAMMAL	0	300	0	42
PERSON	0	180	0	20

Figure 5.17b: Distribution with respect to mode of transport

	WATER	LAND	AMPHIBIAN
LIVING THING	675	675	150
MOLLUSC	80	15	5
BIRD	25	130	16
MAMMAL	10	302	30
PERSON	0	200	0
ANIMAL	450	450	100
REPTILE	5	42	10

Figure 5.17c: Distribution with respect to habitat

	PACIFIST	NON-PACIFIST
PERSON	60	140
CHRISTIAN	24	36
QUAKER	7	3
REPUBLICAN	16	64
DEMOCRAT	44	76

Figure 5.17d: Distribution with respect to beliefs

	AFRICAN	EUROPEAN
PERSON	40	160
REPUBLICAN	5	75
DEMOCRAT	35	85

Figure 5.17e: Distribution with respect to ethnic origin

6   Discussion

In this thesis I have described an evidential formalization of semantic networks. The formulation prescribes how an agent should perform inheritance and recognition so as to arrive at conclusions that are *optimal* in a certain sense, and leads to a principled treatment of exceptions, multiple inheritance and conflicting information during inheritance, and the best match or partial match computation during recognition. I have also shown that the above formalization may be realized as an interpreter-free connectionist network that computes solutions to inheritance and recognition problems very efficiently.

This work should be of interest to researchers, both in artificial intelligence and cognitive science; it formalizes a class of inference that people seemingly perform with extreme facility, and goes on to demonstrate that these inferences may be realized with equal facility using a computational architecture that is inspired in part by the neural architecture. The work may also be interesting because it stipulates certain constraints on the organization of conceptual information that if satisfied, lead to an efficient connectionist implementation.

In this chapter we discuss some insights precipitated by this research, mention some unresolved issues, point out limitations of this work, and indicate possible directions that one may take in pursuing the line of research described in this thesis.

6.1 Structure and inference

Seeking a computationally effective solution to inference made explicit the direct correspondence between the structure of knowledge and effective inference, namely,

> Having information is not sufficient to guarantee its utilization; for it to be used effectively in the reasoning process, information must be represented in an appropriate *form* and occupy an appropriate *place* in the conceptual structure.

This work suggests what this *form* and *place* might be. We have shown that knowledge about property values of concepts may be represented and used very efficiently provided it is expressed in terms of #C[P,V]'s. However, it is difficult to represent correlations *between* property values of concepts in a way such that they may be used effectively during inference[28,29]. Limited amounts of such information may be encoded by making the computational behavior of the connectionist nodes and their interconnections more complicated, but soon the network becomes too complex to be plausible. The easiest way of encoding such information, while keeping the nodes and interconnections simple, involves introduction of "intermediate concepts". For example, in order to make effective use of the information "most red apples are sweet", one must either introduce a node "red apple" and attach to it the appropriate information about the taste of such apples, or alternately, introduce a node "sweet apple" and attach to it the information about the color of such apples. This does not require that all such intermediate concepts be linguistic terms, but it does entail that appropriate computational machinery (concept nodes and binder nodes) be dedicated to make this information accessible during inheritance and recognition.

The above suggests that a possible goal of a concept formation mechanism may be as follows:

If significant information about correlations *between* property values of a concept is available, and if this information is to be used in drawing extremely fast inferences, then *new* concepts must be created so as to allow this information to be expressed in the form of $\delta(C,P)$'s[30].

---

[28]In our formulation, correlations correspond to $\#C[P_i,V_i][P_j,V_j]$

[29]Here "effectively" is being used in the strong sense of "within a few computational steps" or equivalently, "automatically - without attentional intervention, and certainly without props such as paper and pencil".

[30]This is equivalent to saying that a concept formation mechanism should create new Types so that information that was earlier expressible as internal matrix elements of the concept matrices (vide section 4.1) can now be expressed as row or column sums of concept matrices.

The above requirement seems reasonable given that whenever a large amount of *significant* information about some concept is available, we specialize the concept in order to better encode this information: all specialized domains have multiple concepts to represent that which in common parlance is represented by a single concept. Thus, whereas, we may be happy to apply the term "rock" to a large class of "relatively hard naturally formed mass of mineral or petrified matter", a geologist has numerous concepts to capture the subtle distinctions and interrelations in the properties of such substances. It is hypothesized that it would be difficult to make effective use of these interrelations unless they were encapsulated into appropriate concepts.

The above observations suggest a criterion for creating concepts based on an information-theoretic measure that evaluates the effectiveness of a conceptual structure in predicting properties of objects (inheritance) and classifying objects based on partial information (recognition). For work along these lines refer to [Gluck & Corter 85].

6.2 Structure and anomalous inference

The direct relationship between inference and the structure of knowledge also explains why an agent is often unable to use all relevant information during reasoning and decision making, and why the answers produced by an agent are sometimes anomalous and contradictory. We have already observed that knowledge - probabilistic or otherwise - can only be used effectively if it is embedded at the appropriate place in the conceptual structure. If the knowledge is not situated at the appropriate place then one would expect the system to "punt" and give approximate and possibly anomalous answers.

In section 5.7 we introduced the constraint WFR-parallel-6 from which it followed that the choice of REF determines the subset of information that gets used in solving a recognition problem; only information available at concepts below REF affects the outcome of a query. With reference to the Multiple Views Organization, the condition implies that if the reference concept lies within one of the views then only information from that view will be used in solving the recognition problem. For example, consider the Quaker example (refer to figure 5.7) where one of the views is organized along religious divisions while the other along political affiliations. This constraint implies that if the question "Name a politician who is a pacifist" is posed to the system, only information at concepts "Democrat" and "Republican" will be used in selecting an answer - the information at concepts "Christian", "Quaker" or "Mormon" will be ignored even though it may be relevant to the problem. The converse will happen if the question "Name a Christian who is a pacifist" is posed. Information from both the views will be used only if the question is: "Name a person who is a pacifist". Observe that the same information is relevant in each of the three cases, but it is only in one of these, that the system takes all the relevant information into account. This undesirable trait of the system is a direct consequence of a constraint that is required to achieve an efficient parallel solution. This constraint may have some psychological significance and may shed some light on why, sometimes, people *ignore* relevant information and arrive at anomalous conclusions.

In addition to the above, there are other reasons why relevant information may not get used during reasoning. The connectionist realization presented in this paper deals effectively with inferences only if they have a specific *form* in relation to the conceptual structure. For example, consider inheritance queries. These queries inquire about the most likely value of some "property" P of some instance/class C. For the system to provide an optimal (or correct) answer, C must be a concept in the conceptual structure, and P must be a property that applies to C. If the "property" and "concept" referred to by the query do not correspond to a property and concept in the conceptual structure, a correct answer will not be obtained. Such a situation may arise more often than one might expect. Consider the question:

"Are red things more likely to be sweet or sour?"

Even though the above may appear to be a perfectly well formed inheritance query, it may not necessarily be so; the agent may have chosen to represent the information about color of objects using property values (vide section 3.2), and may not have an explicit concept to denote the set of red colored objects. In the above situation, the Memory network will be unable to process the above inheritance query. Of course, a more elaborate system would be able to answer the query by using a more complex inferential process. Such a process would answer the query in three steps. In the first step it would locate all concepts that have RED as the value of the property has-color by posing the recognition query "[has-color, RED]". In the second step it would pose appropriate inheritance queries to retrieve the value of the has-taste property of the concepts selected in the first step. In the third step it would accumulate the results of the second step to ascertain the final answer. Notice, however, that the second step would involve serial - case by case - processing, and one would expect the process to focus only on a few major Types selected in the first step and return an answer based on such a *partial analysis*. Such an "approximate" behavior would be exhibited by any system that must respond in a limited time. Furthermore, given the complexity of the process and the need for storing partial results, it appears that the above process would not be executable automatically and would probably require attentional intervention.

The preceding discussion also suggests that although the work described here is not intended to be a model of how humans deal with evidential information, it cannot be rejected as a candidate model simply by invoking the results of experiments in which the response of subjects is at odds with an evidential analysis [Tversky & Kahneman 83]. In many cases, such experiments involve queries that have arbitrary forms and complexity - relative to the queries that can be handled by the system described in this work - and should be expected to produce anomalous results.

6.3 Use of winner-take-all networks for answer extraction

The use of a winner-take-all network (WTA) to extract answers from the Memory network offers a clean computational account of decision making under uncertainty. In the evidential formulation adopted in this work, certain reasoning tasks are viewed as decision tasks that involve ascertaining the "best" or the most likely alternative given the state of the agent's knowledge. The final act of such a decision task requires that once the best choice has been determined, the agent must *accept* that as the *correct* answer and act accordingly. The Memory network computes the evidence for each choice, but it is the WTA in the answer network that encodes such an acceptance procedure: in a WTA the best answer wins, the other answers are subdued. Recently, Goldman [Goldman 86] has also argued that the WTA answer extraction mechanism offers an "integrated model of *acceptance* as well as uncertainty".

What makes the use of WTA's even more interesting, however, is that besides the set of possible answers (i.e., those listed in C-SET or V-SET), the WTA mechanism also includes two *don't know* possibilities, namely - *no-info* and *conflict*. The WTA returns *no-info* as an answer if there happens to be insufficient evidence for *all* the choices. It returns *conflict* as the answer if none of the answers is a clear winner[31]. The explicit use of *don't know* answers not only helps in modelling indecision, but it also suggests ways of encoding complex reasoning behavior. For example, one may imagine a complex routine that works as follows. At first it initiates a simple (i.e., a quick and dirty) form of reasoning. If a *don't know* response wins the competition, it either initiates an action that gathers additional information from the environment, or trigger additional - more elaborate - reasoning steps. We have already seen an example of the latter when we discussed inheritance queries in section 5.4.3. At first, a inheritance query looks up the locally available property values of a concept, if no activation arrives at nodes in V-SET (i.e., the *no-info* answer gets selected), the IS-A links are activated so as to "inherit" the values from concepts higher up in the IS-A hierarchy.

6.4 Representation issues

The representation language described in chapter 3 addresses a number of issues. These include dealing with partial information and the representation of necessary as

---

[31]What constitutes a clear winner and what constitutes insufficient evidence, can be specified by setting the values of certain parameters of the nodes that make up the WTA network.

well as evidential properties. Furthermore, the language admits both a probabilistic as well as an exemplar model of concepts. Needless to say, the language is very restricted in a number of ways. For example, it only admits limited forms of evidential information, it does not handle relations having overlapping domains, and it cannot represent relationships such as those captured by the structural dependency links in KL-ONE. In evaluating these restrictions, however, it must be borne in mind that the goal of this work was to determine how a *limited* form of inference could be performed with extreme efficiency. It must also be remembered that unrestricted evidential reasoning is as intractable as any other form of reasoning, and restrictions must be placed on evidential as well as non-evidential information in order to achieve computational effectiveness. The following sections discuss some of these questions.

6.4.1 Finer structure of property-values

A simplifying assumption made in this work is that all property values are disjoint. For example, "red" and "green" are assumed to be disjoint values of the property has-color. This is not always the case, and there are property-values that do not fit this simplistic picture. For example, the taste "sweet and sour" is a combination of "sweet" and "sour".

Property-values may also be organized in an hierarchical manner: an artist would tell us that there are many different kinds of "red", each of which may be treated as a subtype of "red". Even in common usage, "pink" is at a lower level of abstraction than "red". It is not clear how evidence for "red" should be distributed among its various subtypes. This seems to be more of a question of *typicality* than frequency of occurrence. If one observes the range of the visual spectrum that is classified as "red", it may range from what would be described as "blood-red" to "pink", some colors within this range being more typical instances of "red" than some others. Therefore, one may want to distribute evidence for "red" according to some measure of typicality. Among existing proposals, the work on fuzzy logic by Zadeh [Zadeh 83] seems relevant for dealing with the notion of typicality. In the framework of fuzzy logic, RED would be a fuzzy predicate and different instances of "red" would have varying degrees of "redness" associated with them; thus Rose may be red with degree 0.8 while Brick may be red only with degree 0.7. The major criticism of fuzzy logic is the manner in which certainty factors are combined when analyzing compound terms: it handles disjunctions by taking the maximum, and conjunctions by taking the minimum. Such a combination rule often leads to counterintuitive results. For example, a guppy may be a very atypical fish and also a very atypical pet, yet it would be inappropriate to infer that guppy is a very atypical pet fish.

An alternative to the use of fuzzy predicates is the use of "exploded values". It may be argued that property values are much more fine grained than their "names" might suggest. Normal usage of language often belies the complexity of the information being communicated. In some cases detailed information may not be articulated because it is considered irrelevant to the situation. Oftentimes, however, a speaker may not make certain distinctions - even though they may be relevant - because he may rely upon the hearer to infer these from contextual and world knowledge. For instance, while referring to the color of an apple and that of a brick as "red" one seldom means that they are one and the same color. One assumes that the hearer is aware of the difference between the two colors and hence will be able to interpret the two usages of "red" appropriately. In view of the above we ought to use exploded color values such as APPLE-RED, ROSE-RED and BRICK-RED. It is important to make these distinctions in a knowledge representation scheme in spite of the surface uniformity of language. Traditional knowledge representation systems do not have to represent these distinctions explicitly as they can shift this burden to the interpreter; the interpreter may be programmed to treat differently the value "red" when it is associated with distinct objects. The absence of an interpreter in the present formulation, however, makes it necessary to explicitly represent concepts in a finer grain. The relationship between concepts such as APPLE-RED and RED may be the same as that between RED and COLOR, and the properties associated with color - HUE, BRIGHTNESS and SATURATION - may be used to make classifications like RED and GREEN and also to make finer distinctions like BRICK-RED and APPLE-RED. These issues are addressed within a connectionist framework in [Cottrell 85].

6.4.2 Representation of relations

One potential extension of the representation language is the representation of relations. Figure 6.1 shows the representation of the predicate LOVES. It is easy to see the similarity in the notion of properties as used in this formulation and case roles that denote relations between predicates and noun phrases [Bruce 75][Fillmore 68]. The simplified representation in figure 6.1 suggests that a PREDICATE has two case roles namely, HAS-AGENT and HAS-PATIENT. For the more specific predicate LOVES these case roles get mapped into HAS-LOVES-AGENT and HAS-LOVES-PATIENT which in turn are filled by JOHN and MARY in the representation of "John loves Mary".

In a similar fashion, the network in figure 6.2 encodes the following information:

> "ON is a kind of spatial relation.
> ON has two arguments: the thing on top and the thing at the bottom.
> A is a ball and B is a cube.
> A is on B."

The representation of a relation is similar to that of a concept and the arguments of a relation are analogous to the properties of an object. Thus the representation of a two place relation such as ON may be characterized as an object with two properties (arguments): *on-top and on-bottom.*

Although no evidential information may be required to represent relations such as PARENT-OF and ON - these either hold or do not hold - some other relations are best viewed as *graded* relations and may require an evidential treatment. An example of this is the relation LOVES, as in "John likes Mary". There are at least two ways in which a degree of strength may be associated with the representation of this relation. First, "liking" itself may have a degree of strength associated with it; John may "like Mary a lot" or "like her just a little". Second, an agent's belief in the various degrees of John's liking for Mary may also vary; the agent may *strongly* believe that "John likes Mary a *little*". Representation of such distinctions may serve as a point of contact between probabilistic or evidential approaches and formalisms such as fuzzy logic.

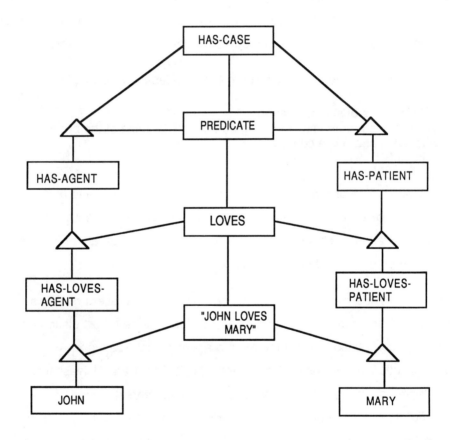

Figure 6.1: "John loves Mary"

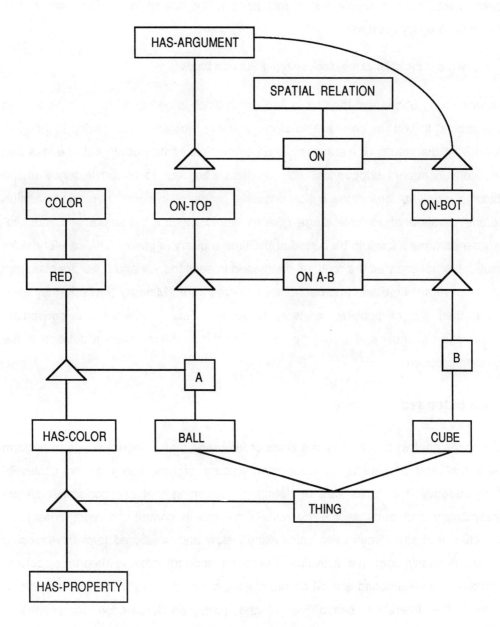

Figure 6.2: "A is on B"

The above encoding does not work if a relation has overlapping domains. In such cases WFR-parallel-1 and WFR-parallel-2 are violated and hence the resulting answers are incorrect. Furthermore, even the simplest of relations directly suggests queries that appear simple but in fact need to be solved in multiple stages. For example, a query such as:

What is the color of the block on top of the blue block?

requires two subqueries: the first to find which block is on top of the blue block, and the second to find the color of this block. The key problem is to develop techniques for saving the results of a subquery and communicating it to other (sub)routines that initiate subsequent subqueries. This problem turns out to be an instance of the *binding problem* - one of the critical unsolved problems in connectionism. A solution to the problem of multiple stage queries would require "parameterized routines" whose parameters would be bound at the time a query is posed. The careful reader may have noticed that the routines mentioned in sections 1.4 and 5.4.3 are assumed to be fully hardwired and appropriately connected to the Memory Network (they even have their set of possible answers wired in). This is obviously a convenient assumption for now and a realistic solution to this problem awaits a solution to the binding problem.

6.4.3 Extended inference

Our initial goal was to identify the kinds of inference that an agent needs to perform very fast and provide a computational account of how this may be achieved. Consequently, the focus was on forms of reasoning that are performed almost instinctively and automatically by human beings. In contrast, a more conscious, directed, and sometimes even painstakingly slow and belabored form of reasoning underlies many cognitive activities. Examples abound: proving theorems, solving puzzles, troubleshooting a VLSI circuit, playing chess and the likes. It is possible to extend the inference capabilities of the proposed knowledge representation framework by using more elaborate routines. Although the work is preliminary in nature, some progress has been made [Shastri & Feldman 86].

6.5 Treatment of evidential information

The representation language described in chapter 3 assumes that if an agent knows $\delta(C,P)$ then he knows #C[P,V] for all $V \in \Lambda(P)$. This eliminates the possibility of representing one form of ignorance. Assume that the agent knows that 40% of the apples are red, 30% are green and 20% are yellow, but he is unsure about the remaining 10%. In the evidential treatment outlined in chapter 4, there is no explicit way of taking such information into account. One possibility is to posit a special value θ_p - denoting "unknown", for every property P, and include #C[P,θ_p] in the specification of $\delta(C,P)$. This raises the question of distributing the ignorance represented by θ_p among the values of P. Should the count assigned to #C[P,θ_p] be distributed equally among all $V \in \Lambda(P)$ or should it be distributed equally to all V such that #C[P,V] = 0? The answer would depend on whether the count #C[P,θ_p] denotes the observations made by the agent about miscellaneous values of P not represented in δ because they were insignificant, or whether the count denotes the agent's belief that there exist other instances of C that may have values other than those observed by him. In the former case, the count #C[P,θ_p] would be distributed to all V such that #C[P,V] = 0, while in the latter case it would be distributed to all #C[P,V].

In addition to the kind of ignorance discussed above, there is another form of ignorance that ought be considered[32]. This form of ignorance may arise because the agent may not have observed sufficient instances of a class to be confident about its distributions recorded by him. In other words, #C may be so small that the agent may not want to use #C[P,V]'s to infer property values of instances of C. It seems plausible to assume that in such situations an agent may prefer to make use of distribution information of a more general class, if such information is available and is thought to be more reliable. An explicit representation of ignorance may help in modeling this situation. For example one may posit that if the ignorance θ_{CP}

---

[32]The significance of this form of ignorance was pointed out by Gary Dell.

associated with $\delta(C,P)$ is very high, then #C[P,V] be estimated on the basis of $\delta(C,P)$ as well as $\delta(D,P)$, where D is some concept higher up in the conceptual hierarchy for which θ_{DP} is very low. It remains to be seen how such a strategy may be incorporated within the framework developed in this thesis.

A related issue is that of treating likelihoods as intervals rather than point values. There are many arguments in favor of using intervals. One of the more forceful being that intervals enrich our capacity to express ignorance. If probabilities express uncertainty, then intervals allow us to express uncertainty about probabilities. For example, if one was certain of one's belief in the probability of some event as being p, then one would express this probability as [p,p]. However, if one's belief about this probability was itself uncertain, one might express this probability as [p-ε, p+ε]. With reference to the example about apples and grapes in section 4.1 (figure 4.1), the number of red and sweet apples must lie between 30 and 60, and therefore, Pr(red & sweet| Apples) must lie in the interval [0.3, 0.6]. Using the maximum entropy formalism we reduced this to a single point value of 0.42. We did so because given the information about apples and grapes in that example, the value 0.42 is the most likely value from among the set of possible values in the interval [0.3,0.6] (vide section 4.1). However, the introduction of θ_p in the set of values of P introduces a complication that needs to be resolved.

Another suggestion due to Rollinger [Rollinger 83] involves using a dimensional representation for uncertainty. One of the dimensions represents positive evidence while the other represents negative evidence. It is argued that a single value does not distinguish between "strong positive evidence in conjunction with some negative evidence" and "some positive evidence and no negative evidence". Thus [1,0] means the proposition is true, [0,1] means that the proposition is false, while [1,1] means that there is a contradiction.

The problem of evidential reasoning becomes extremely complex if the nature of information available to the agent includes inequality constraints. For example, an agent may know that there are more red and sweet apples than there are green and sour ones, without knowing how many such apples there are. In the presence of inequality constraints, the maximum entropy computations become as complex as general optimization problems.

Before considering any of the extensions listed above, their impact on computational effectiveness will have to be evaluated.

6.6 Learning

There has been an undercurrent of issues related to learning throughout this thesis - the knowledge encoded in δ was supposed to be based on the observations made by the agent and it was mentioned time and again that Types "evolve" when certain things happen. It is therefore only natural to discuss some issues related to learning. If one examines the encoding of knowledge as described in section 5.4, one will notice that most of the weights drawn between links have a very simple explanation. If we view nodes in the network to be active elements - as indeed they are - then the weights on the links emanating from δ nodes (both δ_{inh} and δ_{rec}) and incident on other ξ-nodes and δ-nodes have the following interpretation:

> the weight on a link is a measure of *how often the destination node was active when was the source node also active.*

This interpretation relates extremely well to a Hebbian interpretation of synaptic weights in neural nets [Hebb 49] and these weights are based on purely local information. Thus the weight on a link from a δ_{inh} node [C,P -> V] to V is precisely the fraction: "how often was [C,P -> V] also firing when V was firing". If V is RED, P is has-color and C is APPLE, then the weight on the link from APPLE to RED via the binder node would be equal to the fraction of red colored things that are apples.

The above explanation may sound plausible for computing the weights on individual links, but it does not tell us how structures such as concepts evolve. The following is a preliminary attempt at answering this question. Although the problem is far from solved, it does provide a general idea of how learning may occur in connectionist semantic networks. The emphasis is on identifying how pre-existing (innate) structure may give rise to new concepts.

The proposed mechanism for learning in semantic networks is based on the notions of recruitment and chunking [Feldman 82] [Wickelgren 79] and these issues are discussed in brief before a plausible mechanism of concept formation is outlined. Broadly speaking, the idea of chunking may be described as follows: at any given time, the network consists of two classes of nodes:

Committed nodes: These are nodes that have acquired a distinct "meaning" in the network. By this we mean that given any committed node, one can clearly identify sets of other committed nodes, whose activation will result in the former becoming activated. Committed nodes are connected to other committed nodes by "strong" links, and to a host of other free nodes, (see below), via "weak" links.

Free nodes: These are nodes that have a multiplicity of weak links to other nodes, both free and committed. These form a kind of "primordial network" of uncommitted nodes within which the network of committed nodes is embedded.

Chunking involves strengthening the links between a cluster of committed nodes and a free node. Thereafter, the free node becomes committed and functions as the chunking node for the cluster i.e., the activation of nodes in the cluster results in the activation of the chunking node and conversely, the activation of the chunking node activates all the nodes in the cluster. The process by which a free node is transformed to a committed node is called recruitment. The mechanics of recruitment in connectionist networks is described in detail in [Feldman 82]. The basic insight in the solution to the problem of learning through weight change is that certain classes of random connection graphs have a very high probability of containing the sub-network needed for learning a new concept.

The notion of chunking in its generic form only suggests a mechanism whereby nodes can be associated and is not sufficient for explaining how structured relationships arise. In the proposed solution we wish to exploit the non-trivial structure resulting from assuming that knowledge is organized in terms of properties and values thereof. We postulate that learning takes place within a network that is already organized to reflect this structure. For instance, in the context of vision, we

182

specifically assume that concepts that correspond to primitive properties like color, shape, texture, and motion are already present in the semantic network of an agent, together with concepts that represent some basic values of these properties. Simple forms of learning result in the formation of concepts that represent coherent collections of existing properties and values, while more complex forms of learning lead to generalization of concepts and the formation of complex properties that in turn lead to the development of more complex concepts.

We will consider a toy example of a semantic network interacting with a very simple visual system that is capable of detecting the colors blue and green and the primitive shapes round and oval. The initial organization of the semantic network takes into account these characteristics of the visual system. Figure 6.3 is an oversimplified representation of the initial organization of the semantic network. The network has four preexisting concepts namely, the property has-color and its values BLUE and GREEN and the property has-shape and its values ROUND and OVAL. In other words, the nodes representing properties and values are already connected to the visual system and may be activated by it under appropriate conditions. The nodes representing the four concepts are committed nodes embedded in a "primordial network" of free nodes that may be roughly partitioned into three diffuse sub-networks X, Y, and Z. Network X consists of nodes that are primarily connected to the nodes has-color, BLUE, and GREEN, but are also randomly connected to a number of free nodes in network Z. Similarly, nodes in network Y are primarily connected to the nodes has-shape, ROUND, and OVAL, but also receive numerous random connections from free nodes in network Z. Finally, the nodes in network Z are connected to a large number of nodes throughout the semantic network. The existence of networks X and Y indicates that the semantic network is prewired to "know" that BLUE and GREEN are values of has-color, while ROUND and OVAL are values of has-shape.

Figure 6.4 depicts the result of learning an instance of a blue and round object. The figure only shows the committed units and their interconnections. Learning an instance involves two stages of recruitment; the binder nodes B1 and R1 are recruited

184

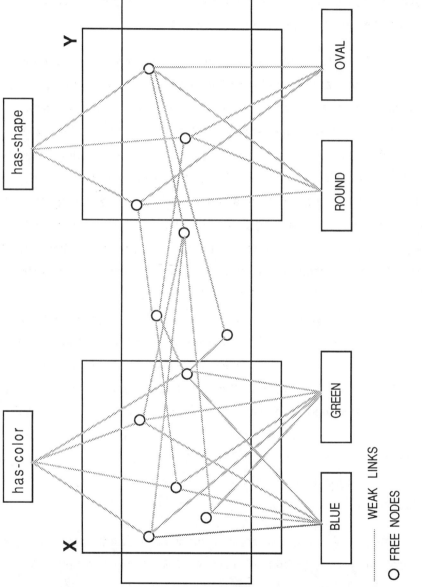

Figure 6.3: Initial organization of the semantic network

first, followed by the concept node BR1. When the visual system detects the color blue in the stimulus it activates the node has-color and BLUE. The coincident activation results in the recruitment of a free node (B1) from the pool of free nodes in network X. The node R1 is recruited in an analogous manner from the pool of nodes in network Y. The simultaneous activity in B1 and R1 leads to the recruitment of the node (BR1) from network Z. Thereafter, the nodes B1 and R1 act as binder nodes and BR1 represents the newly acquired concept. B1 is activated by the coincident activity of has-color and BLUE while R1 is activated by the coincident activity of has-shape and ROUND. The activity of the concept node BR1 is strongly correlated with the activity of B1 and R1.

The working of the scheme depends on the assumptions we made about the pre-existing structure of the semantic network. It was crucial to assume the existence of property and value nodes with appropriate connections to the visual system. The organization of free nodes into networks X, Y, and Z was equally important. Networks X and Y provided binder nodes in order to associate properties with their values, and the network Z provided a pool of nodes that could be recruited to "chunk" binder nodes in order to form concepts.

Figure 6.5 depicts the semantic network with three instances (BR1, BR2 and BR3) of blue round objects and one instance (GO1) of a green oval object. In this situation a second kind of concept formation may occur and result in the formation of the concept "blue and round object" which is a generalization defined over BR1, BR2 and BR3. The resulting network is shown in figure 6.6. The new concept is represented by the node BR that owns the binders B and R that indicate its property values. These property values correspond to the shared property values of the instances.

The transformation from the network in figure 6.5 to that in figure 6.6 is best explained with the help of the simpler networks shown in figure 6.7. The network shown in figure 6.7b is the result of a similar transformation of the network in figure 6.7a. The three instances A, B, and C have the same value (V) for the property P and this forms the basis for the formation of the more general concept D. The transformation occurs in two phases.

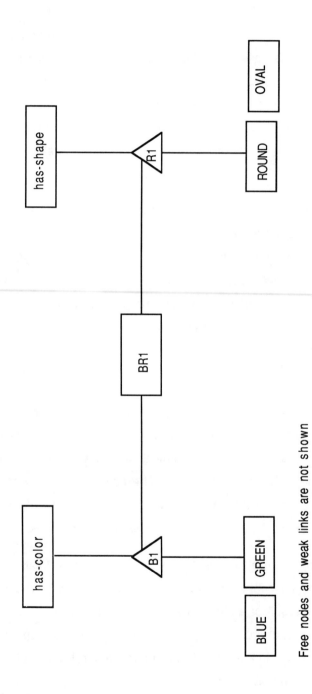

Free nodes and weak links are not shown

Figure 6.4: A blue and round object represented in the semantic network

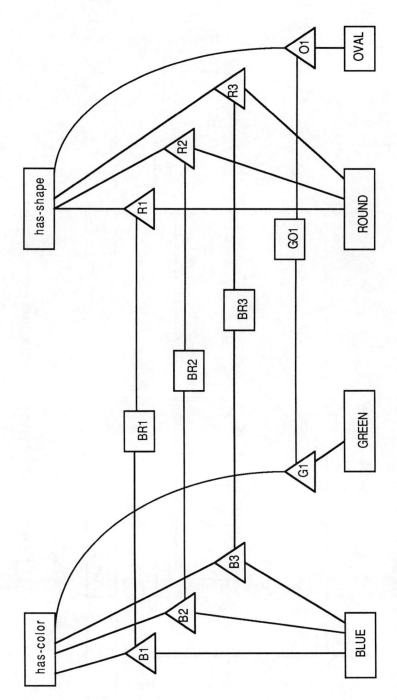

Free nodes and weak links are not shown

Figure 6.5: Multiple blue and round objects represented in the semantic network

188

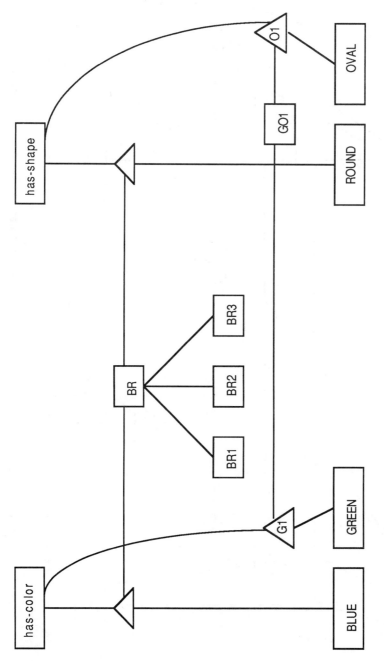

Free nodes and weak links are not shown

Figure 6.6: A new Type representing blue and round objects

Phase-I
  1. A chunking node for b1, b2, and b3 is recruited from a pool of free nodes that serves the same function as network Z in the previous example, i.e., provides a potential concept node.

Phase-II
  1. Over a longer period of time, the multiple paths between P and V via b1, b2 and b3 collapse into a single path via b, where b is one of the existing binder nodes b1, b2 or b3. The collapsing of links does not mean that the links disappear, but rather that the weights of links get reduced in such a way that all binder nodes besides b gradually become free nodes (are released).
  2. The connection between b and D remain strong but the connections between other binder nodes and D become weak.
  3. The links x,y and z (in effect) now emanate from D rather than the binder nodes.

(All changes described in phase II happen during the same time interval).

The net effect of phases I and II is that the network shown in figure 6.7a behaves like the network shown in figure 6.7b. The scheme that we have just described characterizes learning as network transformations that minimize the complexity of the network (number of links and nodes) while maintaining the cause effect relationships between existing concept nodes. Thus the nodes P, V, A, B, and C have roughly the same effect on each other in the two networks shown in figures 6.7a and 6.7b. The complexity of networks is substantially reduced by formation of more general concepts although this may not be evident from this simple example. In general, if the generalization takes place over p properties and c instances (the values of p and c were 1 and 3 in the example of figure 6.7, and 2 and 3 in the example of figure 6.6), then the number of links and nodes saved is of the order of $p \times c$.

Referring back to figure 6.6, BR, a node in network Z, will be recruited as a chunking node of B1, B2, B3 as well as R1, R2, and R3. The release of binder nodes and the collapsing of links will occur separately for the two properties has-color and has-shape. Thus B1, B2, and B3 will collapse into B while R1, R2 and R3 will collapse into R.

190

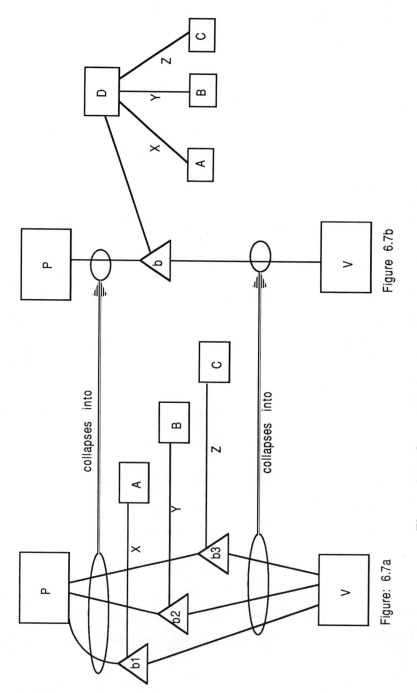

Figure: 6.7a

Figure 6.7b

Figure 6.7: Generalization viewed as network compaction

The above is intended to be a crude description of how the recruitment of free nodes and the release of committed nodes leads to the representation of new instances and the development of novel concepts that are generalizations of existing ones. Recently, Warren [Warren 87] has implemented this idea and shown that not only generalization, but also specialization of concepts can be achieved by a system built along the lines described above.

6.7 Biological plausibility

A discussion of a connectionist system often leads to the question of its biological plausibility. The proposed encoding is certainly not intended to be a blueprint for building "wetware". Yet it does satisfy nearly all the constraints proposed in [Feldman & Ballard 82]. The only serious violation of biological plausibility is the requirement that nodes perform high precision multiplication. A promising research strategy may be to interpret the connectionist system described here as an idealization and try and identify "approximations" of this system that are biologically more plausible, and study the manner in which their response deviates from the prescribed behavior. Such an exercise may point out further constraints that govern the organization of conceptual structure.

6.8 Conclusion

This thesis demonstrates that certain problems in knowledge representation and reasoning have elegant solutions within an evidential framework. I hope that this work will provide a point of contact between researchers who adopt traditional approaches - (i.e., various non-monotonic logics), and researchers who adopt an evidential approach to deal with partial and uncertain knowledge. I also hope that this will lead to a greater interaction between the two groups that have largely worked independently.

This thesis also demonstrates the efficacy of developing efficient connectionist solutions to problems that are considered to be "too difficult" for an apparently "low-level" approach. My experience has been otherwise - "thinking" in connectionist terms gave rise to the intuitions that lead to this thesis.

It has often been argued that a deep understanding of what is intelligence, why is it that we view the world to be structured as we do, and why are we good at certain tasks while inept at some others, will accrue only if we adopt an integrated approach that synthesizes computational, behavioral, as well as neurobiological issues. It is hoped that the work described here is a small step in this direction.

Appendix A   Network Behaviour:
A Proof of Correctness

In this appendix we provide a detailed proof that the network computes solutions to the inheritance and recognition problems in time proportional to the depth of the conceptual hierarchy, and in accordance with the evidential theory developed in chapter 4.

The proof proceeds by establishing that if one focuses only on concept nodes (the ξ-nodes), then the structure of the network is such that with reference to any query, the network can be partitioned into two subparts. In each subpart, activation spreads in a single direction - top to bottom or bottom to top, the directions being defined with reference to the partial ordering $<<$. The two subparts interact via binder nodes (i.e., δ_{inh}-nodes and δ_{rec}-nodes). This interaction, however, is also strictly unidirectional; activation flows from one of the subparts to the other, but not vice versa. Consequently, there are no cycles and the potentials of nodes stabilize at the appropriate value in time proportional to the depth of the conceptual hierarchy. As stated in section 5.7, certain additional conditions need to be imposed on the conceptual structure and on the manner in which inheritance and recognition queries are posed, in order to establish convergence of the connectionist solution. These conditions are:

WFR-parallel-1: For any $P \in \Phi$, if $V \in \Lambda(P)$, then $P \notin \lambda(V)$. Furthermore, for any A, if $A << V$, then $P \notin \lambda(A)$. I.e., a property should not be applicable to its own values or the descendents of its values. In other words, property values and the concepts they apply to, should belong to *distinct* ontological Types.

WFR-parallel-2: For any $P_i, P_j \in \Phi$, if P_i and P_j are distinct and there exists a concept C such that both P_i and $P_j \in \lambda(C)$, then $\Lambda(P_i)$ and $\Lambda(P_j)$ are disjoint. I.e., Properties that apply to the same concept should have distinct values.

WFR-parallel-3: For any $V_i, V_j \in \Lambda(P)$, neither $V_i << V_j$, nor $V_j << V_i$. I.e., all values of a property should be at a similar level of abstraction.

193

WFR-parallel-4: The ordering graph defined by C/C,P and << should be a tree.

WFR-parallel-5: This constraint is with reference to inheritance queries and requires that REF should be such that C is not << REF.

WFR-parallel-6: This constraint is with reference to recognition queries. Let ω be the leaf of the ontological tree that is the ancestor of all members of C-SET. Then if all the relevant information in the conceptual structure is to be utilized, REF should be such that ω << REF.

The proposed network essentially operates in two modes: the inheritance mode and the recognition mode, and therefore, the proof of correctness of the network's behavior may be split into two parts: one for inheritance and the other for recognition.

A.1 Proof of correctness for inheritance

Recall the definition of the inheritance problem and the manner in which it is posed to the network.

Inheritance

Given: a concept C and a property P such that $P \in \lambda(C)$.

a set of possible answers V-SET, i.e., V-SET = $\{V_1, V_2, ...V_n\}$, such that each element of V-SET is also a member of $\Lambda(P)$ - the set of possible values of P, and

a reference concept REF for V-SET such that for all V_i, $1 \le i \le n$, there exists a unique path from V_i to REF in the ordering graph defined by C and <<.

Find: $V^* \in$ V-SET such that, relative to the values specified in V-SET, V^* is the most likely value of property P for concept C.

The above query is posed as follows:

1. The nodes C, P, and INHERIT are activated by setting the external inputs - i.e., the inputs to the site **QUERY** - of these nodes to 1.0.

2. If one or more members of V-SET reach an **active** state within two time steps, REF is activated by setting its external input to 1.0 and the ↓ links leaving REF are enabled.

3. If none of the members of V-SET receive any activation then not only is REF activated and the ↓ links leaving REF enabled, but the ↑ links leaving C are also enabled.

Theorem-A.1: After $d + 4$ time steps - where d is the longest path in the ordering graph defined by **C** and << - the potentials of nodes will be such that the following holds for any two nodes V_i and $V_j \in$ V-SET:

$$\frac{\text{potential of } V_i}{\text{potential of } V_j} = \text{the best estimate of } \frac{\#C[P,V_i]}{\#C[P,V_j]}$$

The proof of this theorem can be broken down into two distinct cases: the local inheritance case and the non-local inheritance case. In the case of local inheritance, $\delta(C, P)$ is known (i.e., for all V_i members of $\Lambda(P)$, $\#C[P,V_i]$ is known) and therefore, there exists a δ_{inh}-node $[C,P \to V_i]$ connecting C, P, and V_i. In the case of non-local inheritance, $\delta(C, P)$ is unknown and $\#C[P, V_i]$'s have to be estimated based on the distributions available at concepts above C in the conceptual hierarchy. In terms of the parallel network, δ_{inh}-nodes associated with ξ-nodes that are above C in the conceptual hierarchy have to take part in the inheritance process.

Before we proceed, recall that throughout the inheritance mode INHERIT is active while RECOGNIZE is inert. Thus *all* the δ_{rec}-nodes remain inert throughout the inheritance mode because they never receive an input from the RECOGNIZE node at site ENABLE. Furthermore, all δ_{inh}-nodes receive an input from INHERIT node at site ENABLE, and hence, in order to become active these nodes only require inputs from the appropriate ϕ-node and ξ-node at this site. (In future we will refer the inputs from a ϕ-node and a ξ-node to a δ_{inh}-node at site ENABLE as the ϕ-input and the ξ-input respectively.)

A.1.1 Proof for the local case of inheritance

Lemma-A.1: Besides C and P, the only other nodes active at the end of step 1 of the inheritance process are δ-nodes $[C,P \to V_i]$'s and ξ-nodes V_i's , where V_i's are the members of $\Lambda(P)$.

Proof: At the onset of step 1, nodes C and P are activated as a result of the input they receive at site QUERY. As per the potential function of ξ-nodes and ϕ-nodes described in section 5.4.2, C and P acquire a potential of 1.0. As none of the $\uparrow$ and $\downarrow$ links are enabled, activation from C and P spreads only along links leading into δ_{inh}-nodes. Clearly, only δ_{inh}-nodes of the form [C,P -> V_i] receive the ξ-input (from C) as well as the ϕ-input (from P) at site ENABLE, and hence, switch to the active state.

Active δ_{inh}-nodes [C,P -> V_i] send outputs to the ξ-nodes V_i's, and possibly, to other δ_{inh}-nodes of the form [B,P -> V_i], where C << B, but C $\neq$ B. However, these δ_{inh}-nodes will not receive any input from a ξ-node at site ENABLE, and hence, will not become active.

The addition of the nodes V_i's to the set of active nodes does not cause any new nodes to become active. To see this, consider an arbitrary node V_i. Because the $\uparrow$ and $\downarrow$ links leaving V_i are not enabled, none of the ξ-nodes receive direct activation on account of V_i. Furthermore, as P is the only active ϕ-node and P does not apply to V_i (by virtue of WFR-parallel-1), no new δ_{inh}-nodes can become active on account of receiving a ξ-input from V_i. This is because none of the δ_{inh}-nodes that receive their ξ-input from V_i will receive their ϕ-input.

Thus the only nodes active at the end of step 1 of the inheritance process are: nodes C, P, and for every $V_i \in \Lambda(P)$, the ξ-node V_i and the δ_{inh}-node [C,P -> V_i]. Furthermore, it will only take 2 time steps for these nodes to become active. Q.E.D.

Lemma-A.2: At the end of step 1 of the inheritance process the potential of δ_{inh}-nodes [C,P -> V_i] is 1.0, while that of ξ-nodes V_i is #C[P, V_i] / #V_i. As before, V_i's refer to members of $\Lambda(P)$.

Proof: First consider the δ_{inh}-nodes [C,P -> V_i]. None of these nodes receive any inputs at site EC. This is because inputs to a node [C,P -> V_i] at site EC can only originate from δ_{inh}-nodes of the form [B,P -> V_i], where B << C, and B $\neq$ C. However, no such B is active. (Lemma-A.1).

Thus the potential, and hence, the output of nodes [C,P -> V_i]'s, will be 1.0.

Next consider the ξ-nodes V_i's. Each ξ-node V_i receives an input from the δ_{inh}-node [C,P -> V_i]. If C is such that, there exists a D such that C << D and δ(D,P) is known, then the link from [C,P -> V_i] will be incident at site **CP** of V_i. However, if such a D does not exist, the link will impinge on site **HCP**. In either case, the weight on the link connecting [C,P -> V_i] to V_i is #C[P, V_i] / #V_i. Thus the input to V_i from [C,P -> V_i] will be 1.0 * #C[P, V_i] / #V_i. As this is the only input received by V_i, its potential will be #C[P, V_i] /#V_i. **Q.E.D.**

At the end of step 1, nodes V_i will be active and hence step 2 will ensue. This will lead to the activation of REF, and the enabling of the $\downarrow$ links emanating from REF.

Lemma-A.3: No additional δ_{inh}-nodes become active during step 2.

Proof: For a δ_{inh}-node to become active, it must receive coincident inputs from an appropriate ξ-node and an appropriate ϕ-node. WFR-parallel-1 guarantees that P does not apply to REF or its descendants, and hence, none of the δ_{inh}-nodes that receive a ξ-input from REF or its descendants receive activation from P. But P is the only active ϕ-node. It follows that none of the δ_{inh}-nodes receiving activation from REF or its descendants become active. **Q.E.D.**

Lemma-A.4: As a result of step 2, each V_i member of V-SET, receives exactly one new input. This is incident along a $\downarrow$ link (at site **RELAY**), and has a magnitude of #V_i / #REF. Furthermore, the time taken for this input to arrive at V_i is at most d, the depth of the conceptual hierarchy.

Proof: Recall that V-SET is a subset of Λ(P). As a consequence of Lemma-A.3, the only possible inputs to V_i's may come from ξ-nodes activated as a result of the activation of REF and the enabling of $\downarrow$ links. By definition, REF is such that for each $V_i \in$ V-SET, there exists a *unique* path from REF to V_i via $\downarrow$ links. Thus, activating REF and enabling the $\downarrow$ links results in a *single* input to each V_i along a $\downarrow$ link. Let the path from REF to V_i be via ξ-nodes D_1, D_2,...D_k. The weights along this path will be #D_1/#REF, #D_2/#D_1, ... #D_k/#D_{k-1}, #V_i/#D_k. Thus the input to V_i along this path will be

output of REF * Π (the weights along the path to V_i)

which is

$$1.0 \times \frac{\#D_1}{\#REF} \times \frac{\#D_2}{\#D_1} \times \ldots \frac{\#D_k}{\#D_{k-1}} \times \frac{\#V_i}{\#D_k}$$

which reduces to $\#V_i / \#REF$.

As the input is along $\downarrow$ links, it will be incident at site **RELAY**. Finally, the time taken for the activation to propagate from REF to V_i along a chain of $\downarrow$ links will be at most d. **Q.E.D.**

Combining the results of Lemma-A.2 and Lemma-A.4, and noting that the potential of each $V_i \in$ V-SET will be equal to the product of the inputs to V_i, we find that the potential of each $V_i \in$ V-SET at the end of step 2 is given by

$$\frac{\#C[P,V_i]}{\#V_i} \times \frac{\#V_i}{\#REF} = \frac{\#C[P,V_i]}{\#REF}$$

Ignoring the common factor, #REF, in the denominator which will occur in the potential of each V_i, it is clear that each V_i has the desired potential. Specifically, for V_i, $V_j \in$ V-SET,

$$\frac{\text{potential of } V_i}{\text{potential of } V_j} = \frac{\#C[P,V_i]}{\#C[P,V_j]}$$

as desired.

Finally, the total time taken for the inheritance process to complete is the time taken by step 1 together with the time taken by step 2, i.e., $d + 2$. This completes the proof for the local case of theorem A.1. **Q.E.D.**

A.1.2 Proof for the non-local case of inheritance

As $\delta(C,P)$ is not known, there are no δ_{inh}-nodes encoding $\delta(C,P)$. Hence the activation of C and P alone does not activate any δ_{inh}-nodes. Furthermore, because neither the $\uparrow$, nor the $\downarrow$ links are enabled, no ξ-node gets activated. Thus, at the end of step 1, only nodes C and P are active, and consequently, step 3 will ensue. This step will lead to i) the enabling of ↑ links at C and ii) the activation of REF and the enabling of the ↓ links at REF.

We will consider the effects of the two actions i) and ii) separately and then show that as far as the nodes in V-SET are considered, these effects are independent. Finally, we will show that the combined effect of actions i) and ii) leads to the desired behavior.

Lemma-A.5: If C and P are active, then the following δ_{inh}-nodes are activated as a result of enabling the ↑ links at C: for all $X \in$ **C/C,P** and for all $V_i \in \Lambda(P)$, the δ_{inh}-nodes [X,P -> V_i].

Proof: By the definition of projection, each $X \in$ **C/C,P** is such that C << X. Hence, if C is active and the ↑ links at C are enabled, each $X \in$ **C/C,P** will be activated.

Furthermore, if $X \in$ **C/C,P**, then $\delta(X,P)$ is known. This in turn implies that for every member V_i of $\Lambda(P)$, there exist δ_{inh}-nodes of the form [X,P -> V_i]. Because P is already active, the activation of X causes nodes [X,P -> V_i] to become active, and consequently, all δ_{inh}-nodes that encode $\delta(X,P)$, for some $X \in$ **C/C,P**, will become active. **Q.E.D.**

Lemma-A.6: If C and P are active, then the ξ-nodes that become active as a result of enabling the ↑ links at C are *exactly those* that either lie above C, or are members of $\Lambda(P)$.

Proof: The ξ-nodes activated as a result of enabling the ↑ link at C may be divided into two categories: ones that receive activation from C along a chain of ξ-nodes connected by ↑ links (let this category be *set1*), and others that receive activation along a path that includes one or more δ_{inh}-nodes (let this category be *set2*).

The nodes in *set1* are exactly those ξ-nodes that are above C. We next consider the category *set2*.

Consider the nodes in *set2* that are activated via a path that includes only *one* δ_{inh}-node. Clearly, the solitary δ_{inh}-node in such a path must be one that gets its ξ-input from a ξ-node in *set1*, and hence, must be of the form $[X,P \rightarrow V_i]$, where X is a member of $C/C,P$, and V_i is a member of $\Lambda(P)$ (recall that the only active φ-node is P). It follows that the nodes in *set2* that are activated via a path that includes some (zero or more) ξ-nodes followed by *exactly one* δ_{inh}-node are none other than the ξ-nodes V_i's - the members of $\Lambda(P)$. Furthermore, by virtue of WFR-parallel-1, no member of $\Lambda(P)$ lies above C, and hence, the ↑ links emanating from the members of $\Lambda(P)$ will not get enabled. Consequently, no new ξ-nodes receive activation along a chain of ↑ links from ξ-nodes that are members of $\Lambda(P)$. Hence, it follows that the nodes in *set2* that are activated via a path that includes *only one* δ_{inh}-node are *exactly* the ξ-nodes V_i's, the members of $\Lambda(P)$.

Finally, P is the only active φ-node and P does not apply to members of $\Lambda(P)$. Therefore, no additional δ_{inh}-nodes become active on account of ξ-nodes that are members of $\Lambda(P)$, and hence, no ξ-nodes can become active on account of activation arriving via paths that include more than one δ_{inh}-nodes. Thus only ξ-nodes that are members of $\Lambda(P)$ constitute the set *set2*. **Q.E.D.**

Lemma-A.7: If C and P are active, then every δ_{inh}-node activated as a result of enabling the ↑ links at C is of the form: $[X,P \rightarrow V_i]$, where $X \in C/C,P$ and $V_i \in \Lambda(P)$.

Proof: Any active δ_{inh}-node must receive a ξ-input and a φ-input. By virtue of Lemma-A.6, the only active ξ-nodes are either those that are above C, or those that are members of $\Lambda(P)$. Furthermore, P is the only active φ-node and WFR-parallel-1 entails that P does not apply to any member of $\Lambda(P)$. Therefore, the only δ_{inh}-nodes that receive both the ξ-input and the φ-input must be those that get their ξ-input from ξ-nodes that lie above C, and their φ-input from P. But these are exactly the δ_{inh}-nodes of the form $[X,P \rightarrow V_i]$, where $X \in C/C,P$, and $V_i \in \Lambda(P)$. **Q.E.D.**

Lemma-A.8: If C and P are active, then enabling the ↑ links at C results *exactly* in the following δ_{inh}-nodes becoming active: for all $X \in C/C,P$ and for all $V_i \in \Lambda(P)$, the δ_{inh}-nodes $[X,P \rightarrow V_i]$.

Proof: This lemma directly follows from Lemma-A.5 and Lemma-A.7.

Lemma-A.9: The set of δ-nodes activated as a result of nodes C and P being active and the ↑ links at C being enabled, does not include REF, or any ξ-node that lies between REF and a member of V-SET.

Proof: By virtue of Lemma-A.5, the only ξ-nodes that become active under the conditions defined in this Lemma are either those that lie above C or those that are members of $\Lambda(P)$. By virtue of WFR-parallel-5, C is not below REF. Hence, no node above C can either be REF or any node below REF. Consequently, no node above C can either be REF or any node that lies between REF and members of $\Lambda(P)$. Therefore, any active ξ-node situated between REF and members of $\Lambda(P)$ must be a member of $\Lambda(P)$. However, by virtue of WFR-parallel-3, there exists no V_i, $V_j \in \Lambda(P)$ such that $V_i << V_j$. Therefore, there exists no member of $\Lambda(P)$ that lies between REF and some other member of $\Lambda(P)$.

We have established that none of the ξ-nodes activated as a result of nodes C and P being active and the ↑ links at C being enabled, lie between REF and members of $\Lambda(P)$. Now V-SET is a subset of $\Lambda(P)$, therefore none of the activated nodes lie between REF and members of V-SET. **Q.E.D.**

Lemma-A.10: Given that C and P are active, the activation incident at members of $\Lambda(P)$ as a result of activating REF and enabling the ↓ links at REF, is not modified by enabling of the ↑ links at C.

Proof: Lemma-A.3 proved that activating REF and enabling ↓ links at REF does not activate any δ_{inh}-nodes, and activation originating at REF reaches members of V-SET along a path consisting solely of ξ-nodes connected via ↓ links. Lemma-A.9 proved that none of the ξ-nodes activated as a result of enabling the ↑ links at C lie between REF and members of V-SET (nor do the nodes thus activated include REF).

Thus, enabling the ↑ links at C has no effect on the activation reaching member nodes of V-SET as a result of activating REF and enabling the ↓ links at REF. **Q.E.D.**

Lemma-A.11: Given that C and P are active, the activation incident at members of V-SET due to activating the ↑ links at C is not modified by activating REF and enabling the $\downarrow$ links at REF.

Proof: The effect of activating the $\uparrow$ links at C on the members of V-SET is via ξ-nodes that lie above C; these nodes activate δ_{inh}-nodes which in turn activate members of V-SET. Activating REF and enabling the $\downarrow$ links at REF does not activate any δ_{inh}-nodes (Lemma-A.3). Furthermore, none of the ξ-nodes affected by activating REF and the enabling of $\downarrow$ links at REF lie above C (this follows from WFR-parallel-5). Hence none of the nodes that affect the members of V-SET - as a consequence of C being active and the $\uparrow$ links at C being enabled - are modified by activating REF and enabling the $\downarrow$ links at REF. **Q.E.D.**

Lemma-A.12: With C and P active, the effect on the members of V-SET due to activating REF and enabling the $\downarrow$ links at REF is independent of the effect of enabling the $\uparrow$ links at C.

Proof: This lemma directly follows from Lemma-A.10 and Lemma-A.11. **Q.E.D.**

In Lemma-A.4 we established that each $V_i \in$ V-SET receives an input of magnitude #V_i / #REF at site **RELAY** as a result of activating REF and enabling the $\downarrow$ links at REF. We now consider the effect of activating the $\uparrow$ links at C on the members of V-SET.

Lemma-A.13: For each V_i, member of $\Lambda(P)$, the interconnections between δ_{inh}-nodes of the form [X,P -> V_i], where X is a member of **C**/C,P, are isomorphic to the ordering graph defined by **C**/C,P and <<.

Proof: This lemma follows from the definition of projection and the encoding rules for δ_{inh}-nodes described in section 5.4.1. A δ_{inh}-node [X,P -> V_i] exists for every X that is a member of **C**/C,P. Furthermore, there is a link from [X,P -> V_i] to [Y,P-> V_i] if and only if Y is a parent of X in the ordering induced on **C**/C,P by <<. **Q.E.D.**

Recall that the ordering diagram defined by **C**/C,P and << is a tree (WFR-parallel-4). In view of Lemma-A.13, the interconnections between δ_{inh}-nodes of the form [X,P -> V_i], where X is a member of **C**/C,P, also define a tree structure. Furthermore, by virtue of Lemma-A.8 all these δ_{inh}-nodes become active during step 3.

Lemma-A.14: During step three, the tree of δ_{inh}-nodes referred to in Lemma-A.13 computes BEST-ESTIMATE(Ξ,P,V_i) / #V_i, for each $V_i \in$ V-SET. In the above expression BEST-ESTIMATE (henceforth B.E.) is the function described in section 4.4.3 and Ξ is such that, there exists no D such that $\Xi \ll D$ and $\delta(D,P)$ is known.

Proof: Except for the case where the recursion bottoms out, a call to B.E. (ξ, ϕ, ν) performs the following computations:

$$\#\xi(\phi,\nu) \times \prod \frac{B.E.(\xi_i,\phi,\nu)}{\#\xi(\phi,\nu)}$$

The division operation (op1) follows each recursive call - one for each son of ξ - and divides the value returned by the recursive call by $\#\xi(\phi,\nu)$. A second operation (op2) computes the product over all the recursive calls, and finally, a multiplication operation (op3) multiplies the result of op2 by $\#\xi(\phi,\nu)$. In the ground case, the function simply returns $\#\xi(\phi,\nu)$.

Now consider figure A.1. We argue that the process enclosed in the dotted region surrounding the δ_{inh}-node $[X,P \rightarrow V_i]$ corresponds to a call to B.E.(X,P,V_i). Each input link into $[X,P \rightarrow V_i]$ corresponds to a recursive call to B.E. made from within B.E. (X,P,V_i). For example, the input link from $[X_S,P \rightarrow V_i]$ into $[X,P \rightarrow V_i]$ corresponds to a recursive call B.E.(X_S,P,V_i) made from within the call B.E.(X,P,V_i). However, there is one difference - an input received along an incoming link not only corresponds to the value returned by the recursive call, but also includes the effect of performing op1. For example, the input coming into $[X,P \rightarrow V_i]$ along the link $[X_S,P \rightarrow V_i]$ corresponds to the value returned by B.E.(X_S,P,V_i) divided by #$X[P,V_i]$. Thus, instead of being performed by B.E.(X,P,V_i), op1 - which in this case is a division by #$X[P,V_i]$ - is being performed by B.E.(X_S,P,V_i). However, as shown below, this preemptive computation of op1 is performed consistently.

To further the correspondence between $[X,P \rightarrow V_i]$ and B.E.(X,P,V_i), note that $[X,P \rightarrow V_i]$ computes its potential by multiplying all its inputs and this step corresponds to op2 in the definition of B.E.

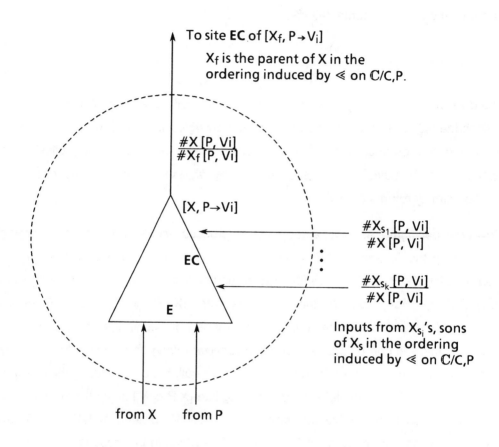

To site **EC** of $[X_f, P \rightarrow V_i]$

X_f is the parent of X in the
ordering induced by $\ll$ on $\mathbb{C}/C,P$.

$\dfrac{\#X\,[P,\,Vi]}{\#X_f\,[P,\,Vi]}$

$[X, P \rightarrow Vi]$

EC

E

$\dfrac{\#X_{s_1}\,[P,\,Vi]}{\#X\,[P,\,Vi]}$

$\vdots$

$\dfrac{\#X_{s_k}\,[P,\,Vi]}{\#X\,[P,\,Vi]}$

Inputs from X_{s_i}'s, sons
of X_s in the ordering
induced by $\ll$ on $\mathbb{C}/C,P$

from X   from P

Figure A.1: Computation performed by a δ_{inh}-node

Finally, the output of $[X,P \rightarrow V_i]$ is multiplied by $\#X[P,V_i] / \#X_f[P,V_i]$ before it appears as an input to its parent $[X_f,P \rightarrow V_i]$. The numerator corresponds to op3, and the denominator corresponds to the preemptive computation of op1.

The recursion bottoms out when a call is made to B.E. with a relevant concept as the first argument. In this case, the call $B.E.(X,P,V_i)$ returns $\#X[P,V_i]$. In the tree structure defined by δ_{inh}-nodes, the ground instances of calls to B.E. correspond to the lowest level δ_{inh}-nodes. A lowest level δ_{inh}-node $[X,P \rightarrow V_i]$ does not receive any inputs at site EC, and hence, its potential and output equals 1.0. However, before this output is incident at a higher level node, it is multiplied by a weight of $\#X[P,V_i] / \#X_f[P,V_i]$, where the numerator corresponds to the desired result and the denominator corresponds to the preemptive computation of op1.

It remains to be shown where the very first call to B.E. is performed. Thus far, the highest node in the tree of δ_{inh}-nodes does not perform op3. (Recall that op3 is performed when the output of a node is multiplied by the weight of the outgoing link). The problem is solved by the presence of the link that goes from the highest δ_{inh}-node to the site HCP of V_i. This link has a weight of $\#X[P,V_i] / \#V_i$. The multiplication by $\#X[P,V_i]$ performs the required op3 but also introduces an extra division by the factor $\#V_i$.

Thus the input to V_i at site HCP equals $B.E.(\Xi,P,V_i) / \#V_i$, where Ξ is a ξ-node such that, there exists no D such that $\Xi << D$ and $\delta(D,P)$ is known.

This completes the proof of Lemma-A.14. **Q.E.D.**

In order to complete the proof we need to show that

$$\frac{\text{potential of } V_i}{\text{potential of } V_j} = \frac{B.E.(\Omega,P,V_i)}{B.E.(\Omega,P,V_j)}$$

Thus far we have established that

1. As a result of activating REF and enabling the $\downarrow$ links at REF, each $V_i \in$ of V-SET receives an input of magnitude $\#V_i / \#REF$ at site **RELAY**.

2. As a result of enabling the ↑ links at C, each $V_i \in$ of V-SET receives an input of magnitude B.E.(Ξ,P,V_i) at site **HCP**.

3. Each $V_i \in$ V-SET, also receives inputs at site **CP** from active δ_{inh}-nodes of the form $[X,P \rightarrow V_i]$ where $X \in$ **C/C,P**.

As per the potential function of ξ-nodes, inputs at site **CP** will be ignored because site **HCP** is active, and the potential of each member node of V-SET will be given by the product of the inputs at site **HCP** and **RELAY**. (There are no inputs at site **QUERY**). Thus the potential of each $V_i \in$ V-SET is: B.E.(Ξ,P,V_i) / #REF.

The factor 1/#REF occurs in the potential of all $V_i \in$ V-SET. Hence for any V_i, $V_j \in$ V-SET

$$\frac{\text{potential of } V_i}{\text{potential of } V_j} = \frac{\text{B.E.}(\Xi,P,V_i)}{\text{B.E.}(\Xi,P,V_j)}$$

We now need to show that: B.E.(Ξ, P, V_i) = B.E.(Ω,P,V_i).

Recall that WFR-parallel-4 requires that the ordering induced by $<<$ on **C/C,P** result in a tree. Hence, if there exists an Ω that is a reference concept for $\Gamma(C,P)$, it follows that the ordering induced on **C/C,P** by $<<$ is as shown in figure A.2. In particular, there is a single chain of nodes linking Ω and Ξ. From the definition of B.E. it follows that if A has only one son, say A_s, then

$$\text{B.E.}(A,P,V_i) = \#A[P,V_i] \times \frac{\text{B.E.}(A_s,P,V_i)}{\#A[P,V_i]} = \text{B.E.}(A_s,P,V_i)$$

As there is a linear sequence of nodes from Ω to Ξ, it follows that B.E.(Ξ,P,V_i) = B.E.(Ω,P,V_i).

The time taken in step 3 will be at most $d + 2$; all ξ-nodes in **C/C,P** will be activated within d time steps, it will take an additional time step for all δ_{inh}-nodes attached to these ξ-nodes to be activated, and yet another time step for all nodes in V-SET to be activated. In parallel to this spread of activation, activation will spread from REF to nodes in V-SET. This process will also take at most d steps. Thus the total time taken in step 3 will be at most $d + 2$. Step 1 takes 2 time steps, giving a total time of $d + 4$

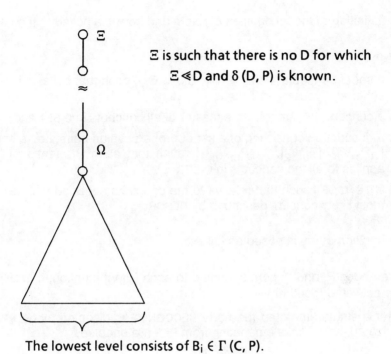

Ξ is such that there is no D for which
$\Xi \ll$ D and δ (D, P) is known.

The lowest level consists of $B_i \in \Gamma$ (C, P).

Figure A.2: Relation between the nodes Ω and Ξ

for the non-local case of inheritance. (Recall that the local case took $d + 2$ time).
Q.E.D.

A.2 Proof of correctness for recognition

Recall the definition of the recognition problem and how it is posed to the network.

Recognition

Given: a set of concepts, C-SET = $\{C_1, C_2, ... C_n\}$, such that concepts in C-SET are either all Types or all Tokens,

a concept, REF, that is an ancestor of all concepts in C-SET and

a description consisting of a set of property value pairs, i.e., a set DESCR = $\{ [P_1,V_1], [P_2,V_2], ... [P_m,V_m] \}$, such that each P_j mentioned in DESCR applies to all the concepts in C-SET.

Find: $C^* \in$ C-SET such that relative to the concepts specified in C-SET, C^* is the most likely concept described by DESCR.

The recognition query is posed as follows:

1. The nodes P_j and V_j corresponding to each $[P_j,V_j]$ mentioned in DESCR are activated together with the node RECOGNIZE.
2. After a single time step the node RECOGNIZE is disabled, node REF is activated, and $\downarrow$ links emanating from REF are enabled.

There are two distinct cases of the recognition problem: Type recognition and Token recognition. We will deal with each of these in turn.

A.2.1 Proof for Type recognition

In order to prove that the network computes the correct solution we have to show that at the end of the recognition process the potential of each C_i, $1 \leq i \leq$, (i.e, each C_i in C-SET) equals

$$\#C_i \times \prod_{j=1}^{m} \frac{\#B_{ij}[P_j,V_j]}{\#B_{ij}}$$

208

where P_j, $1 \leq j \leq m$, are properties mentioned in DESCR and B_{ij} is the concept relevant to C_i with respect to P_j. (Vide section 4.7.3).

Towards this end we prove the following theorem:

Theorem-A2: After $d + 2$ time steps the potential of each C_i, $1 \leq i \leq n$, equals:

$$\alpha \times \#C_i \times \prod_{j=1}^{m} \frac{\#B_{ij}[P_j,V_j]}{\#B_{ij}}$$

where α is a common factor in the potential of all C_i, $1 \leq i \leq n$.

Lemma-A.15: The set of δ_{rec}-nodes that become active during recognition consists exactly of the nodes of the form: $[P_j,V_j \rightarrow Y]$, where $[P_j,V_j] \in$ DESCR, and $Y \in$ **C**.

Proof: In order to become active a δ_{rec}-node requires a ξ-input, a ϕ-input and an input from RECOGNIZE. During the first time step after the recognition problem is posed, the only active nodes besides RECOGNIZE are ϕ-nodes P_j's and ξ-nodes V_j's, for $1 \leq j \leq m$. Thus, only δ_{rec}-nodes that receive their ϕ-input from one of the P_j's and their ξ-input from one of the V_j's can become active. Clearly, all δ_{rec}-nodes of the form $[P_j,V_j \rightarrow Y]$ will receive the appropriate inputs and become active. Now WFR-parallel-2 entails that $\Lambda(P_i)$ and $\Lambda(P_j)$ are disjoint, if $P_i \neq P_j$ and both P_i and P_j apply to the same concept. Therefore, there do not exist any δ_{rec}-nodes of the form $[P_k,V_l \rightarrow Y]$, where $1 \leq k,l \leq m$, and $k \neq l$. If such nodes do not even exist, they clearly cannot become active. Thus, the only δ_{rec}-nodes active after the first time step will be nodes of the form $[P_j,V_j \rightarrow Y]$ for $1 \leq j \leq m$, and $Y \in$ **C**.

After the first time step RECOGNIZE is disabled, and hence, no new δ_{rec}-nodes can become active thereafter. However, all the P_j's and V_j's continue to remain active throughout the recognition process, and therefore, all the δ_{rec}-nodes active at the end of the first time step will remain active throughout this process. Hence the only δ_{rec}-nodes that remain active during the recognition process are the ones specified in Lemma-A.15. Q.E.D.

Lemma-A.16: The following ξ-nodes become active during the recognition process:

i) V_j for $1 \leq j \leq m$.

ii) All nodes Y such that their exist δ_{rec}-nodes of the form $[P_j, V_j \rightarrow Y]$, $1 \leq j \leq m$.

iii) REF and all nodes reachable from REF via $\downarrow$ links (i.e., all nodes Z such that Z << REF.)

Proof: Nodes in i) are activated during step 1 as part of the initialization process. Lemma-A.15 established that all δ_{rec}-nodes of the form $[P_j, V_j \rightarrow Y]$, $1 \leq j \leq m$, will be active, These δ_{rec}-nodes will in turn activate nodes Y listed in ii). In step 2 REF is activated and $\downarrow$ links emanating from it are enabled. This explains why nodes mentioned in iii) will become active. **Q.E.D.**

Lemma-A17: The ξ-nodes activated during the recognition process are exactly those specified in Lemma-A.16.

Proof: A ξ-node becomes active if it receives activation along any one of its six input sites: QUERY, RELAY, CP, HCP, PV, and INV. During recognition the sites CP and HCP are irrelevant as these receive inputs only from δ_{inh}-nodes, none of which are active.

The only ξ-nodes receiving activation at site QUERY are nodes P_j and V_j $1 \leq j \leq m$, and REF. But these nodes are already included in the set of nodes specified in Lemma-A.16.

Inputs at site PV of a ξ-node are provided by δ_{rec}-nodes. But the only active δ_{rec}-nodes are of the form $[P_j, V_j \rightarrow Y]$, $1 \leq j \leq m$, and therefore, the only ξ-nodes receiving activation from δ_{rec}-nodes at site PV are nodes such as Y. But nodes such as Y are already included in the set of active nodes specified by Lemma-A.16.

By definition of the interconnection pattern, a ξ-node Y has an incoming link at site INV from a δ_{rec}-node $[P_k, V_l \rightarrow X]$, if and only if, it also has an incoming link at site PV from another δ_{rec}-node $[P_k, V_l \rightarrow Y]$. But if $[P_k, V_l \rightarrow X]$ is active then $[P_k, V_l \rightarrow Y]$ must also be active. Thus any ξ-node receiving inputs at site INV must also receive inputs at site PV. Hence, we need not consider separately, the set of ξ-nodes activated as a result of receiving inputs at site **INV**; these nodes are covered by the nodes activated as a result of receiving inputs at site **PV**. This still leaves the site **RELAY**.

During recognition, all inputs at site **RELAY** arrive along $\downarrow$ links. But the only enabled $\downarrow$ links are the ones that lie below REF. Therefore, any ξ-node receiving activation along $\downarrow$ links must be reachable from REF via $\downarrow$ links. But all such nodes are already claimed to be active by Lemma-A.16. Hence all the ξ-nodes that can possibly be active during the recognition process are accounted for by Lemma-A.16. This establishes Lemma-A.17. **Q.E.D.**

Because each C_i, $1 \leq i \leq n$, is a Type, WFR-mv-1 (cf. section 4.7.3) entails that for any P_j, $1 \leq j \leq m$, there is exactly one concept - B_{ij} - relevant to C_i with respect to P_j. WFR-parallel-6 entails that for each B_{ij}, $C_i << B_{ij} <<$ REF. This is because B_{ij} can be no higher than ω - the ontological type to which C_i belongs - and WFR-parallel-6 requires that $\omega <<$ REF. Furthermore, WFR-parallel-6 together with the Multiple Views Organization entails that there is a unique path Ψ_i from REF to each C_i made up of ξ-nodes connected via $\downarrow$ links. Let the nodes in this path be: REF, D_{i1}, D_{i2}, ... D_{is}, C_i. (Note that we are including REF and C_i in Ψ_i). Clearly, each B_{ij} lies in Ψ_i.

It is also the case that the paths Ψ_i's, share a common initial segment of one or more nodes. This segment begins at REF and terminates at ω. (I.e., either REF or one of the D_{ik}'s is ω). This follows from the fact that $\omega <<$ REF and ω is the ontological Type to which all the C_i's belong.

The activation arriving at C_i may be viewed as originating at REF and travelling down $\downarrow$ links along the ξ-nodes in Ψ_i. Along the way, the activation is modified in two ways: i) it is multipied by the weights on the $\downarrow$ links between nodes in Ψ_i and ii) it is multiplied by the activation arriving from δ_{rec}-nodes at sites **PV** and **INV** of the nodes in Ψ_i.

Given the multiplicative effect of the above modifications, the effect of each of them may be decoupled and later combined by taking their product. The modification due to weights along $\downarrow$ links is given by

$$1.0 \times \frac{\#D_1}{\#REF} \times \frac{\#D_2}{\#D_1} \times \ldots \frac{\#D_s}{\#D_{s-1}} \times \frac{\#C_i}{\#D_s}$$

which reduces to $\#C_i / \#REF$.

The modification due to inputs from δ_{inh}-nodes are due to inputs at the sites PV and INV. However, the interconnection pattern for δ_{rec}-nodes is such that if X and Y are two nodes in Ψ_i, and Y is the parent of X in the ordering defined by $\ll$ on $C/C_i, P_j$, then the activation provided by $[P_j, V_j \rightarrow Y]$ to the site PV of Y is *cancelled* by the activation provided by it to the site INV of X. The activation provided by $[P_j, V_j \rightarrow Y]$ to the site PV of Y will not get cancelled *if and only if*, there exists no X in Ψ_i such that Y is the parent of X in the ordering defined by $\ll$ on $C/C_i, P_j$. In other words, activation provided by $[P_j, V_j \rightarrow Y]$ at site PV of Y will contribute to the activation reaching C_i if and only if, Y is relevant to C_i with respect to P_j, i.e., $Y = B_{ij}$. Furthermore, this contribution will equal the output of $[P_j, V_j \rightarrow B_{ij}]$ (always 1.0 when active) times the weight on the link from it to B_{ij}. I.e.,

$$1.0 \times \frac{\#B_{ij}[P_j, V_j]}{\#B_{ij}} = \frac{\#B_{ij}[P_j, V_j]}{\#B_{ij}}$$

From the argument outlined above, it also follows that the activation provided by a node such as $[P_j, V_j \rightarrow Y]$ to the site INV of a node X in Ψ_i will affect the activation arriving at C_i if and only if, Y is the parent of X in the ordering defined by $\ll$ on $C/C_i, P_j$ *and* Y is not in Ψ_i. It also follows that the above can occur only if both REF and $\omega \ll Y$. In fact X, Y, REF, and ω can be partially ordered, the ordering being given by $\omega \ll X \ll REF \ll Y$. It follows that X lies in the segment common to all Ψ_i's, and therefore, the contribution of $[P_j, V_j \rightarrow Y]$ will have the same effect on the activation that reaches all the C_i's. We will refer to the contribution of all such (undesired) activation arriving at the INV sites of nodes in Ψ_i's as β.

The product of all the activation arriving at C_i, and hence, the potential of C_i can be expressed as:

$$\beta \times \frac{\#C_i}{\#REF} \times \prod_{j=1}^{m} \frac{\#B_{ij}[P_j, V_j]}{\#B_{ij}}$$

where β and 1/#REF are common factors and appear in the activation arriving at all members of C-SET. These factors may therefore be grouped together as α.

Finally, observe that the time taken for the appropriate activation to reach C_i would equal the length of the path from REF to C_i and this time will at most be d. Notice that all relevant δ_{rec}-nodes would be activated in the very first time step and their outputs will become available to nodes in Ψ_i in the next time step. Hence the total time required to compute the solution will be no more than $d + 2$.

This concludes the proof for the case of Type recognition. **Q.E.D.**

A.2.2 Proof for Token Recognition

To prove the correctness of the network behavior during Token recognition it must be shown that the potential of each C_i, $1 \le i \le n$, equals

$$\prod_{j=1}^{m} \prod_{k=1}^{q} \beta_{ij}^{k}$$

where P_j, $1 \le j \le m$, are the properties mentioned in DESCR, q refers to the number of views defined below ω - the ontological Type to which the C_i's belong, and

$$\beta_{ij}^{k} = \frac{\#B_{ij}^{k}[P_j, V_j]}{\#B_{ij}^{k}} \quad \text{; if there exists a concept } B_{ij}^{k} \text{ in view } H_k \text{ that is relevant to } C_i \text{ with respect to } P_j$$

$$\qquad\qquad 1 \qquad\qquad \text{; otherwise.}$$

Towards this end we prove the following theorem.

Theorem-A.3: After $d + 2$ time steps, the potential of each C_i, $1 \le i \le n$ equals:

$$\gamma \times \prod_{j=1}^{m} \prod_{k=1}^{q} \beta_{ij}^{k}$$

where γ is a common factor appearing in the potential of all C_i, $1 \le i \le n$, and β_{ij}^{k} are as defined before.

Proof: This result is a generalization of the result derived for Type recognition. In the case of Type recognition there was a single path, Ψ_i, from REF to C_i. However, in the case of Token recognition there will be multiple paths from REF to C_i - one through each view defined over C_i. Specifically, if C_i's belong to the ontological Type ω and there are q views defined under ω, then there will be q paths, Ψ_{il}, $1 \leq l \leq q$, from REF to C_i.

Activation arriving along each path Ψ_{il} can be analyzed in a manner analogous to that adopted for analyzing the activation arriving along the path Ψ_i during Type recognition. Recall that the activation arriving along Ψ_i during Type recognition was

$$\beta \times \frac{\#C_i}{\#REF} \times \prod_{j=1}^{m} \frac{\#B_{ij}[P_j,V_j]}{\#B_{ij}}$$

where β and $1/\#REF$ were undesired factors in the activation arriving at C_i. But because these factors were common to the activation arriving at each C_i, they did not have any impact on the solution produced by the network. In case of Token recognition, however, there can be an additional undesired component in the activation arriving at C_i along a path Ψ_{il}. To observe this, consider two views, H_k and H_l, such that there exists a concept $B_{ij}{}^l$ in H_l that is relevant to C_i with respect to P_j, but there exists no concept $B_{ij}{}^k$ in H_k that is relevant to C_i with respect to P_j. The presence of $B_{ij}{}^l$ implies that ω - the ontological Type to which the C_i's belong - is not relevant to C_i with respect to P_j. Hence, the activation contributed by $[P_j,V_j \rightarrow \omega]$ at site PV of ω is undesirable and should be ignored. Indeed, the presence of $B_{ij}{}^k$ implies that this activation will be cancelled by the activation contributed by $[P_j,V_j \rightarrow \omega]$ to the site INV of some concept D_l in Ψ_{il}, where $B_{ij}{}^k \ll D_l \ll \omega$. Such a cancellation, however, will not occur for the activation propagating along the path Ψ_{ik}. The absence of a concept relevant to C_i with respect to P_j implies that there does not exist a node D_k in H_k such that $\delta(D_k,P_j)$ is known, and hence, there does not exist any node in Ψ_{ik}, between ω and C_i, which receives activation at site INV from $[P_j,V_j \rightarrow \omega]$. Thus the activation arriving at C_i along a path Ψ_{ik} will contain an undesired factor of the form $\#\omega[P_j,V_j] / \#\omega$ - for each P_j for which no concept $B_{ij}{}^k$, relevant to C_i with respect to P_j, exists in H_k.

In view of the above discussion the activation arriving at each C_i along a path Ψ_{ik} may be expressed as:

$$\beta \times \frac{1}{\#REF} \times \prod_{j=1}^{m} \beta_{ij}{}^k$$

where β is the undesired factor common to all C_i's (analogous to the one in the expression for Type recognition), $\#C_i$ has been replaced by 1 (in the case of Token recognition, $\#C_i = 1$ for all C_i), and where:

$$\beta_{ij}{}^k = \frac{\#B_{ij}{}^k[P_j,V_j]}{\#B_{ij}{}^k} \quad ; \text{ if there exists a concept } B_{ij}{}^k \text{ in view } H_k \text{ that is}$$

relevant to C_i with respect to P_j

$$\frac{\#\omega[P_j,V_j]}{\#\omega} \quad ; \text{ otherwise.}$$

By virtue of WFR-mv-3, however, if there does not exist a concept relevant to some C_i with respect to P_j in view H_k, then there does not exist a concept relevant to *any* C_i with respect to P_j in view H_k. Hence, if one C_i receives an undesirable contribution from a node such as $[P_j,V_j \rightarrow \omega]$, then so do all C_i's. Specifically, the activations arriving at each C_i, $1 \le i \le n$, along paths Ψ_{ik}, $1 \le i \le n$, respectively, will all contain the same undesirable but common extra factors contributed by nodes such as $[P_j,V_j \rightarrow \omega]$. Therefore, we may factor out these undesirable but common factors and rewrite the activation arriving at C_i along a path Ψ_{ik} as

$$\varepsilon \times \prod_{j=1}^{m} \beta_{ij}{}^k$$

where:

$$\beta_{ij}{}^k = \frac{\#B_{ij}{}^k[P_j, V_j]}{\#B_{ij}{}^k} \qquad \text{; if there exists a concept } B_{ij}{}^k \text{ in view } H_k \text{ that is}$$

relevant to C_i with respect to P_j

$$1 \qquad \text{; otherwise.}$$

in the above expression, ε incorporates β, $1/\#REF$, as well as the undesired but common contributions of nodes such as $[P_j, V_j \rightarrow \omega]$.

The product of all the activation arriving at C_i, and hence, the potential of C_i can now be expressed as

$$\varepsilon^q \times \prod_{k=1}^{q} \prod_{j=1}^{m} \beta_{ij}{}^k$$

where:

$$\beta_{ij}{}^k = \frac{\#B_{ij}{}^k[P_j, V_j]}{\#B_{ij}{}^k} \qquad \text{; if there exists a concept } B_{ij}{}^k \text{ in view } H_k \text{ that is}$$

relevant to C_i with respect to P_j

$$1 \qquad \text{; otherwise.}$$

If we equate the common factor ε^q to γ and reorder the product terms, we have the result we set out to prove.

Finally, observe that the activation propagates from REF to C_i's via all paths Ψ_{ik}'s in parallel, and therefore, the time taken by the activation to reach from REF to members of C-SET is no greater than d. Hence, as was the case with Type recognition, the time taken to solve the recognition problem is at most $d + 2$. **Q.E.D.**

References

[Ackley et al. 83] Ackley, D.H., G.E. Hinton, and T.J. Sejnowski. A learning algorithm for Boltzmann Machines, *Cognitive Science*, 9 (1): 147-169, 1985.

[Allen 83] Allen, J.F. Maintaining knowledge about Temporal Intervals. *Commun. ACM* 26: 832-843, 1983.

[Allen & Frisch 82] Allen, J.F. and A.M. Frisch. What's in a Semantic network? In *Proc. 20th Annual Meeting, Assoc. of Computational Linguistics*, pp 19-27, 1982.

[Anderson 83] Anderson, J. R. *The Architecture of Cognition*. Harvard University Press, Cambridge, MA, 1983.

[Ballard 86] Ballard, D.H. Parallel Logical Inference and Energy Minimization. In *Proc. AAAI-86*, pp 203-208.

[Bobrow & Winograd 77] Bobrow, D.G. and Terry Winograd. An overview of KRL: A Knowledge Representation Language. *Cognitive Science* 1 (1): 3-46, 1977.

[Brachman 85] Brachman, R. J. "I lied about the trees". *The AI Magazine*, vol. 6, no. 3, Fall 1985, pp. 80-93.

[Brachman & Schmolze 85] Brachman R.J. and J. Schmolze. An overview of KL-ONE Knowledge Representation System. *Cognitive Science* 9 (2): 171-216, 1985.

[Bruce 75] Bruce B.C. Case systems for natural language. *Artificial Intelligence*, 6: 327-360, 1975.

[Cercone & Schubert 75] Cercone, N, and L.K. Schubert. Toward a State Based Conceptual Representation. In *Proc. IJCAI-75*, pp 83-90.

[Charniak 83] Charniak, E. The Bayesian Basis of Common Sense Medical Diagnosis,. In *Proc. AAAI-83*, pp 70-73.

[Charniak 83a] Charniak, E. Passing markers: A theory of contextual influence in language comprehension. *Cognitive Science*, 7(3): 171-190, 1983.

[Charniak 81] Charniak, E. A common representation for problem solving and language comprehension information. *Artificial Intelligence*, 16: 225-255, 1981.

[Cheeseman 83] Cheeseman, P. A Method of Computing Generalized Bayesian Probability Values for Expert Systems. In *Proc. IJCAI-83*, 198-202.

[Collins & Loftus 75] Collins, A. M. and E.F. Loftus. A Spreading Activation Theory of Semantic Processing. *Psych. Rev.*, 82 (6): 409-428, 1975.

[Cottrell 85] Cottrell, G.W. A connectionist approach to word-sense disambiguation. Ph.D. Dissertation, Dept. of Computer Science, University of Rochester, 1985.

[Derthik 86] Derthik, M. A connectionist Knowledge Representation System. Thesis Proposal, CMU, June 1986.

[Etherington & Reiter 83] Etherington, D. W. and R. Reiter. On inheritance hierarchies with exceptions. In *Proc. AAAI-83*, pp 104-108.

[Fahlman 82] Fahlman, S. E. Three flavors of parallelism. In *Proc. CS-CSI-82*, pp 230-235

[Fahlman et al. 81] Fahlman, S. E., D.S. Touretzky, and van Roggen Walter. Cancellation in a parallel semantic network. In *Proc. IJCAI-81*, pp 257-263.

[Fahlman 79] Fahlman, S.E. *NETL: A System for Representing and Using Real-World Knowledge*, The MIT Press, Cambridge, MA, 1979.

[Fanty 85a] Fanty, M.A. Connectionist network building tools. Internal Document, Computer Science Department, University of Rochester, 1985.

[Fanty 85b] Fanty, M.A. Connectionist network simulation tools. Internal Document, Computer Science Department, University of Rochester, 1985.

[Feldman 85] Feldman, J.A. (Ed.) Special Issue on Connectionism. *Cognitive Science*, 9 (1), 1985.

[Feldman 82] Feldman, J. A. Dynamic connections in neural networks, *Bio-Cybernetics*, 46: 27-39, 1982.

[Feldman & Ballard 82] Feldman, J. A. and D.H. Ballard. Connectionist models and their properties. *Cognitive Science*, 6 (3): 205-254, 1982.

[Fillmore 68] Fillmore, C.J. The case for Case. In *Universals in Linguistic Theory*, E.W. Bach and R.T. Harms (Eds.), pp 1-88, Holt, Rinehart, & Winston, New York,

1968.

[Fox 79] Fox, M.S. On Inheritance in Knowledge Representation. In *Proc. IJCAI-79*, pp 282-284.

[Frisch & Allen 82] Frisch, A.M. and J.F. Allen, Knowledge retrieval as limited inference. *Lecture notes in Computer Science: 6th Conference on Automated Deduction*, D.W. Loveland (Ed.), Springer-Verlag, New York. 1982.

[Goldman 86] Goldman, A.I. *Epistemology and Cognition.* Harvard University Press, Cambridge, MA, 1986.

[Gluck & Corter 85] Gluck, M.A. and J.E. Corter. Information and Category Utility. In *Proc. of the Seventh Annual Conference of The Cognitive Science Society*, pp 283-287, 1985.

[Hart & Duda 77] Hart, P.E. and R.O. Duda. PROSPECTOR - A computer-based consultant system for mineral exploration. TN 155, SRI International, Menlo Park, California. 1977.

[Hayes 79] Hayes, P.J. The logic of frames. In *Frame conception and Text Understanding*, D. Metzing (Ed.), pp 46-61. Walter de Gruyter, Berlin, 1979.

[Hebb 49] Hebb, D.O. *The Organization of Behavior,* Wiley, New York, 1949.

[Hillis 85] Hillis, W.D., *The Connection Machine*, The MIT Press, Cambridge, MA, 1985.

[Hinton 81] Hinton, G.E. Implementing Semantic Networks in Parallel Hardware. In *Parallel Models of Associative Memory.* G.E. Hinton and J.A. Anderson. (Eds.), pp 161-187. Lawrence Erlbaum Associates, Hillsdale, NJ, 1981.

[Hopfield 82] Hopfield, J.J. Neural Networks and Physical Systems with Emergent Collective Computational Abilities. In *Proceedings of the National Academy of Sciences*, vol. 79: 2554-2558, 1982.

[Jackendoff 83] Jackendoff, R. *Semantics and Cognition.* The MIT Press, Cambridge, MA, 1983.

[Jaynes 57] Jaynes, E.T. Information Theory and Statistical Mechanics. Part I, *Phy. Rev.*, vol. 106, pp. 620-630, March 1957; Part II, ibid., vol. 108, pp 171-191, October 1957.

[Jaynes 79] Jaynes E.T. Where Do We Stand on Maximum Entropy. In *The maximum entropy formalism*, R.D. Levine and M. Tribus (Eds.), MIT Press, Cambridge, MA, 1979.

[Keil 79] Keil, F.C. *Semantic and conceptual development.* Harvard University Press, Cambridge, MA, 1979.

[Kohonen et al. 81] Kohonen, T., E. Oja, and P. Lehtio. Storage and Processing of Information in distributed associative memory systems. In *Parallel Models of Associative Memory*, G.E. Hinton and J.A. Anderson (Eds.), pp 105-143, Lawrence Erlbaum Associates, Hillsdale NJ, 1981

[Kyburg 83] Kyburg, H.E. Jr. The reference class. *Philosophy of Science*, 50: 374-397, 1983.

[Levesque 84] Levesque, H.J. A Fundamental Tradeoff in Knowledge Representation and Reasoning. In *Proc. CS-CSI-84*, pp 141-152.

[McAllester 80] McAllester, D.A. "An Outlook on Truth Maintenance". AI Memo 551, MIT AI-Lab, August, 1980.

[McClelland & Rumelhart 86] McClelland, J.L. and D.E. Rumelhart. (Eds.) *Parallel Distributed Processing: Explorations in the Microstructure of Cognition.* Vol II. Bradford Books/MIT Press, Cambridge, MA, 1986.

[McCulloch & Pitts 43] McCulloch, W. S., and W. Pitts. A logical calculus of the ideas immanent in neural nets. *Bulletin of Mathematical Biophysics*, 5: 115-137, 1943.

[Pearl 85] Pearl J. Bayesian Networks: A model of self-activated memory for evidential reasoning. In *Proc. of the Seventh Annual Conference of The Cognitive Science Society*, pp 329-334, 1985.

[Quillian 68] Quillian R.M. Semantic Memory. In *Semantic Information Processing*, M. Minsky (Ed.), pp 216-270, The MIT Press, Cambridge, MA, 1968.

[Reiter 80] Reiter, R. A Logic for Default reasoning. *Artificial Intelligence*, 13: 81-132, 1980.

[Reiter & Criscuolo 81] Reiter, R. and G. Criscuolo. On interacting defaults. In *Proc. IJCAI-81*, pp 270-276.

[Roberts & Goldstein 77] Roberts, B. and I. Goldstein. The FRL Manual MIT AI memo 409, 1977.

[Rollinger 83] Rollinger, Claus-Rainer. How to represent Evidence - Aspects of Uncertain Reasoning. In *Proc. IJCAI-83*, pp 358-361.

[Rosenblatt 62] Rosenblatt, F. *Principles of Neurodynamics.* Spartan, New York, 1962.

[Rosch 75] Rosch, E. Cognitive Representations of Semantic Categories. *Journal of Experimental Psychology: General*, 104: 192-233, 1975.

[Rumelhart & McClelland 86] Rumelhart, D.E. and J.L. McClelland. (Eds.) *Parallel Distributed Processing: Explorations in the Microstructure of Cognition.* Vol I. Bradford Books/MIT Press, Cambridge, MA, 1986.

[Shafer 76] Shafer, G. *A mathematical theory of evidence.* Princeton University Press, Princeton, NJ, 1976.

[Schubert et al. 83] Schubert, L.K., M.A. Papalaskaris, and J. Taugher Determining Type, Part, Colour, and Time Relationships. IEEE Computer 16 (10): 55-60, October 1983.

[Shastri & Feldman 86] Shastri, L and J.A. Feldman. Neural Nets, Routines, and Semantic Networks. In *Advances in Cognitive Science 1*, N.E. Sharkey (Ed.), pp 158-203, Ellis Horwood Limited, England/John Wiley & Sons: New York. 1986.

[Smith & Medin 81] Smith, E. E., D.L. Medin. *Categories and Concepts.* Harvard University Press, Cambridge, MA, 1981.

[Sommers 65] Sommers, F. Predicability. In *Philosophy in America*. M. Black (Ed.), Cornell University Press, Ithaca, NY, 1965.

[Touretzky 86] Touretzky, D. S. *The Mathematics of Inheritance Systems.* Pitman Publishing Company, London, 1986.

[Tversky and Kahneman 83] Tversky, A. and D. Kahneman. Extensional versus intuitive reasoning: the conjunction fallacy in probability judgement. *Psych. Rev.*, 90 (4): 293-315, 1983.

[Vilain 85] Vilain, M., An Approach to Hybrid Knowledge Representation. In *Proc. IJCAI-85*, pp 547-551.

[Wickelgren 79] Wickelgren, W.A. Chunking and Consolidation: A Theoretical Synthesis of Semantic Networks, Configuring in Conditioning, S-R Versus Cognitive Learning, Normal Forgetting, the Amnesic Syndrome, and the Hippocampal Arousal System. *Psych. Rev.*, 86 (1): 44-60, 1979.

[Warren 87] Warren C. Hierarchical Learning in a Massively Parallel Machine, Senior Thesis, University of Pennsylvania, April, 1987.

[Willshaw 81] Willshaw, D. Holography, associative memory, and inductive generalization. In *Parallel models of associative memory*, G.E. Hinton and J.A. Anderson (Eds.), pp 83-104, Lawrenc Erlbaum Associates, Hillsdale, NJ, 1981.

[Zadeh 83] Zadeh, L.A. Commonsense Knowledge Representation Based on Fuzzy Logic, *IEEE Computation*, 16(10): 61-66, 1983.

819